GENDER IDENTITY

IT HAPPENED TO ME

Series Editor: Arlene Hirschfelder

Books in the It Happened to Me series are designed for inquisitive teens digging for answers about social issues, certain illnesses, or lifestyle interests. These books feature up-to-date information, relatable teen views, and thoughtful suggestions to help you figure out stuff. Besides special boxes that highlight singular facts, each book is enhanced with the latest reading lists, websites, and other recommendations.

The following titles may also be of interest:

Activism: The Ultimate Teen Guide, by Kathlyn Gay
ADHD: The Ultimate Teen Guide, by John Aspromonte
Adopted: The Ultimate Teen Guide Revised Edition, by Suzanne Buckingham Slade
Autism Spectrum Disorder: The Ultimate Teen Guide, by Francis Tabone
Bigotry and Intolerance: The Ultimate Teen Guide, by Kathlyn Gay
Bullying: The Ultimate Teen Guide, by Mathangi Subramanian
College: The Ultimate Teen Guide, by Lisa Maxwell Arter
Creativity: The Ultimate Teen Guide, by Aryna Ryan
Depression: The Ultimate Teen Guide, by Tina P. Schwartz
Divorce: The Ultimate Teen Guide, by Kathlyn Gay
Eating Disorders: The Ultimate Teen Guide, by Jessica R. Greene
LGBTQ Families: The Ultimate Teen Guide, by Eva Apelqvist
Parental Death: The Ultimate Teen Guide, by Michelle Shreeve
Self-Injury: The Ultimate Teen Guide, by Judy Dodge Cummings
Sexual Assault: The Ultimate Teen Guide, by Olivia Ghafoerkhan
Sexual Decisions: The Ultimate Teen Guide Second Edition, by L. Kris Gowen
Shyness: The Ultimate Teen Guide, by Bernardo J. Carducci, PhD, and Lisa Kaiser
Siblings: The Ultimate Teen Guide, by Olivia Ghafoerkhan
Substance Abuse: The Ultimate Teen Guide, by Sheri Bestor

GENDER IDENTITY

THE ULTIMATE TEEN GUIDE

SECOND EDITION

CYNTHIA L. WINFIELD

ROWMAN & LITTLEFIELD
Lanham • Boulder • New York • London

Published by Rowman & Littlefield
An imprint of The Rowman & Littlefield Publishing Group, Inc.
4501 Forbes Boulevard, Suite 200, Lanham, Maryland 20706
www.rowman.com

6 Tinworth Street, London, SE11 5AL, United Kingdom

British Library Cataloguing in Publication Information Available

Library of Congress Cataloging-in-Publication Data

Names: Winfield, Cynthia L., 1960– author.
Title: Gender identity : the ultimate teen guide / Cynthia L. Winfield.
Description: Second Edition. | Lanham, MD : Rowman & Littlefield Publishing
    Group, Inc. [2019] | Series: It happened to me | Revised edition of the
    author's Gender identity, 2007. | Includes bibliographical references and
    index.
Identifiers: LCCN 2018051311 (print) | LCCN 2019003001 (ebook) | ISBN
    9781442278370 (electronic) | ISBN 9781442278363 (cloth : alk. paper)
Subjects: LCSH: Intersexuality—Social aspects. | Gender identity—United
    States. | Intersexuality—Psychological aspects. | Gender identity—Social
    aspects. | Sexual orientation. | Intersex people—Identity.
Classification: LCC RC883 (ebook) | LCC RC883 .W56 2019 (print) | DDC
    616.6/94—dc23
LC record available at https://lccn.loc.gov/2018051311

♾️™ The paper used in this publication meets the minimum requirements of American National Standard for Information Sciences—Permanence of Paper for Printed Library Materials, ANSI/NISO Z39.48-1992.

For all young people seeking to understand themselves and their world,
and for their families, friends, allies, and advocates.
For my pastor, who only preaches love
and works tirelessly to inspire understanding, acceptance, and radical inclusion
across the country and around the world.
And for my spouse, without whom this work would not exist.

Contents

Acknowledgments

While many resources were used to compile this book, several people deserve recognition.

Sincere thanks to Arlene Hirschfelder, It Happened to Me series editor, for her careful, deliberate attention to the manuscript and for her support through circumstances that necessitated deadline extensions. Thanks to Phyllis Winfield, whose offhand suggestion one morning many years ago—"Why don't you do a book about gender?"—was the genesis of the first edition of this book. Genuine thanks to Jamie Shupe, the first person in the United States to be granted a non-binary gender in the courts, for the time they devoted to discussing issues related to skeletal physiology (and how having a male skeleton may provide a transgender female athlete with advantages despite a lack of testosterone) and concerns about how adolescents transitioning affects future fertility. Grateful thanks to Hans Lindahl, intersex activist for interACT Advocates for Intersex Youth, for her thoughtful editing of chapter 5 about intersex bodies, her patient explanations about why the words *penis* and *vagina* were preferable over the vague *male body* and *female body*, and her tireless work in finding other interACT advocates to obtain permission to use their photographs.

Many thanks to the young transgender, genderqueer, and nonbinary persons who submitted writings and photographs for this edition. Having to select which pieces to include was challenging, especially in the face of young people (all adults, yet young to me) baring their souls and sharing their photographs for the greater good. I wish you all the best. And, thanks to Jack James, once a student at the middle school where I taught, who shared his thoughts about contemporary film—and encouraged my work on this book.

Further, thanks to Zoe Perry-Wood, gifted social documentary photographer, who has created a body of work photographing the Boston Alliance of Gay and Lesbian Youth (BAGLY) Prom over the last decade. Her series "Hanging in the Balance: Portraits from the BAGLY Prom" documents lesbian, gay, bisexual, transgender, queer, questioning, and nonbinary youth at their prom—the prom where they may come as they are to celebrate and be celebrated.

Finally, thank you to the multitude of authors of young adult fiction who are busily publishing stories featuring transgender, nonbinary, intersex, lesbian, gay, bisexual, queer, and questioning characters. How I wish I could have included more of your titles within these pages. Your stories make an important difference. And thank you to the myriad television and movie producers creating more shows than I could possibly watch, review, or include herein. That shows featuring transgender actors and characters are becoming the norm is good. I may still have a soft spot in my heart for Corporal Max Klinger from the old television show *M*★*A*★*S*★*H*, but his cross-dressing in search of a Section 8 discharge from the US Army during the Korean War is far from what it means to be transgender in today's military. Your stories, in the face of continued divisiveness across the country and around the globe concerning issues of gender and sexuality, gives me hope for the future.

INTRODUCTION

··

This book is about gender identity—the sense a person has of whether he or she is a boy or a girl, or both—and what happens when this sense of self conflicts with the person's anatomical sex. This book examines how hormones affect a developing fetus and how male and female brains may differ, considers the wealth of language that exists around these issues, investigates the presence and prevalence of intersex persons, briefly travels the road of transgender history—including current laws and protections—and concludes with ways anyone might help to make the world a better place for all of us, including those whose gender identity differs from the norm. Although issues faced by the trans community often overlap with those of the lesbian, gay, and bisexual (LGB) community, and while the two communities are often lumped together as one—the lesbian, gay, bisexual, and transgender (LGBT) community—this book is not about sexual identity. Additionally, although the intersex community is often included in the same mix—lesbian, gay, bisexual, transgender, and intersex (LGBTI)—it has a different viewpoint and goals. Lumping together sexual and gender minorities provides convenient political alliances, but they represent at least three distinct communities, each with unique issues. For those interested in learning more about gender identity, see the "Resources" section at the back of the book.

For centuries, male and female gender roles were distinct—for the most part, men worked and provided for their families while women tended to hearth, home, and child rearing. While there have been popular culture representations of men appearing as women—and women appearing as men—for the most part, they have been for entertainment purposes rather than the education and enlightenment of the masses. But garnering an audience for theatrical productions is a far cry from achieving acceptance in daily life. Ellen DeGeneres has given visibility to and normalized lesbians who prefer masculine attire, but acceptance of Ellen on television does not always translate to acceptance of others like her in person. Our twenty-first-century society may imagine itself as having transcended many of the social limitations of our predecessors; however, gender identities, roles, and expectations still shape both our behaviors and the ways in which we are perceived by others, and the gender binary is still accepted as wholly factual by many.

A decade ago, *transgender* was a word heard infrequently by the general population in the United States, and even more rarely in the news. Today, *transgender* is so common as to be heard in the news at least weekly, generally more often. Why the change? Many reasons account for this, including

- The progress of our social consciousness, as the civil rights movement has shifted from the black and African American community to the lesbian, gay, bisexual, transgender, queer or questioning, intersex, and asexual (LGBTQIA) community.
- The backlash from conservative religious and political groups against the legalization of same-sex unions—especially the legalization of the unions as marriages.
- The public coming-out of celebrities (Caitlyn Jenner comes to mind).
- The increase in popular culture of LGBTQ representations around the world.

Caitlyn Jenner is a television personality and former Olympic gold medalist who was known as Bruce Jenner before transitioning to a woman. She received the Arthur Ashe Courage Award at the 2015 ESPY Awards for coming out as her true self. *E! Entertainment Television / Photofest © E! Entertainment Television*

For young people attending public or private schools, colleges, and universities, the public discussion and awareness has filtered to bathroom facilities on campuses—and who is entitled to use which bathroom. Indeed, after transgender teen Jazz Jennings wrote to President Obama about bathroom access in schools, in 2016 the White House issued a directive to public schools and universities to allow transgender students to use the restroom of their chosen gender. Even the Democratic National Committee included a mention of trans-inclusiveness in the party platform going into the 2016 presidential elections, and changed the signs on women's bathrooms to make them gender neutral. (Which, opponents were quick to point out, immediately doubled the number of restrooms available to men.) Perhaps a decade from now the media focus will have moved on to other hot-button issues, and the question of who uses which restroom will seem trivial in our collective hindsight.

As LGBTQIA awareness and trans-visibility has increased, so have our responsibilities as a society. Despite wishful thinking, one really cannot "un-know" new knowledge. Before the legislation of "bathroom bills" how many nontransgender people ever gave a thought to which restroom a transgender person used? Now that awareness of the restroom issue exists, society is grappling with that knowledge. In 2016, nonbinary gender markers began appearing on legal documents on a case-by-case, state-by-state basis. How long before nonbinary gender markers appear on same-sex marriage certificates, adoption certificates, and so on? Society has been grappling with those issues for over a decade longer, and we continue to wrestle with what we believe is the "right" solution to each question.

Transgender activist Jazz Jennings is a YouTube personality and reality television star best known for her series *I Am Jazz. TLC / Photofest © TLC*

Interestingly, responses to societal and political issues often follow the path of a pendulum. In 2016, when the eight-year Obama administration was winding down, the LGBTQIA community was enjoying long-sought, hard-won freedoms and social, legal, and political gains. Fast forward to 2017, when the Trump administration took office and the new president rushed to negate some of those gains—including workplace protections from discrimination, the move toward single-stall and unisex bathroom facilities, and protections for transgender and gender-nonconforming persons seeking to use the restroom of the gender with which they identify, as opposed to that assigned to them at birth.

From infancy, we are trained into one of two gender roles. Beginning with pastel pink or powder blue baby clothing, we are socialized to fit into either the "girl" role or the "boy" role. (Although gender-neutral clothing items are available for infants and toddlers, the pink-blue dichotomy reigns in the marketplace.) As we grow, we advance beyond simple color codes to basic social behavior patterns. Boys play wars games and girls play house. Boys live rough-and-tumble existences; girls act with more sedate, demure manners.

In the mid-twentieth century, when societal roles were extremely rigid, boys played cops and robbers, or engineered with train sets or building blocks, while girls played hopscotch, jump rope, and house. *Tomboys* were girls who avoided behaving like little ladies, preferring tree climbing to crocheting, and *sissies* were boys who behaved more like girls—perhaps playing with dolls instead of trucks; neither tomboys nor sissies were considered normal. While contemporary society allows boys and girls to play more equal roles, eyebrows are still raised when a boy from a working-class family studies ballet, or when a girl from an upper-class family chooses to work as a truck driver, hauling loads long distances and often being away from home overnight.

Indeed, usually the first question asked in the delivery room is about gender: "Is it a boy or a girl?" This seemingly innocuous question can be fraught with complications. Don't all children deserve to be loved and accepted as they are?

Feelings of being different can be extremely isolating. A person's internal sense of gender may not always agree with that designated by his or her external sexual equipment. In other words, sometimes a boy may feel he is in the wrong body or that people are telling him he's a girl when he knows deep within his core that he is most definitely a boy; or vice versa. Sometimes that mix-up can feel like being trapped inside the wrong body, but not always.

For many readers, language may add confusion to the discussion of trans issues. Readers who find it helpful to insert the pairing transsexual/transgender when encountering *trans* as a single whole word are encouraged to do so; I chose to use *trans* to make reading easier. Also, I use *transgender* in this text, although the words *transgender* and *transgendered* appear throughout the literature.

Born to celebrity parents Sonny Bono and Cher, Chastity Bono underwent female-to-male transition and changed his name to Chaz in 2010. *ABC / Photofest © ABC*

Changes in this second edition of *Gender Identity: The Ultimate Teen Guide* include updated resources, references, language, and images. In the chapter about intersex variations, care was taken to avoid references to "male" and "female" anatomy; instead, readers will find the anatomical descriptors "penis" and "vagina." Yet, this is a reference text for public schools and libraries, and as such, the more publicly palatable euphemisms "male" and "female" anatomy are generally used throughout the other chapters.

I hope readers will find the information on gender as fascinating as I have. You may never look at gender roles quite the same when you are through reading this book.

Enjoy your reading!

GENDER

Is It All in Your Head?

Science of Brain Sex

Consider the number of times you've explained something away because of a person's gender. Wouldn't it be nice to think that males and females behave the way they do because of the ways their brains are wired and that the common strengths and failings of both genders are inevitable and/or inescapable? If science were to prove that "men are from Mars and women are from Venus,"[1] we could, theoretically, stop trying so hard to get members of the opposite sex to understand our point of view.

The best seller *Brain Sex: The Real Difference between Men and Women* (1992) builds a strong argument behind this theory. The work remains controversial because the scientific community has yet to decisively settle the matter. The authors of *Brain Sex* argue that the brain's sex is determined in utero. Simply put, they contend that exposure to testosterone over a period of time during the first trimester of pregnancy causes a female brain to become male.

Although the authors want readers to believe that brain sex is wholly developed by birth, other researchers have since documented additional brain sex differentiation in humans between two and four years of age. Furthermore, in late 2003, Dr. Eric Vilain and colleagues identified fifty-four genes that play a role in the expression of sex in a fetus before hormones are ever released.[2] Whether brain sex—the functional structure of the brain along gender lines—is determined in the womb or at a later stage is still a matter for debate among scientists, as is the theory that male and female brains do, in fact, differ structurally along gender lines.

Researchers in Amsterdam doing postmortem brain studies determined that the hypothalamus influences sexual behavior. In male and female brains, the hypothalamus (a region in the forebrain that controls some functions of the autonomic nervous system) develops differently, and in transsexual brains the hypothalamus more closely resembles that of the opposite sex from which it was born.[3] A 2017 study analyzed forty-six other studies that collectively examined the brains of over 6,700 persons and determined that there is no significant difference in amygdala volume between males and females.[4] (The amygdala, located in the frontal portion of the temporal lobe, helps people to feel certain emotions—such as fear—and to perceive them in other people.) A *Science Daily* article says this study strengthens the case for gender similarity in the brain.[5] Some scientists go beyond brain structure to say this study suggests the gender with which one identifies (gender identity) and the sex(es) to which one is physically attracted (sexual orientation) may be seated in the mind; however, no scientific consensus has yet been reached.

In addition to the simple male-female dichotomy to which many in the United States adhere, some multidimensional theories of gender exist. Psychotherapist Carl W. Bushong suggests gender consists of five attributes. Two of these—genetic and physical—are addressed in chapter 5, "Boy or Girl? Delivery Room Decisions and Intersex Bodies." The other three are based in the brain or mind and develop "from a few weeks after conception until two or three years of age." One is brain sex, or "how we perceive sex, relationships and goals along male or female" lines. Another is brain gender, or "how the brain is wired along gender lines." The third is gender identity, or "how we perceive ourselves as male or female." Bushong says these five attributes operate semi-independently of one another, meaning each person is a unique combination of these variables and that the vast majority of people are a mixture of attributes and not homogeneously male or female.[6]

What prompts our self-perceptions of gender, or gender identity, is not well understood, but it is undeniable that our perception is strong. This makes it very difficult for transgender persons, whose gender identity does not match their physical sex. The resulting state of psychological unease, often distress, is currently known as *gender dysphoria*. A 2016 study estimated the transgender population in the United States to be 0.58 percent.[7] That means over 1.3 million people in this country deal with that sense of psychological discomfort.

There is growing evidence that genetics play a significant role in gender identity and sexual orientation. While some people believe sexuality—be it homosexuality, heterosexuality, bisexuality, or asexuality—is a choice, others disagree. After conducting postmortem research on the brains of gay men who had died of AIDS, Simon LeVay published a paper noting that the structure of the hypothalamus in homosexuals differs from that in heterosexuals. LeVay's research findings were among those that led to the popular media discussion of the possibility of a "gay gene."[8]

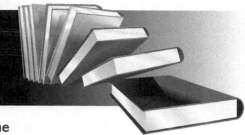

Contemporary Nonfiction: The Gene *by Siddhartha Mukherjee (2016)*

To learn more about genetic research, read the bestselling book *The Gene: An Intimate History* by cancer physician, researcher, and Pulitzer Prize–winning author Siddhartha Mukherjee. Although Mukherjee devotes few pages to the issue of gender identity, his exploration of the genetics of humankind reads like a fascinating detective novel. Interweaving his family's medical history with the history of how humans have understood genetics over the centuries, case histories, newer findings, and directions for future research, Mukherjee tells the gene's story thoroughly and wonderfully. For those daunted by in-depth science, the audiobook may allow you to enjoy the story more easily.

A 2017 study conducted by scientists in Canada supports this possibility. The study looked at native Zapotec people indigenous to the Istmo region of Oaxaca in Mexico. Among the Istmo Zapotec a third gender exists: men who are sexually attracted to men and are known as *muxes*. Comparable to what are known as gay men in the United States, the *muxe nguiiu* tend to appear masculine, whereas the *muxe gunaa* are feminine in their appearance and behavior, akin to transgender women.[9]

Another study by the same research team found that the Istmo Zapotec *muxes* had more relatives who were *muxes*. This is similar to studies of Samoan *fa'afafine* (a third gender of feminine men who are attracted to men) and of Euro-American gay men. Since all studies cited found a consistent proportion of either gay male relatives, or male-to-female transgender relatives who are sexually attracted to men, these authors conclude that both "share a similar biological foundation."[10] Whatever the cause of homosexuality, it should have no bearing on a person's right to being treated equally.

In *The Gene: An Intimate History*, physician and researcher Siddhartha Mukherjee writes, "Genes are vastly more influential than any other force in shaping sex identity and gender identity,"[11] adding that some aspects of gender can be developed with hormones and training. Further, he recognizes the medical community's growing understanding that intersex babies should be raised in their chromosomal (genetic) sex regardless of their external genitalia, and given the opportunity to make choices when they are older. Of sex determination, he observes that the Y chromosome, which determines maleness and has information packed into it, is the smallest and most vulnerable chromosome.

While sex is determined by simply flipping the switch of the SRY gene on the Y chromosome—*on* (for male) or *off* (for female), gender determination and gender identity are much more complex. SRY must turn on and off an entire cascade of genes, which are then impacted by all manner of occurrences—input from the self and the environment, including "hormones, behaviors, exposures, social performance, cultural role-playing, and memory—to engender gender."[12] This cascade recognizes that who we are is ultimately a combination of both nature (genes) and nurture (environment). Mukherjee believes "the existence of a transgender gender identity provides powerful evidence for this geno-developmental cascade."[13]

If you've heard that gender variance occurs only within the human population and that sex and gender roles in nature are either male or female and always heterosexual, you've been misinformed. For reproductive purposes, some plants rely on cross-pollination (male and female intermixing) but others self-pollinate—reproducing by themselves. In the ocean, the male seahorse carries the eggs, births the young, and then raises them. On land, earthworms are both male and female (in one worm), and some snails reproduce by mating with themselves.

Researcher Paul Vasey has documented many animals that engage in homosexual sex—including female Japanese macaques, male fruit flies, and male flour beetles—without forming long-term same-sex partnerships. Female Laysan albatrosses on the Hawaiian Islands form lifelong partnerships; however, with a dearth of male albatrosses available, the female pairings make sense for raising young. Both male and female bonobos, in the ape family, and bottlenose dolphins also exhibit homosexual behavior, but ultimately pair with a member of the opposite sex to produce offspring. All of these animals are better described as bisexual. To date, only two species have been discovered that demonstrate lifelong homosexual preferences—humans and domesticated sheep.[14]

Homosexuality as a Disease?

Until 1973, the American Psychiatric Association (APA) considered homosexuality a mental illness and a treatable deviation from the norm. The diagnosis was included in the first and second editions of the APA's *Diagnostic and Statistical Manual (DSM)* of mental illnesses. Psychiatrist Jack Drescher writes that theories of homosexuality generally fall into one of three types: (1) homosexuality as a result of pathology; (2) homosexuality as a demonstration of immaturity; and (3) homosexuality as a natural phenomenon.

For many years, homosexuality was viewed as a pathology, or illness, by the medical community. According to Drescher, those who ascribe to the theory of pathology may see homosexuality as morally bad or evil. The medical community may no longer consider homosexuality a disease, and cultural attitudes about homosexuality have shifted in countries that accept scientific authority on the subject, including the United States. Yet, many people continue to think homosexuality is morally wrong. The second theory, immaturity, is based in psychoanalysis and views homosexuality as a phase a person passes through at a young age before developing into an adult heterosexual. This theory does not carry the weight of moral failings, but it does suggest the homosexual is not mature. The final theory, normal variation, considers homosexuality to be a state of being that occurs naturally, like left handedness or having red hair. Drescher writes, "Such theories see no place for homosexuality in a psychiatric diagnostic manual."[15]

Even after homosexuality was removed as a diagnosis, the *DSM-II* printed after 1973 continued to designate some forms of homosexuality as abnormal conditions or diseases. The diagnosis of homosexuality was replaced by a new diagnosis: sexual orientation disturbance (SOD). This applied to persons who were troubled by their attraction to persons of the same sex and wanted to change. When homosexuality was viewed as a curable illness, many went to great lengths to either cure themselves or to get help for a family member or friend. Conversion therapies, while outlawed in a few states, continue to be legal in the United States. (See chapter 8, "Legal Issues," for more information.)

When the next edition was published in 1980, the *DSM-III* included the diagnosis of ego dystonic homosexuality, for those distressed about having homosexual feelings. After much debate, this diagnosis was also removed, and the 1987 revised edition held only the slightest trace of it with the diagnosis of sexual disorders not otherwise specified. This could be used when a patient experienced continued distress about unremitting homosexual attractions. By not viewing homosexuality as an abnormal condition, the medical community can now focus on the physical and mental health needs of the LGBT population.

Transsexualism as a Disease?

According to transgender psychology professor Madeline H. Wyndzen, the 1980 *DSM-III* included the diagnosis of transsexualism for those distressed by their gender assignments from birth and "who demonstrated at least two years of continuous interest in removing their sexual anatomy and transforming their bodies and social roles."[16] Two other forms of gender identity disorder were included in that edition: gender identity disorder of adolescence or adulthood nontranssexual type and gender identity disorder not otherwise specified. Wyndzen points out that the media overlooked these latter diagnoses in favor of the more inflammatory term *transsexual*.

The 1994 *DSM-IV* replaced the diagnosis of transsexualism with that of gender identity disorder (GID). The GID diagnosis was to be used for "those with a strong and persistent cross-gender identification and a persistent discomfort with his or her sex or a sense of inappropriateness in the gender role of that sex."[17] As such, having a diagnosed case of GID earned transgender patients the stigma of having a mental illness.

In the fourth edition of the *DSM*, criteria for the diagnosis of GID remained the same. The *DSM-IV-TR* also specified that a gender dysphoric child must demonstrate at least four of the following five criteria to qualify for the diagnosis GID of childhood:

1. Repeatedly stated desire to be, or insistence that he or she is, the other sex
2. In boys, preference for cross-dressing or simulating female attire; in girls, insistence on wearing only stereotypical masculine clothing
3. Strong and persistent preferences for cross-sex roles in make-believe play or persistent fantasies of being the other sex
4. Intense desire to participate in the stereotypical games and pastimes of the other sex
5. Strong preference for playmates of the other sex[18]

The behaviors described in these diagnostic criteria are those seen in and experienced by transgender children around the world.

Gender Dysphoria

In 2013, when the *DSM-5* was published, the diagnosis of gender identity disorder was replaced by that of gender dysphoria. The change, while still identifying a mental concern, "shifted the emphasis in treatment from fixing a disorder to resolving distress over the mismatch."[19] It also removed some of the stigma associated with having a mental disorder. Since transgender individuals do not necessarily feel distress about the mismatch between the sex assigned to them at birth and the one with which they identify, many would not qualify as gender dysphoric. Like the 1973 decision to remove homosexuality as a mental illness, this shift recognizes that a person can be homosexual (or, in this case, transgender) and psychologically distressed *or* psychologically healthy. The sexual orientation or gender identity is not the problem; rather the problem is the distress felt by some of those persons.[20]

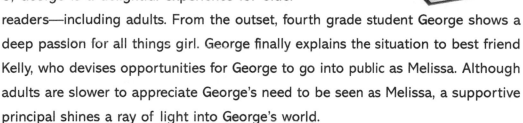

Contemporary Literature: George *by Alex Gino (2015)*

While aimed at readers in grades 4 through 6, *George* is a delightful experience for older readers—including adults. From the outset, fourth grade student George shows a deep passion for all things girl. George finally explains the situation to best friend Kelly, who devises opportunities for George to go into public as Melissa. Although adults are slower to appreciate George's need to be seen as Melissa, a supportive principal shines a ray of light into George's world.

Feature Film: Boys Don't Cry *(1999)*

In *Boys Don't Cry*, Hilary Swank's portrayal of Brandon Teena earned her several awards for best actress—including an Oscar. Based on the true story of Teena Brandon's troubled life (1972–1993) in Nebraska, the film documents a young person's life spiraling out of control. While born into a female body and raised as Teena Brandon, this person's gender identity and gender expression were distinctly male, and the sexual preference was for females, thus the name change to Brandon Teena. *Boys Don't Cry* is a love story, and a story of both hope and tragedy. The film's violence is disturbingly strong and includes sexual violence in a graphic rape scene.

Challenging Gender in Schools

Challenging perceptions of gender in schools is an ongoing issue. In 2006, the *Broward-Palm Beach New Times* shared the story of a five-year-old Floridian assigned male at birth who claimed to be female.[21] The child was to enter kindergarten that fall, where she would be addressed with a feminine version of her name and referred to with female pronouns. Free to dress as she liked, within uniform restrictions, she would have a supportive teacher working with her family to be sure that she was happy. Most students and some teachers would have been unaware of her anatomical sex.[22] At that time, such stories about young children were more newsworthy. Today, transgender issues appear frequently in the news. While schools may not feel ready to deal with transgender and gender-nonconforming students, resources to help are readily available.

In 2013, California's governor, Jerry Brown, signed legislation making California the first state to guarantee certain rights for transgender students in K–12 schools, by allowing transgender students access to their choice of restrooms and locker rooms. According to one article, the Los Angeles Unified School District has had a similar policy for "nearly a decade" without incident. The article reported that while both Massachusetts and Connecticut have had policies granting such statewide protections in place, California has now enshrined them in a statute.[23]

Several schools around the country are now moving to introduce the concept of gender neutrality. A middle school in Nebraska instituted gender-neutral classrooms using guidelines from Gender Spectrum, an organization that works to create a gender-sensitive and inclusive world for all children and teens. By excluding gendered language—"ladies and gentlemen" or "boys and girls"—and using the students' preferred names and pronouns, they hoped to create more inclusive classrooms and reduce bullying. While the Lincoln Public Schools superintendent and some other administrators support the changes, some parents and teachers do not. Similar initiatives are underway in New York, Minnesota, and Colorado.[24]

Extensive support for schools desiring to become more gender inclusive, and for families needing to help those schools, is readily available online. You can find several in the "Resources" section of this book.

Resources for Schools

Several organizations provide extensive online materials that schools can use to guide their ventures into becoming more gender inclusive. Two are listed briefly here. Check the "Resources" section in the back of this book for more info.

- The Education section of the Gender Spectrum website at www.gender spectrum.org/resources/education-2/
- The website of GLSEN, an educator resource network, at www.glsen.org/ educate/resources

Self-Perception

A person's gender identity is an integral part of the self. When it conflicts with the physical sex of the body and with the messages a person receives about society's expectations for the individual's gender expression, it can leave someone feeling unaccepted by others and extremely isolated. One gender-nonconforming person, assigned female at birth, expresses this in the poem "Gender Dysphoria, Abuse," written when the poet was twenty-one years old, and which opens with a quote from a Tumblr post.

Personal Reflection: "Gender Dysphoria, Abuse," by Caroline T., Age 21

"Please stop destroying what is left of your heart by constantly thinking about things that have broken you."—Nikita Gill

I'm pulling out all the emergency stops
Anything to stop the disaster that's ahead of me.
I'm going through emergency procedures
And flipping through the manuals of what self-care is supposed to be
But page after page, there's no stopping the tornado;
The maelstrom of emotions that is wrecking me up inside.
No matter how many times I've been calmer than the ocean,
Chiller than a warm Sunday with no responsibilities—
These moments are hurricane systems,
They are sudden destruction,
They come and go
Leaving nothing but coldness inside of me.
But there has been a pattern,
A reoccurring theme
A red flag to what's to come.
It starts with the clothes that line the curves too well
It's the "she/hers/hers" and the "damn gurrrrl."
It's the sense of everyone staring at the way

You walk, you talk, you present.

And with that it's the wave of the tsunami

With everything crashing down on you at once

As your body is stripped and carved by

Heteronormativity and the gender binary.

And suddenly it's worse than the monthly visitor

Because at least you know in 3–5 days

She goes away.

But no, with each wrong assumption

Hell's demons are knocking on my door

Reminding me that

You can't possibly be thriving outside of the binary

When you're assigned as a girl

But don't feel like one.

Dysphoria that's a name to put to

My soul shriveling into misery

That there is no escape, no distraction

From that wrongness of what you see in the reflection.

And it's as if you're thrown back to fifth grade

Plagued with memories of

Not being able to do anything right

Dang, how can anyone be such a failure that

Even your own body can't stand who you are

In fact it's hard to understand how a person

Can be filled with such anger, shame, disappointment and disgust

Brokenness from being entirely the wrong thing

But I guess it is understandable if

That's all you ever felt from those that society said loved you
    unconditionally.

And I guess it's harder to apply the framework of self-love

When going back home is a constant assault on who you are and who
    you can be

From a woman who will only love you by her standards

And even then you're found lacking.

So I look at my reflection and I move on.

I move on even as disappointment seeps through my entire being.

Acutely aware of the flesh pushing down on my chest

Too stubborn to live in a state of self-harm and self-medication

Unwilling to stand on the precipice of abysmal failure

And determined to say blast it and so what if

Satan has my mind on a grill—

You don't own me Satan.

And that's what I'm doing—

I'm saying

Not today, Satan, not today.

I'm saying

I'll never be your prince or princess,

Because saving myself from your expectations

And my dysphoria

Is my happy ending.[a]

The people with whom I spoke while researching this topic, including those who contributed personal narratives, all spoke of feeling an enormous sense of isolation when seeking to bring incongruent gender identities, roles or expectations, and expressions into line. Our self-perceptions of sexual identity and orientation are such integral parts of who we are that many spend a lifetime seeking acceptance in society—simply for being ourselves.

Indeed, adolescence and early adulthood are a time of self-discovery and self-determination, a time when people often decide who they are (and what they stand for) and seek to accept themselves. Unfortunately, in the process of self-definition, we often resort to overly simplistic labels readily available—for biological sex: male, female, and intersex; for sexual orientation: straight, gay, lesbian, bisexual; for gender identity: male, female, transgender; for political affiliation or leanings: Democrat, Republican, Independent, left, right, center; for religion: Christian, Muslim, Hindu, Jew; and so on. The catch is that by using these labels we mislead ourselves and others through vastly oversimplifying who we are. Acceptance, of oneself or another, based on such arbitrary labels unjustly pigeonholes the labeled person into a box that just might not fit and gives the

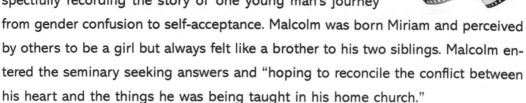

Documentary: Call Me Malcolm (2005)

Call Me Malcolm is a ninety-minute documentary film respectfully recording the story of one young man's journey from gender confusion to self-acceptance. Malcolm was born Miriam and perceived by others to be a girl but always felt like a brother to his two siblings. Malcolm entered the seminary seeking answers and "hoping to reconcile the conflict between his heart and the things he was being taught in his home church."

Producers Joseph Parlagreco and Kierra Chase travel with Malcolm on a road trip across the United States, where he calls on a variety of people who share their views of gender, faith, and love with him. On the way, he finds acceptance and gains understanding that will help to shape his life path.[b]

observer a distorted, stilted view of the labeled person's identity or beliefs. Also, such labels provide roles that we may allow to limit us. Finally, if our upbringing taught us that being X, Y, or Z is undesirable—even bad—how are we to accept and love ourselves when we wear that label?

Contemporary Film: Freak Show (2018)

Freak Show is the film adaptation of James St. James's young adult novel of the same name. Billy Bloom is a gender-expansive youth with a strong feminine bent and delightful theatrical abilities. When his mother disappears, Billy moves to his father's estate and enrolls in a new high school, where he feels hated by all. Every school day becomes an exercise in psychological torture, even after Mary Jane quietly befriends him and provides her take on their fellow classmates. You will laugh, cry, shudder, and cheer because *Freak Show* affects readers and viewers deeply.

Unconditional Love

When the first edition of this book was being written around 2006, Peter, a five-year-old anatomical boy, told his younger sister Emily, "I'm a girl."[25] Was this a passing phase? An afternoon of make-believe? Or was it the statement of a deeply rooted sense of self?

At the time I knew Peter; he was a gentle child. Based on his play behavior, his mother expected that her son might grow up to be effeminate or gay. Emily's rough-and-tumble play made Peter's absence of boy behaviors even more noticeable. Peter's mother had always said she was ready to love him however he might grow up, and she recognized that her son might face discomfort, even pain, if his eventual choice did not meet society's expectations for him. When she told me about his declaration to his sister, she acknowledged that he could have greater hurdles in his future than she had previously envisioned.

Some young people who contributed to this book and its predecessor asserted that they knew their gender identity clearly before entering elementary school and were confused by the adults who insisted that the child's gender must align with his or her anatomical sex. My friend, Peter and Emily's mother, was aware that gender identity may be in place in a child's early years. Even so, she was not ready to draw any conclusions when Peter was but five years old. At the time, she planned to continue listening to her children and watching their behavior; maintaining an open, loving home for them; and using care to avoid pressuring either Peter or Emily into stereotypical gender roles. Although we have since lost touch, I firmly believe that both Peter and Emily, no matter what has happened in their lives, reside in a devoted home. My friend's children are lucky to be raised with such unconditional love, but isn't that all any of us want? To be accepted and loved for who we are?

Documentary: Being Me (2014)

Being Me reports on the life experiences of three transgender Australians: two transgender girls, Isabelle and Jamie, who are still in school, and one trans male adult named Paige. The documentary presents various aspects of the transgender youth journey, with a specific emphasis on the Australian experience. Yet, beyond the court requirements, the experiences shared are universal. Anyone with an interest in the subject will find the forty-three minutes required for viewing *Being Me* to be time well spent.[c]

TRANS HISTORY THROUGH THE AGES AND ACROSS CULTURES

Transgenderism is not a new phenomenon, although the *concept* of transgender is relatively new. Indeed, transgender individuals have been with us for centuries, and perhaps for as long as people have roamed the earth. Biblical laws against transvestism appear in Deuteronomy: "A woman shall not wear a man's apparel, nor shall a man put on a woman's garment; for whoever does such things is abhorrent to the Lord your God" (22:5, New Revised Standard Version [NRSV]). Deuteronomy 23:1 further states, "No one whose testicles are crushed or whose penis is cut off shall be admitted to the assembly of the Lord" (NRSV).[1] Although the date these laws were laid down is uncertain, they were written before the sixth century BCE. Clearly taboos against crossing gender roles have been part of human society for thousands of years—and why include such rules unless someone crossed a boundary for acceptable gender role behavior during ancient times?

Transgender Historical Figures

In the fifteenth century BCE, Egypt was ruled for more than twenty years by King Hatchepsut, a woman who served her country in the role of divine pharaoh. Alternatively remembered in history as queen or king, Hatchepsut preferred to be viewed as male and successfully conducted business as pharaoh during Egypt's eighteenth dynasty. Dressing as a king, Hatchepsut wore the pharaoh's traditional fake beard. Although much of Hatchepsut's rule has been lost to history and although she is often depicted as a traditional king, some remaining sculptures show this individual dressed as a male but having distinctly female breasts.[2]

In the fifteenth century CE, during the Hundred Years War in France, a seventeen-year-old female peasant donned the garb of military men, mounted a horse, and ultimately rode to sainthood in the eyes of her adoring public. Her stated goal was to lead an army of peasants and expel the occupying English troops. This woman, known to us as Joan of Arc, incited furor and fear among members of the ruling class; in time, she saw Prince Charles crowned as King of France. Shortly thereafter, she was captured by allies of the English feudal lords. Because her role as a successful female military leader of peasants, whom she had helped gain power, actually threatened the French nobility the nobles declined to come to her aid. Denounced for her gender identity and expression—not just her cross-dressing, but her cross-gendered appearance in general—Joan spoke on her own behalf at the trial held by the Inquisition. At her hearings, Joan was accused of "following the custom of the Gentiles and the Heathen."[3] She refused to take an oath that she would stop acting and dressing as a man, and so Joan of Arc was burned at the stake in 1431; she was nineteen.

If the peasantry prized transgender expression, only to face brutal punishments as did Joan of Arc, the wealthy and powerful did not. As continues to be true today, wealth buys one a certain amount of social comfort and behavioral latitude denied to persons in poverty. A wealthy eccentric is just that—a wealthy eccentric—but an impoverished eccentric is often seen as deviant. The word *deviant* carries only negative connotations, while the word *eccentric* implies deviance but has connotations that include a measure of tolerance or acceptance and understanding for the individual who is different.

Throughout history, the unusual behavior of the wealthy and powerful has been tolerated. In the sixteenth century, King Henry III of France often cross-dressed. When the king was dressed as a woman, courtiers referred to him as "her majesty." In the seventeenth century, Queen Christina of Sweden relinquished her throne to dress as a man; she renamed herself Count Dohna. In the same century, the woman Nzinga ruled as king of Angola for nearly three decades. In the 1670s, the male-to-female transsexual Abbe Francois Timoleon de Choisy attended the pope's inaugural ball dressed as a woman; his memoirs provide the earliest first-person documentation of cross-dressing.

In the early nineteenth century, the renowned French author George Sand, a female who often wore men's clothes, was as famous for her affairs as for her writing. She scandalized her peers by being the first woman in modern European history to dress this way. Toward midcentury, in Wales, a group of male-to-female cross-dressers banded together in Robin Hood fashion, calling themselves "Rebecca and her daughters." Much like Robin Hood's merry men, the Rebeccas destroyed road toll barriers to benefit the poor. Later in the century, during the US Civil War, female-to-male cross-dressing flourished, as women who wished to serve the cause disguised themselves as men to join the fight. Upon their deaths, about four hundred soldiers, on both the Union and Confederate sides, were found to be women.

Today, although the male-female gender role dichotomy continues to thrive in US culture, other cultures—both on this continent and around the world—recognize, accept, and even celebrate transgender persons. Eunuchs, the name derived from the Greek *eunoukhos* or bedroom guard, were castrated males given important historical roles. Employed as harem attendants or charged with important affairs of state in Asian courts and under Roman emperors, these emasculated males held favored positions in royal households. The *hijras* of India, whose history dates back 2,500 years, are known as a "third gender" caste today. While some *hijras* are born intersex, others choose to become *hijra*. Although mostly marginalized by society, *hijras* bless children and exercise symbolic powers in Indian culture.[4] In Europe, the *castrati* (from the Italian *castrare*, to castrate) were adult male singers who had been castrated in their youth to retain a childlike soprano or alto voice. The *mahu* of Hawaii were respected before Christianity came to the islands, and while they are far less visible today, they continue to have a role in Hawaiian culture.[5] In the Dominican Republic, the *guevedoche* are recognized as a third sex. Born with the intersex trait of 5-alpha-reductase deficiency, they are often assumed to be female at birth but develop male characteristics at puberty (much like the character Cal Stephanides in Jeffrey Eugenides's 2002 novel *Middlesex*). In fact, the name *guevedoche* translates to "balls at twelve."[6]

Gender across Cultures

Annual Festival in Koovagam, India

Each April, as part of an annual rite in the town of Koovgam, India, thousands of men gather to honor the warrior god Aravan, whose life was sacrificed to win a war.[7] Indeed, some *hijras* prefer to be called *arvani*.[8] Dressed as brides, they ceremoniously wed their god husband and remain his new bride for the night. Although *hijras* live at the margins of Indian society, in which conversation about cross-dressing is taboo and homosexuality can result in imprisonment, this annual ceremony celebrates the brief marriage of the eunuch Aravan to the god Krishna. Krishna is said to have temporarily transformed into a woman for the marriage, and then had Aravan beheaded the next day. Men of all sexual orientations partake in this ritual. Men who are homosexual, bisexual, transgender, *hijra*, and even heterosexual with wives and children wear dresses, makeup, and jewelry for the celebration.

While some people see this behavior as bizarre and may offer ridicule or cat-calls, hordes of male "sexual tourists" also flock to the town for the Koovagam Festival. There, they are ceremoniously wed to one of the temporary brides. One

Unidentified transgender people take part in a religious ritual to mourn the death of Lord Aravan in their annual festival of transgender people held at Koothandavar temple in Koovagam, Tamil Nadu, India. © *iStock / ajijchan*

or both parties entering the ceremonial union may already be married, and it is understood that their one-night marriage will be consummated. In the morning, the brides have their jewelry and garlands of flowers cut off and become widows who return to their usual lives. For those who live on the fringes of society throughout the year, this annual ritual provides affirmation and a place to belong.

Explore Further: Koovagam Festival

Short films of India's Koovagam Festival can be found online. Although brief, the videos add sound, movement, and color to one's understanding. The following videos come from recent gatherings.

- "Koovagam Festival 2017," www.youtube.com/watch?v=v-aCy84Idml.
- "Indian Transvestites Gather for the Koovagam Festival in Tamil Nadu," www.youtube.com/watch?v=VgFNKMbvtqO.
- "Koovagam Transgenders Festival 2017," www.youtube.com/watch?v=pkt2NDKZC6M.

On Facebook, find Koovagam Festival 2017.

Native American Two-Spirit People

On this continent, Native American cultures recognize that gender is not simply an either-or, male-female experience. Just as a diversity of Native American cultures exists, so, too, the Native views of gender encompass diversity—and they do seem to agree that transgender, or other than either male or female, is an option. In Native culture, the berdache, or two-spirit individual, is accepted as a third sex. In fact, transgender Natives were often respected or revered and held positions of power in the tribe. The tribal shamans, or healers, were frequently transgender individuals. Examples of Native views of gender roles can be found throughout all tribes, and given the vast number of tribal languages, many words exist to describe transgender Native people.

Among the Navajo people, gender was not assigned when a child of indeterminate gender was born. Rather, they allowed the child a voice in the determination of its own gender in an unusual ritual: they put "a child inside a *tipi* with [a] loom and a bow and arrow—female and male implements respectively. They set fire to the *tipi*, and whatever the child grabbed as he/she ran out determined the child's gender."[9]

When the Europeans came to colonize the Americas, they used *berdache* as a derogatory word to describe any Native person who did not fit their narrow gender role expectations. As the colonizers explored the Americas, reports of transgender Native peoples were common, and often disparaging. In time, the European colonizers sought to impose their own standards of behavior upon Native peoples. As we know today, their efforts at colonization amounted to genocide and extreme cultural suppression.

The imposition of European or Christian standards did not end when the United States achieved independence from British rule. In the 1850s, white Western travelers to Montana and Wyoming were shocked to encounter Barcheeampe, the Crow nation "woman chief" who was famous for both prowess in war and for polygamy. In 1886, We'wha, a six-foot-tall two-spirit Zuni artisan, is reported to have visited President Grover Cleveland in Washington, DC, without being recognized by the president as having been born male. In the late nineteenth century, the US government subjected the Crow nation's *badé* (or *boté*) to demeaning treatment and punishment in its attempts to change their behavior.[10] Although today the term *berdache* is not generally derogatory, Native peoples may prefer the gentler, more compassionate term *two-spirit* be used to describe persons having diverse gender expressions.[11]

Although Native Americans allow for gender diversity, throughout the history of the United States, diversity of either sexual preference or gender within the settlers' population has always been viewed as suspect. However, a tradition of transgender expression does appear as part of certain US holiday celebrations such as Mardi Gras, mummer's parades, and Halloween

Explore Further: Gender in Native American Cultures

Learn more about the Native American berdache people through books and videos.

Books

The Spirit and the Flesh by Walter Williams (1986) chronicles as many types of berdache people as there were different tribes. An important milestone in trans cultural history, this book includes the voices of Native two-spirit people.

Changing Ones: Third and Fourth Genders in Native North America by Will Roscoe (1998) provides a comprehensive exploration of the tribal roles of berdache Native North Americans.

An earlier work by Roscoe, *The Zuni Man-Woman* (1991), reveals the story of We'wha (pictured on page 27) and examines berdache roles among Pueblo Indians.

Videos

"Our Families: LGBT/Two-Spirit Native American Stories," a short film by Basic Rights Oregon, shares personal stories of struggle, acceptance, and family. Visit www.youtube.com/watch?v=geFgT-X7Ajc.

"As They Are: Two-Spirit People in the Modern World," a short film by the University of Southern California Department of Anthropology, interviews three two-spirit persons from different tribes—Navajo, Kiowa, and Paiute—who share some of their experiences growing up. Visit www.youtube.com/watch?v=AYGxZL87OZE.

"Two Spirit—This Is Family" is a clip from a feature-length documentary. Shot in a two-spirit planned community in Denver, Colorado, the clip depicts the two-spirit community reaching out to reintegrate itself with the broader Native community. Visit www.youtube.com/watch?v=_9LtyY-2YCl.

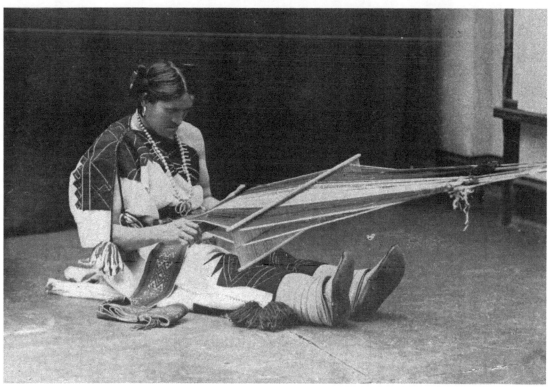

We'wha, a Native American (Zuni), sits and weaves a belt on a backstrap loom, Zuni Pueblo, New Mexico. We'wha is a berdache, a man who prefers women's work and adopts female dress. We'wha is dressed as a woman and wears a woven manta, moccasins, and squash blossom necklace. *Denver Public Library, Western History Collection; History of the American West, 1860–1920; Reproduction Number X-30150*

Gender in the Twentieth Century

The Institute for Sexual Science in Germany was founded in 1919 by sexologist and homosexual reformer Magnus Hirschfeld (1868–1935), who described homosexuals as "the third sex." Hirschfeld, a known cross-dresser, also coined the term *transvestite*. By the end of his life, the climate toward gender-variant individuals had become distinctly frostier.

Although homosexuals were targeted by the Nazis during World War II and vilified and ostracized elsewhere in the world, transsexuals were practically invisible to society—of necessity. Then, in 1952, an ex-GI from the Bronx underwent transsexual surgery in Sweden and became the center of a media circus for some time. Christine Jorgensen's sex change titillated the public, but her story signaled to many transgender people, who may have felt uncomfortably different and isolated, that they were not alone.

Jorgensen's life provided hope and inspiration for other transgender and transsexual people.[12]

Some transgender people manage to avoid detection. When Billy Tipton, a notable jazz musician and band leader of the 1940s and 1950s, died in 1989, his female body surprised the medical technicians who arrived on the scene. Tipton lived for more than half a century as a man, was married a number of times, and raised children—although he neither fathered nor bore these children. For readers who imagine his wives *must* have known, consider how well a person's modesty was respected at the time, and how a clever man—who was perhaps shy and liked the lights turned down—could pull off such a stunt. If you're still skeptical, or simply curious, the biography of Tipton's life, *Suits Me* (1998), would be a good place to start; it includes quotes from people who knew Billy well.

Some transgender people pass successfully for a time, only to be outed in their lifetimes. One of the beautiful women from the James Bond movies, Caroline "Tula" Cossey, worked as an actress and model until she was outed by the British press in the late 1980s. Watch *For Your Eyes Only*; can you pick out which Bond girl she is?

Overall, the second half of the twentieth century brought a greater openness to and visibility of gender-bending. Transvestism hit prime time, and in such a way that many viewers supported cross-dressing by TV characters. The character Corporal Klinger on *M★A★S★H* (1972–1983) dressed in women's clothes hoping for a Section 8 discharge from the military. Viewers knew his behavior only served to prove his sanity to the psychiatrist who periodically visited the 4077th Mobile Army Surgical Hospital near the Korean War front. In the early 1980s, *Bosom Buddies*, a popular television sitcom, featured two heterosexual, masculine young men who cross-dressed in order to secure housing. By the time the sitcom *Ally McBeal* hit the airwaves in 1997, the show starring a single lawyer with eccentric colleagues featured transgender characters who were "portrayed with understanding, pathos, and acceptance."[13]

By the 1990s, a full-scale gender revolution was under way. This is not to say that gender-bending and gender-blending were wholly accepted in society. With the publication of *Midnight in the Garden of Good and Evil* (1994)—a history of Savannah, Georgia—Lady Chablis (1957–2016) achieved national acclaim and a good measure of respect. Dr. Renée Richards, a world-class tennis player who competed as a woman following her transition, went on to have a successful career as an ophthalmic surgeon. Jennifer Finney Boylan, an English professor from Colby College, wrote of her transition in *She's Not There: A Life in Two Genders*. Even David Palmer, the former arranger and keyboard player for the 1970s band Jethro Tull, announced his gender switch after the death of his wife; in his mid-sixties, he became "Dee."[14]

On the islands of Hawaii, a cultural melting pot exists with Hawaiian, Filipino, Japanese, Chinese, Laotian, Portuguese, and Polynesian cultures as the basis, though the resulting mix has been heavily influenced by Western and Christian

Spoken Narratives: 'O Au No Keia by Andrew Matzner (2001)

'O Au No Keia: Voices from Hawaii's Mahu and Transgender Communities discusses the *mahu* and transgender communities of Hawaii. In his study, Matzner recorded oral narratives of some of Hawaii's contemporary male-to-female transgender persons. Each personal narrative begins with a photo of the speaker.

ways. The stories in Andrew Matzner's book (see above) reflect how these latter influences impacted the visibility of Hawaii's *mahu* population. The narratives relate not only each person's current reality but also much cultural history about the Hawaiian Islands.

At one time, Hawaiians viewed gender along a continuum that was inclusive of differences. They believed everyone is born androgynous and that as we mature either the male or the female side becomes stronger, more prominent—except in *mahu*, who develop their male and female strengths equally. Thus, the *mahu* were seen as strong people; they could do all the things that both men and women do and were not restricted by identifying with just one gender. Further, *mahu* were keepers of the culture. They knew its history and secrets; they knew where to find healing plants and how to appease the gods and goddesses. Western and Christian influences have since marginalized the *mahu* in Hawaii.

Memoir: Redefining Realness (2014) and Surpassing Certainty (2017)

For an in-depth view of one multi-racial transgender Hawaiian woman's experiences, read Janet Mock's memoirs. *Redefining Realness: My Path to Womanhood, Identity, Love, and So Much More* (2014) and *Surpassing Certainty: What My Twenties Taught Me* (2017) are openly candid explorations of Mock's experiences, including her insights about engaging in sex work as a means for survival for many impoverished transgender persons.

In Iran, where homosexuality is condemned by Islam and punished by lashing, transsexuals are gaining a level of acceptance with some Muslim clerics. In 1978, an early transsexual activist, Maryam Hatoon Molkara, who had previously been a man named Fereydoon, wrote a letter seeking religious guidance from the Ayatollah Ruhollah Khomeini. The ayatollah, who lived in exile at the time but later became the leader of the Islamic Revolution, replied that Molkara had his blessing as her case differed from that of a homosexual. Yet, when the revolution occurred in 1979, transgender and transsexual men were harassed, jailed, even tortured. Molkara was forbidden to continue dressing in women's clothes and was forced to take hormones to look like a man.

The Islamic government repressed transgender people for many years, but now Muslim clerics who dominate the judiciary are better informed and more accepting; some even recommend sexual reassignment surgery where they feel it is warranted. Even with supportive clerics, transgender people face numerous obstacles in the male-dominated society where many cannot understand why a man of social standing would seek to become a woman of lower social status. In Iran, the process of obtaining the proper documents for surgery and a new birth certificate is lengthy, requires the surgical candidate to carry a medical diagnosis of gender identity disorder, and is expensive, much as it is in the United States.[15]

In the traditionally patriarchal society of rural Albania and some parts of Bosnia and southern Serbia, where gender roles are inflexible, the practice of becoming "sworn virgins" is rooted in laws that date back to the fifteenth century. By traditional law, only men could own property and wives would become the husband's property upon marriage; however, becoming a sworn virgin allows a woman to live her life as a man, with the rights and privileges of a man. This is an important social role for families that do not have enough able-bodied men for the family to survive economically. Sworn virgins remain celibate throughout their lifetime, as the culture only recognizes traditional heterosexual relations. Life in the rural north is far removed from the bustling Albanian capital of Tirana, where

Explore Further: Women Who Become Men

Read about the sworn virgins of Eastern Europe in Antonia Young's *Women Who Become Men: Albanian Sworn Virgins (Dress, Body, Culture)* (2000). The National Geographic Channel followed Young in Albania for a segment of "Sexuality," a 2002 episode of the channel's series *Taboo*.

Explore Further: Trans People Who Paved the Way

The Massachusetts Transgender Political Coalition (MTPC) website offers a plethora of materials for those interested in transgender history. A sampling follows.

MPTC is part of the I AM: Trans People Speak project, which offers over sixty videos of trans people speaking about their lived experience. The videos run around five minutes in length. Visit www.transpeoplespeak.org/.

A 2014 blog post by Aaron, an MTPC intern, honors five black trans women important to trans history:[a]

- Lucy Hicks Anderson—Lucy was a pioneer in the fight for marriage equality.
- Carlett A. Brown—Carlett learned she was intersex during physical exams while serving in the US Navy in the 1950s.
- Sir Lady Java—Lady worked as a female impersonator in Los Angeles in the 1960s.
- Marsha P. Johnson—Marsha was one of the first instigators of the Stonewall Riots and a leader of the transgender community in Greenwich Village. Find a one-hour documentary about her life at www.youtube.com/watch?time_continue=188&v=rjN9W2KstqE.
- Miss Major Griffin-Gracy, better known as Miss Major—Miss Major was revered as a guiding elder of the transgender community and "one of the most significant pioneers of today's trans rights movement." *Major!* is a ninety-minute documentary about her life; it garnered nineteen festival awards and may be found on some streaming services. Learn more at www.missmajorfilm.com/.

Find the full blog post at www.masstpc.org/5-who-paved-the-way/.

women are becoming independent in such areas as their choice of career; in Tirana, the phrase *sworn virgin* is dimly recognized but has little meaning.[16]

Given the myriad social changes the world weathered during the twentieth century, the undercurrent of societal tension as the new millennium approached is understandable. Amid a flurry of media hype, messages of gloom and doom were broadcast. The "millennium bug" was said to be lying dormant in the world's computers, set to awake with the dawning of the new century. The forecast was grim. The bug could shut down our now-computerized society, causing home computers to crash and disabling networked systems the world over. Everything from transportation to power stations and hospital equipment was threatened, and individuals were urged to be prepared.

Gender beyond the Year 2000

Needless to say, the millennium bug did not cause the world's computers to crash. Traffic did not come to a standstill; life support systems continued sustaining life. Some of us who wondered if such a disaster was really possible may have felt a little foolish. Lives continued without disruption, as did societal change.

Explore Further: Transgender Politics

In 2004 the Democratic National Convention (DNC) made history when a contingent of openly transgender delegates attended the event in Boston, Massachusetts. Although one delegate had identified as such in the past, a contingent of five wore special DNC buttons incorporating a US flag, a Revolutionary War silhouette, and a prominently displayed transgender logo.

Fast forward to 2017, when at least twenty transgender candidates were running for office around the country, from local school board seats to state and national positions. According to Victory Fund president Aisha Moodie-Mills, "We have more transgender candidates running in this cycle than in almost all other cycles combined."[b]

To date, only two transgender candidates have been elected to the state legislature: Althea Garrison, elected in Massachusetts in 1992, and Stacie Laughton, who was elected to the New Hampshire State Legislature in 2012 but later resigned.[c]

Television Brings LGBT Characters into Our Living Rooms

In the twenty-first century, television shows, especially those available through cable and internet channels, embraced LGBTQ society. When *Queer Eye for the Straight Guy*, a Bravo reality series (2003–2007), introduced five stereotypical gay men who "made over" straight men by advising them on clothing, decorating, grooming, and more, the show gave millions of viewers opportunities to appreciate the artistic and aesthetic sensibilities from which gay male stereotypes have grown. The show's tag line was "Five gay men, out to make over the world—one straight guy at a time," and the campy, energetic team prided itself on turning one cisgender heterosexual male into a well-dressed, stylish, and cultured gentleman living in neat and attractive surroundings, within a sixty-minute time frame. An immediate hit, the show spawned international versions as well as a short-lived spinoff *Queer Eye for the Straight Girl*, and it garnered an Emmy Award for Outstanding Reality Program in 2004. After a ten-year hiatus, in 2017, Netflix announced plans to revive the show and has commissioned an eight-episode season focused in the southern states to "turn red states pink . . . one makeover at a time."[17]

Showtime's Canadian-American coproduced lesbian television drama *The L-Word* (2004–2009) brought the intertwined storylines of a set of Southern California lesbians to the screen. No longer did viewers need to guess at any character's sexual orientation, looking for a possible lesbian. *The L-Word* brought lesbian drama to television without question—out and proud. Only five years before the show's debut, its creator, Ilene Chaiken, had pitched such a similar show without receiving "a shred of receptivity" from potential producers. But the century turned and LGBT issues became visible—even hip. Rosie O'Donnell came out and Ellen DeGeneres became a daytime talk show host. From its first season, *The L-Word* was enormously popular, and Showtime continued it for six seasons. After that, *The L-Word* was picked up by Logo TV.[18]

In 2005, Viacom launched Logo TV, a satellite and digital cable television station catering to an LGBT audience,[19] although it broadened its base in 2012 to reach a more general audience. In 2009, cultural icon RuPaul, America's most famous drag queen, moved from simply stunning audiences as a hot, sexy woman to being the highly accomplished host of the LOGO multiseason reality competition *RuPaul's Drag Race*, which moved to VH1 in 2017 to reach a wider audience provided by the more mainstream network. While most of the contestants are cisgender men in drag, several are transgender women.

Also in 2005, the Sundance Channel premiered *TransGeneration*, an original documentary series following four transgender college students as they transition on campus. The premier and concluding episodes run an hour each, while the other six episodes run thirty minutes each. *TransGeneration* features two male-to-female students, Raci and Gabbie, and two female-to-male students, T.J. and Lucas. During the series, each student explains his or her personal struggle to find the appropriate gender identity and how family, friends, and the medical community fit into their lives. Directed by Jeremy Simmons and rated TV-14 for mild violence, adult language, and adult content, *TransGeneration* allows viewers to glimpse various aspects of life for transgender youth at college.

In 2013, Netflix introduced a comedy-drama about inmates in a women's federal correctional facility in upstate New York. *Orange Is the New Black* was well received from the moment it aired, fast becoming the platform's most-watched show ever. As a women-in-prison storyline, *Orange Is the New Black* may be perceived as a lesbian TV series—indeed, the *Advocate* magazine characterized it as possibly "the greatest lesbian TV series ever"—but the show's relevance here is that openly transgender actress Laverne Cox was hired to play the role of transgender character Sophia Burset. Speaking with the *Advocate*, Cox observed that her character had beautiful and rich storylines, unlike any she had seen a trans woman of color play on television before this show.[20]

In 2014, *Transparent*, a comedy-drama made for Amazon Studios changed the landscape for American viewers by providing a web-television series that focused around the title character of Maura Pfefferman, played by Jeffrey Tambor, a transgender parent—formerly known as Morton, or Mort—in the process of transitioning from male to female. The family's children, now grown, were raised by Mort and Shelly; although the couple divorced before the series opens, they remain amicable. Writer Jill Soloway changed the television studio landscape for the show's production, too—first by taping general-neutral signage over the male and female restroom signs and then by enacting a "transfirmative action program" wherein transgender candidates were preferentially hired over nontransgender applicants. By August 2014, "20 trans people had been hired in the cast and crew, and more than 60 had been employed as extras." In 2017, the show was in its fourth season and still going strong, only now it showcased the storylines of all members of a Jewish-American family which just happened to have a transgender parent in its midst.[21]

The CBS courtroom drama series *Doubt*, starring Laverne Cox as transgender lawyer Cameron Wirth, premiered in February 2017 only to be cancelled after the second episode due to poor ratings. Even so, the balance of the first season's thirteen episodes was aired during the 2017 summer season, during which time viewers were able to appreciate the show for being a solid courtroom drama. Before the show aired, CBS was proud of the show's diverse casting as being multicultural and multigenerational, reflecting a "broad swath of America." By playing the role of Cam, an "impressive lawyer with an Ivy League background," Cox became the first transgender actress to portray a trans character in a fixed role on a broadcast TV series.[22]

Transgender actress Laverne Cox, shown here in a promo for her show *Doubt. CBS / Photofest © CBS*

In June 2018, the series *Pose* premiered on FX, featuring five transgender women of color—Dominique Jackson, Mj Rodriguez, Indya Moore, Angelica Ross, and Hailie Sahar—and making history for having the largest transgender cast on TV.[23] Set in the 1980s, a decade shadowed by the scourge of AIDS, this ballroom drama focuses on the aspirations of its characters. According to one writer, *Pose* is a show that "demands to be seen" and that "puts its characters, subculture, and history stage center."[24] Translation: prepare to learn much about LGBTQ life during the '80s while watching *Pose*.

To keep abreast of all that's happening on television, surf over to the GLAAD (Gay and Lesbian Alliance Against Defamation) website (glaad.org) "every Sunday for up-to-date coverage in LGBTQ-inclusive programming on TV."[25] Of course, the GLAAD "must-see LGBTQ TV" feature would not have clued you in about watching the Miss Universe competition. Although transgender contestants have been allowed to compete since 2012, GLAAD could not have predicted that during the 2018 LGBTQ Pride month (June), twenty-five-year-old transsexual contestant Angela Ponce would be crowned Miss Universe Spain 2018. Catch a video round-up of her Miss Universe performance at www.youtube.com/watch?v=qHFOuN6k7EA.

Antitransgender Violence

In the twenty-first century across the United States, gender-bending is readily visible on high school and college campuses; guidelines are available for elementary, middle, and high school administrators and teachers that have students transitioning gender identities; and gender-bending can be found in towns and cities, stores and libraries. Yet, as normal as this appears to some Americans, numerous people are not yet accepting. Hate crimes are committed routinely against the LGBTQ community, and the most vicious attacks are often directed at transgender people, particularly transgender women of color.

The transgender murder rate has hit historical highs in recent years. Although numbers are difficult to identify and often vary from source to source, most likely the numbers collected are incomplete. A major reason behind such discrepancies is misgendering of victims in police reports, in news stories, and by family members. A 2015 report by the Human Rights Campaign identified that year as the deadliest on record for transgender people in the United States, stating that more transgender people were killed during the first half of 2015 than in all of 2014; the report included short biographies for each of the twenty-one victims counted by the time the report was published in early autumn.[26] The International Transgender Day of Remembrance website lists the names of persons who have died because of antitransgender violence, whose deaths could be confirmed by news stories in the

Personal Reflection: "I Am Trans," by Pamela

I am Trans.

I am alive and breathing.

I am not afraid or ashamed.

I am neither vulgar, disgusting, gross, perverse, nor a pedophile.

I think, feel, love, and toil, just like you.

I am not confused, or insane.

When I came out as me, all of my guilt, shame, and fear vanished.

I am Pam, and have always been.

I have not changed, you just know more about me now.

I am making my body and my life fit me as it never has before.

My feet are sure and strong, as I know that the road I trudge is the
right one.

I will not retreat, nor will I change course.

Whether I stand with a fist, or cry over foolish whims of fleeting, heart-
felt moments; I am real.

I am sensitive and compassionate, in my mind, heart, and soul.

My life is a journey, it is my journey.

We either walk forward, or we move back;

The only time we stand still, we are dead.

Please don't hate on me; I am good and decent people.

I am alive and breathing, as are you.

Please walk with me, or stand aside.

I will be your friend, if you will be mine.

My road is not easy, but it is worthy; As am I.

Celebrate as I emerge from my cocoon, and take flight.

I am Pam, and I am free.

Please take my hand, and walk a peace [*sic*] with me.[d]

media, and includes the cause of death for each homicide; the site does not include names of transgender individuals who died by suicide or as a result of domestic violence. The 2016 list includes eighty-seven names across nine countries—fifteen of whom were murdered in the United States, and sixty-five of whom were murdered in Brazil. (According to GLAAD, an LGBTQ media advocacy organization, twenty-seven—not fifteen—transgender people were murdered in the United States in 2016. A memorial page of the *Advocate* includes photographs of the victims and clarifies that two were not ruled homicides by police, yet family members remain adamant that their loved ones were murdered.)

The International Transgender Day of Remembrance website list for 2017 includes murders in twenty-two countries. Those countries with dozens murdered included the United States, for which the website lists 24 names; Mexico, for which the list includes 47 names; and Brazil, for which it includes 150 names. The *Advocate* memorial page for 2017 includes photographs and bios of twenty-three transgender persons murdered; the Human Rights Campaign Fund lists names and brief statements for twenty-six transgender persons murdered in the United States in 2017.

To be transgender in the United States, particularly to be a transgender woman of color, is to live knowing that your life is less valued by many and reviled by some. The statistics support this fact. Fear, hate, and prejudice combined with a culture that accepts violence against LGBTQ persons allows perpetrators to turn their demonization of these individuals into a perceived license to kill. Currently, transgender people are being killed in the United States at a rate of at least one every two weeks, and the vast majority of the victims are transgender women of color. Transgender Day of Remembrance, celebrated on November 20, provides an occasion to honor those who have been murdered.

In Memoriam: Transgender Day of Remembrance

The Transgender Day of Remembrance (TDoR) is meant to memorialize persons who were murdered due to antitransgender hate or prejudice. TDoR began as a candlelight vigil in San Francisco in 1999 in honor of Rita Hester, who was murdered on November 28, 1998. Now observed annually on November 20 in cities around the globe, the day allows people to remember and honor the transgender victims lost to senseless, often brutal, violence over the prior year. To find locations for the current year's celebrations visit www.facebook.com/transdayofremembrance/; myriad local groups link their TDoR events to the Transgender Day of Remembrance Facebook page. Rita Hester's murder, like most antitransgender murder cases, has yet to be solved.[e]

LGBT Rights and Political Activism, 1900–Present

In 1949, Dr. D. O. Cauldwell coined the word *transsexualism*, but Dr. Harry S. Benjamin, a New York sexologist and endocrinologist, popularized the word. When Benjamin's book *The Transsexual Phenomenon* was published in 1966, few medical professionals had experience working with transsexualism. Benjamin and his colleague Wardell Pomeroy categorized transvestites separately from transsexuals. Further, Benjamin treated his transsexual patients with hormone therapy to help bring their bodies in line with their gender identities. In 1969 he was recognized as the "grandfather of transsexualism" and honored for his work in the field through the naming of the Harry Benjamin International Gender Dysphoria Association (HBIGDA).[27]

Also in 1969, the Stonewall Riots in New York's Greenwich Village marked the birth of gay activism. Before that, LGBTQ rights were not taken seriously. Homosexual and transgender people were oppressed and marginalized by mainstream society. The riots began on June 27, 1969, when police raided the Stonewall, a gay bar. This time, the patrons did not go quietly; they fought back! When the tactical patrol force arrived, marching together to break up the crowd, it was greeted by a kick-dancing chorus line of transvestites (the terminology then used

Facade of the Stonewall Inn at 53 Christopher Street in New York City, the site of the Stonewall Riots on June 27–29, 1969, and a catalyst for the gay liberation movement. In 2000, the Inn was designated a national historic landmark. © iStock / blackwaterimages

for transgender women and men in drag) singing, "We are the Stonewall Girls, we wear our hair in curls . . . ," a surprising sight. The rioting continued for multiple nights, as increasing numbers of protesters arrived to add their voices to the fray. From this revolution, the gay liberation movement was born.

Although the Stonewall Girls may have kicked off gay liberation efforts, gains in gay rights do not necessarily include similar gains for transgender individuals. Take the issue of gay marriage, for example. A 1993 decision by the Hawaii Supreme Court ruling that a same-sex marriage ban was unconstitutional led to questions about whether all states would have to honor same-sex unions formed in Hawaii. In a move to protect the rights of individual states, President Bill Clinton enacted the federal Defense of Marriage Act (DOMA) in 1996. DOMA not only enabled states to individually decide whether to recognize same-sex unions, but also it defined marriage as only between one man and one woman for the purposes of federal programs and benefits. Attempting to take this stance even further, in 2002 the second Bush administration proposed a Federal Marriage Amendment to the United States Constitution, which failed to pass. After same-sex marriage was legalized in Massachusetts in 2004, individual states flocked to the polls to pass ballot measures either legalizing same-sex unions or defining marriage as only legal between one man and one woman. Eventually, DOMA was overturned in 2015 during the Obama administration. Throughout the evolution of same-sex unions, transgender persons fell under the LGBT umbrella without benefitting directly unless involved in same-gender-loving relationships. Even so, the gay and trans communities continue to unite for the benefit of either or both groups.

Transgender people often live on the margins of society and experience far greater discrimination than do lesbian, gay, or bisexual people with regard to education, employment, housing, health care, and more. In 2005, the TransJustice arm of the Audre Lourde Project, a lesbian, gay, bisexual, two-spirit, trans, and gender nonconforming people of color center for community organizing, created the Trans Day of Action (TDoA) for Social and Economic Justice. This march, held annually during Pride Month in Washington Square Park in New York City, seeks to do more than simply honor and remember the dead. They celebrate those who are alive and urge action for justice for the living. Further, the day is rooted in challenging white supremacy and police violence. The Points of Unity developed by TransJustice for the 2008 TDoA include demands on the behalf of transgender and gender nonconforming persons of color to end police profiling, harassment, and violence; to have equal access to employment and educational opportunities; to have respectful and safe housing; and to have access to health care.[28]

GLAAD, an organization of writers formed in the 1980s in response to virulently defamatory writing in the age of AIDS, works to increase acceptance of the LGBTQ community in the media. Since the early 2000s GLAAD has included

Documentary Miniseries: When We Rise (2017)

When We Rise is an eight-hour miniseries chronicling the personal stories and political struggles of a variety of LGBT persons who "helped pioneer one of the last legs of the US civil rights movement from its turbulent infancy in the 20th century to the once unfathomable successes of today."

Episodes can be streamed via Amazon and other sites.

transgender people on staff. A recent Harris Poll found that while 16 percent of Americans report knowing someone who is transgender, including 27 percent of Millennials, only 9 percent of respondents over the age of forty-five claim this. Citing this poll, the organization believes that most Americans learn about transgender people through the media. GLAAD works with the media to ensure that transgender people are represented fairly and accurately in newspapers and magazines, on television, and in movies. If you witness defamation of transgender people in the media, online, or at a live event, such as at a concert, game, or performance, GLAAD has an online form where you can report the incident and it will follow up. Visit www.glaad.org/reportdefamation.

In 2009, a Colorado jury determined that the murder of eighteen-year-old transwoman Angie Zapata was a hate crime. Although the hate crime conviction in Colorado only added three years to the sentence, the conviction of first-degree murder carried a sentence of life without parole. The application of the hate crimes law in this case marked a milestone along the journey toward equal rights for transgender people.[29] Later that same year, President Obama signed into law the Matthew Shepard and James Byrd Jr. Hate Crimes Prevention Act, extending the coverage of the federal hate crimes law to include attacks based on the victim's actual or perceived sexual orientation or gender identity.[30]

Although in 2010, President Obama signed the bipartisan legislation repealing Don't Ask Don't Tell, effectively allowing lesbian, gay, and bisexual Americans to serve openly in the military, it took another five years for the Pentagon "to consider allowing openly transgender service members." In September 2016, the Defense Department outlined its new policy on service by transgender persons in a seventy-two-page handbook titled *Transgender Service in the U.S. Military*. That same month, Blake Dremann, an openly transgender service member, was

It Gets Better

LGBT youth are at greater risk for suicide than the mainstream population. Being different is difficult, and youth who are perceived as being different are often teased and bullied for these differences. A series of videos has been created to encourage LGBT youth, especially those contemplating suicide, that it does get better; all of the following can be viewed on YouTube.

- President Obama's "It Gets Better" video message delivered from the White House
- An LGBT tribute video titled "It Gets Better, I Promise"
- The It Gets Better Project's YouTube channel devoted to "It Gets Better" video messages
- The L Studio's entire online docuseries of "It Got Better" videos posted with the It Gets Better Project
- The "5 Years Better" series, another set of videos posted in conjunction with the It Gets Better Project

If you only have five minutes to spare and want to know if it does, truly, get better, check out Ryan Cassata's video under the "5 Years Better" series. Ryan was a transgender high school student when the It Gets Better Project first appeared in 2010. His "Did 'It' Get Better?" video is an uplifting message promising that, yes, it does get better.

promoted from navy lieutenant to lieutenant commander. He was the first openly trans service member to be promoted.

In schools, and elsewhere, LGBTQIA students are at risk for bullying that may result in depression and attempted suicide. During the Obama administration, the Department of Health and Human Services collaborated with other departments to establish a federal task force on bullying. One of the outgrowths of this collaboration was a website—www.StopBullying.gov—which includes resources and assistance for LGBT youth. One of the outcomes of the first ever White House Conference on Bullying Prevention was the "It Gets Better" video wherein the president addresses LGBT youth who have been bullied or are at risk for suicide.

Attorney General Eric Holder directed the Department of Justice, in 2014, to include gender identity when considering cases of sex discrimination in employment. Title VII of the 1964 Civil Rights Act made it illegal for employers (at companies with fifteen or more employees) to discriminate against employees "because of sex." Attorney General Holder's memo reversed an earlier departmental decision that had excluded gender identity and transgender discrimination from the Title VII protections.[31] This landmark decision was reversed by Attorney General Jeff Sessions, under the Trump administration, in 2017.

Under the Obama administration, 2015 was a banner year for transgender issues in American politics. In his State of the Union address in January, President Obama mentioned transgender people—something no previous president had done. In July, the Pentagon announced plans to reverse its ban on transgender people being allowed to serve in the military. In August, openly transgender Raffi Freedman-Gurspan was appointed to serve as the president's outreach and recruitment director, making her the White House's first openly transgender appointee.[32] But politics and progress often move as with a pendulum, achieving gains for one side and then swinging to the other—before shifting again.

Whereas in 2016, candidate Trump made a show of inviting openly transgender Caitlyn Jenner to use any bathroom she so desired in Trump Tower, when President Trump took office in 2017, his campaign reassurances of being a friend to the LGBT community vanished. He set about reversing the gains made under the Obama administration. As has happened throughout history, those being targeted fought back and by mid-July *Time* magazine ran an article asking, "Will 2017 Be the Year of the Transgender Candidate?" In it, writer Emma Talkoff reported that the Trans United political organization estimated that over twenty openly transgender people were running for public office across the country.[33] A year after President Trump was elected, a plethora of candidates made history as political "firsts," being elected to positions such as city council, school board, state congress, and mayor.[34]

More milestones in the advancement of transgender visibility have been reached than are included here, many of them in the twenty-first century. With the help of the media, transgender visibility has increased markedly in America

---

Be Aware

Ask yourself: in failing to recognize trans people in history, or in underreporting contributions of LGBTQIA people, does our educational system discriminate against this marginalized segment of our society? As you learn more about underreported persons or groups—LGBTQIA, Native American, anyone of non-European descent—consider sharing your knowledge when the situation allows. You can help create a better-informed society.

over the past decade, and while acceptance has lagged behind this prominence—particularly among older Americans—Millennials and members of Generation Z will shape a more accommodating country. Even as the Trump administration reverses advances made by its predecessor, recent election results prove that it cannot reverse all of the gains made in public opinion. As your own awareness of transgender and gender nonconforming communities and issues grows, you can be a part of the change.

TERMINOLOGY

What Do All Those Words Mean?

The greater knowledge one has of a particular subject, the greater will be his, her, or their grasp of any associated vocabulary. It makes sense that people who have greater experience with variations of gender will have a vocabulary that extends beyond *he* and *she*, *tomboy* and *sissy*. While exploring language, remember that some words carry with them emotional aspects and some can be perceived as hurtful—even when the speaker has no intention to hurt.

Words can be used to build up or tear down the thoughts, actions, or existence of others. Language evolves in response to the knowledge and needs of its users. Over the past decade, since the first edition of this book was written, the language of gender has experienced significant changes. The media has given attention to gender identity, sexual orientation, and intersex issues while managing to avoid dwelling upon many of the finer details of the evolution of language. Indeed, the language of gender identity and personal pronouns managed to evolve significantly—and mostly outside of the mainstream public eye.

In exploring the language of gender identity, let's start with pronouns.

Pronouns

We're all familiar with the masculine and feminine pronouns *he* and *she*, *his* and *her*. Until recently, using *they* and *their* as singular pronouns was considered grammatically incorrect. Until the advent of the first female-authored English grammar book in the eighteenth century, *they* was acceptable as a singular pronoun. Indeed, that grammar book, written by a British schoolmistress and feminist, appears to have been the catalyst for moving English away from using *they* and *their* as singular pronouns and was the impetus behind the use of masculine language as a catchall for *anybody*.[1] Then, in the late-twentieth century, using the term *men* to mean "both men and women" fell out of favor when the feminist movement of the day promoted a shift from such words as *chairman* (or *chairwoman*) to *chairperson*. Confusing though it may be, language does change with the times.

As our culture grew more sensitive to issues of gender bias and to the fact that gender identities exist beyond the simple binary of male and female, alternative pronouns surfaced. In 2014, Facebook offered over fifty choices for gender in one's profile—male, female, and custom—the last of which had a drop-down menu with many choices. By 2016, the Gender category was simplified so that "custom" allows users to write in their gender identity and to specify their personal pronouns.

Pronouns have evolved beyond *she*, *he*, and *they*. Some persons in the trans community prefer the gender-neutral pronouns *hir*, *xe*, *xyr*, *ze* (or *zee*), or *they*. *Hir* and *xyr* are gender-neutral replacements for *her* and *him*, and *xe* and *ze* are gender-neutral replacements for *he* and *she*. Author Leslie Feinberg credits the internet as being the birthplace for both *hir* and *ze*.[2] A decade later, I had a young friend go away to college and come home with both *hir* and *ze* as part of her working vocabulary. Now, universities are posting guides to pronouns because the topic has become far more complex than her/hers and him/his. Search online and you will not only find more variations than are included here, but also you will find that pronoun guides differ one from another. The result can be mind-boggling.

Preferred gender pronouns (PGPs) are important to learn and use correctly. Indeed, in the years since the first edition of this book was published, the standard "Hello, my name is . . ." name tags have grown to include "My pronouns are . . . ," and signature blocks on emails, which routinely include the sender's name and possibly title and/or contact information, now often include a line for the sender's PGPs.

Some will take issue with the use of "preferred" here because it implies choice or other options. For example, I am a woman who was raised using *she/her/hers* pronouns. On the occasions when my hair has been quite short, I have sometimes been referred to using male pronouns, but doing so was incorrect. Generally, one's gender pronouns are fixed and stable; however, one who identifies as gender fluid may have pronouns that change over time—even on a daily basis—and may require your checking in with that person to determine what pronouns they wish you to use. For the vast majority of the population, pronouns will remain stable. As such, although PGPs are important, try referring to them as personal pronouns, rather than preferred pronouns. The acronym PGP also works when referring to personal gender pronouns.

How can one best determine which pronouns to use? Ask. Of course, use discretion when asking. By this I mean, do not potentially out a person in the middle of a group by asking about pronouns out of the blue. When introducing yourself to someone new, try saying, "Hi, I'm [insert your name here]. My pronouns are [insert your pronouns here]." Also, if you find that you have misgendered someone by using an incorrect pronoun, simply apologize, correct yourself, and move on. Dwelling on the mistake or apologizing profusely can be unproductive and may make the misgendered person uncomfortable. Amid the growing diversity of personal pronouns, all one can do is pay attention, be considerate, and try one's best to honor another's pronouns.

Also, realize that not every person will be comfortable sharing pronoun preferences. This is a valid response. You need not question why the person chooses to not provide pronouns. Although having pronoun choices specified makes conversation simpler, honor the decision of the person who chooses to provide none by not using pronouns to refer to that person. Referring to persons without using pronouns is possible, if cumbersome.

Consider the examples in table 4.1. The table provides a few of the more common personal pronouns in use among LGBT and gender-nonconforming communities today—and the correct way to use them. Although one may be

Table 4.1. Pronouns

he	He ran.	I saw him.	His hand waves.	That is his.	He washes himself.
she	She ran.	I saw her.	Her hand waves.	That is hers.	She washes herself.
it	It ran.	I saw it.	Its hand waves.	That is its.	It washes itself.
one	One ran.	I saw one.	One's hand waves.	That is one's.	One washes oneself.
they (singular)	They ran.	I saw them.	Their hand waves.	That is theirs.	They washes themself.
ze, hir	Ze ran.	I saw hir.	Hir hand waves.	That is hirs.	Ze washes hirself.
ze, zir	Ze ran.	I saw zir/zem.	Zir/Zes hand waves.	That is zirs/zes.	Ze washes zirself.

> ## Personal Pronouns on YouTube
>
> Lest the influx of gender-neutral personal pronouns overwhelm you, YouTube is here to help! In the first video, *Seventeen* magazine puts faces to the issue, personalizing it. The second video introduces Ash Hardell, an incredibly sincere, enthusiastic genderqueer/nonbinary twenty-something whose common-sense advice may strike viewers as so appropriate that the viewer may wonder why that nugget of knowledge is actually new to him, her, or them.
>
> - "Why Gender Pronouns Matter," www.youtube.com/watch?v=9iKHjl5xAaA.
> - "All About PRONOUNS!" www.youtube.com/watch?v=4NcMV5dsmgl.

more likely to encounter them commonly on college campuses and in LG-BTQIA+ settings, news stories of kindergartens discussing transgender identities are now easy to find online.

Prefixes

Prefixes vibrantly flavor the meaning of simple root words. Whereas *homo-* means "the same" or "equal," *hetero-* indicates "other" or "different." Thus, a homosexual is primarily interested, sexually, in his, her, or hir own gender, while a heterosexual is primarily interested, sexually, in a partner of another or a different sex. The prefix *bi-* indicates "two," so a bisexual is interested in partners of both sexes—and, yes, this prefix presupposes the gender binary system. In a world where the boy-girl dichotomy rules, one might imagine that these three prefixes could cover the possibilities. Not so. Indeed, some persons are *omnisexual*, sexually interested in any partner (from *omni-* meaning "all"). And, while *asexual* is generally used as a biology term to indicate the absence of reproductive sexuality, when a person calls him-, her-, or hirself *asexual*, the speaker probably means that he, she, or ze has no interest in sexual coupling whatsoever; the asexual are sexually disinterested.

When the preceding prefixes are connected with *sexual*, they refer to one's interest in or choice of sexual companion or partner. The prefixes *inter-* or *trans-* paired with words like *sexual*, on the other hand, refer to the sex assigned based on the shape of one's genitals. The prefix *inter-* indicates being between or among something. For instance, you're familiar with the word *interstate*. The interstate highway system runs between and among states; it includes more than one state. Similarly, an *intersexual* has a body residing between male and female; it includes more than one sex. See chapter 5, "Boy or Girl? Delivery Room Decisions and Intersex Bodies," for more about intersex.

Conversely, the prefix *trans-* before a noun indicates that it is across, beyond, or on the other side of where it began. Sticking with the travel analogy, a trans-continental flight or train trip is one that crosses the continent. *Transsexual* refers to one's sex as crossing from what one was (or is) to what one is (or wishes to be). Thus "trans" or "crossing" sexual lines covers a wealth of differences. Although some people try to simplify matters by using *transgender* for a person who feels he, she, or they is the sex opposite the one assigned at birth and *transsexual* for one who has undergone gender reassignment surgery, the language is murkier than that. Someone who has male genitalia but feels female inside, yet has no intention of making a surgical change, or any change for that matter, may call themselves *transsexual*, for such a person does cross the lines of sexual identity. To determine how any person wishes to be identified, listen closely to how that person identifies hirself, and then model your language to the occasion. Other terms you might encounter to describe one who crosses gender lines and who may or may not identify as transgender or transsexual could include *gender nonconforming*, *genderqueer* or *gender queer*, and *nonbinary* or *non-binary*.

In the transgender community, words such as *transman* or *transwoman* may be used to indicate someone who has crossed into a male or female identity. Another term you may encounter for one who has crossed into a male identity is *boi* (the

What's in a Name?

Our name is our identity. Addressing someone by the wrong name accidentally can be embarrassing for the person speaking. If the person being addressed is transgender and has changed the name chosen by that person's parents, being addressed by the wrong name may "out" them as trans. Purposefully addressing a transgender individual by that birth name is hurtful—and worse. In the wrong setting, misnaming to out a person can put that individual in danger of ridicule and even physical violence. See chapter 3, "Trans History through the Ages and across Cultures," for more about violence against trans people. Using the name assigned to a trans person at birth, or their "dead name," is also called dead-naming. Not only does it open the trans person to the reactions of those within earshot, but also it can trigger gender dysphoria—feelings of extreme discomfort. Respect who a person is today. Use the individual's chosen name.

plural of which is *bois*). Not limited to trans culture, *boi* may be making its way into mainstream culture. In the June/July 2004 *Jane* magazine, bois are listed as one of "six types of guys" that are recommended to women seeking dates.[3] That issue of *Jane* also includes a personal essay titled "My Boyfriend Used to Be My Girlfriend" in its It Happened to Me column. Beyond simply the language, the awareness of the trans community is filtering into mainstream culture.

One way writers represent persons who fall under the trans umbrella is to use *trans*★ because the asterisk allows representation of the variety of identities across the transgender spectrum. *Trans*★ can include cross-dressers, drag kings and drag queens, and those who otherwise identify as transgender and gender nonconforming.

Another prefix pertinent to the discussion of gender is *cis-*. Just as *trans-* indicates something across, beyond, or on the other side of, *cis-* indicates on this side, or on the same side. Thus, a *cisgender* individual is one who is on the same side of the gender from whence that soul began, or one who has not changed genders. Although the majority of persons are cisgender, the assumption that people are all cisgender—an assumption that normalizes cisness to the exclusion of trans-ness—is cisnormative. Cisnormativity is to be avoided in that is marginalizes those who are not cisgender.

! Be Aware: Word Choices Supporting the Gender Binary

Cisgender need not be limited to the gender binary. In *Born Both: An Intersex Life* (2017), author and intersex activist Hida Viloria, points out that an unaltered intersex person is also cisgender. Case in point: her body is literally both male and female, yet she is a cisgender intersex person because she was born intersex and her body is unaltered. If you notice the female pronouns, understand they are used because *she/her/hers* are Viloria's pronouns. Although she is cisgender, Viloria is also a nonbinary person, an identity considered transgender. As it is used today, *cisgender* usually only considers male and female; when you hear someone using the word *cisgender*, the underlying gender binary can be assumed.

In her 2014 essay "Caught in the Gender Binary Blind Spot: Intersex Erasure in Cisgender Rhetoric," Viloria addresses how the word *cisgender*, especially when linked to the notion of a "sex assigned at birth," serves to deny the existence of intersex variations—thus erasing the existence of intersex people. When focusing on language, it helps to be fully aware of the meanings of the words we use.[a]

Table 4.2. Prefixes

Prefix	Meaning	Examples
a-	not, without	agender, asexual, aromantic
bi-	two	binary gender system, bisexual
cis-	on this side	cisgender, cissexual
demi-	half, partially	demisexual
hetero-	the opposite	heteronormative, heterosexual
homo-	the same	homophobic, homosexual
inter-	crossing between	intersex
omni-	all	omnisexual
pan-	all	pansexual, panromantic
poly-	many, multiple, several	polyamorous, polygamous
trans-	across, beyond, through	transgender, transphobic, transsexual

Table 4.2 provides several prefixes often used in conjunction with sex, gender identity, sexual orientation, or romantic inclination. How cool is it to be able to change or amplify the meaning of a root word simply by adding a prefix? Or, for that matter, a suffix?

Suffixes

Beyond the impact of various prefixes on the words they modify, words can be equally impacted by the addition of a suffix. Since an important aspect of transgender or transsexual life may include surgical changes to the body, one cannot overlook the suffixes *-ectomy* and *-plasty*.

The suffix *-ectomy* indicates the removal of some part of the body through surgery. When a tonsillectomy is performed, a person's tonsils are removed.

Hysterectomy refers to the removal of female sex organs. Transsexual surgery—often called gender confirmation surgery (GCS), gender reassignment surgery (GRS), or sexual reassignment surgery (SRS)—may include the removal of some body part(s).

GCS may also include the creation of body part(s). The suffix -*plasty* is related to *plastic*, meaning "malleable," and indicates formation or creation of some part of a body through surgery. When undergoing transsexual surgery, the body changes from one sex to another. In *vaginoplasty*, a vagina is constructed where one did not exist previously. Similarly, *phalloplasty* indicates surgical construction of a penis. More information about surgical changes appears in chapter 7, "Transformations."

Acronyms

Acronyms—abbreviations formed using selected letters or parts of words or phrases and then used as words themselves—abound in the world, and can be confusing. Indeed, long acronyms that do not form pronounceable words, like LGBTQIA+, are sometimes disparagingly referred to as alphabet soup. Yet, acronyms make lengthy oft-repeated phrases much simpler for speakers, writers, and readers because an acronym communicates a whole chunk of information in a shorter form.

The acronym GSA, which stands for Gay-Straight Alliance, is heard on many secondary school and college campuses. The concept of the Gay-Straight Alliance was developed before someone thought to make the name more inclusive. Although today such alliance groups are more inclusive, the acronym GSA is often still used to refer to a group of persons of varying sexual orientations and gender identities or preferences banding together with allies to discuss issues of sexuality and gender. One important aspect of GSAs is the inclusive nature of the group; one need not have any specific sexual orientation, or gender identity or expression, to join a GSA. Groups eschewing the binary language of the GSA nametag have used such identifiers as Pride Club, Queer Students Alliance, and Genders and Sexualities Alliance.

As political correctness impacts language and awareness of the diversity of sexual orientations and gender identities grows, the string of letters used as an acronym to represent this diverse community grows. In the 1980s what was once referred to as "the gay community" began to appear more often as the gay, lesbian, and bisexual (or, as an acronym, the GLB) community. Then, transgender got added and references to GLBT appeared. At some point the *GL* ordering of the acronym was swapped out for *LG*, possibly as a chivalrous nod to "ladies first." When *Q* was added to represent those who identify as queer—in either sexual orientation or gender identity—another *Q* was added to represent those who question their sexual orientation or gender identity. The addition of *I* for intersex introduced the category of sex variations beyond the strict binary to the growing acronym. As of this writing, those who are asexual or aromantic may also be included in this acronym. Often one will encounter the acronym LGBT+. The plus sign allows speakers and writers to be more concise while continuing to imply inclusion. Groups not yet specifically incorporated into the LGBTQIA+ acronym, yet represented by the +, include nonbinary and gender-nonconforming persons.

This conflating of groups into one community is deceptive. While those included do represent minority groups, no LGBTQQIAA community exists. Indeed, the issues faced by one group may be vastly different from those faced by another, although all are lumped under the same umbrella. Also, members of one group may resent being lumped together with other groups, or may feel they do not belong under the extra-large LGBTQQIAA umbrella. Understand that LGBT+ may represent certain political interests, but that the alphabet soup of an acronym does not represent a single, unified community. See table 4.3 for a summary of the current LGBT+ acronyms.

Another acronym gaining ground to describe trans people is TGNC for transgender and gender nonconforming. This acronym also includes persons who identify as nonbinary and genderqueer or gender fluid. The TGNC umbrella covers persons who do not conform to societal gender expectations, yet who may not identify as transgender. TGNC persons are included under the LGBT+ umbrella.

Recently, an acronym surfaced that could eventually replace the entire LGBTQQIA string. SGM stands for sexual and gender minority. These three letters form a wide umbrella. Sexual minorities include lesbian, gay, bisexual, queer (as it refers to lesbian, gay, bisexual), questioning, and asexual persons. Gender minorities include transgender, genderqueer or gender nonconforming, and intersex persons. Although SGM is an efficient acronym, covering much territory without resorting to alphabet soup, the ever-changing LGBT acronym has been in use long enough to be entrenched in public consciousness. Stay alert for references to SGM in the media, around your school, and in your community. Should you hear others asking, "What's that?" with regard to SGM references, you can be the person with the answer!

As noted earlier, surgical gender change can be represented by assorted acronyms. Whether you see the acronym GCS, GRS, or SRS, each refers to the surgical process of changing sex or gender. The first letter of these acronyms—*G* or *S*—either represents *gender*, *genital*, or *sex*. The middle letter—*C* or *R*—can represent *confirmation*, *reassignment*, or *reconstruction*. The last letter, *S*, represents *surgery*. The word choices are personal, but the result is the same. A person who has undergone such surgery has surgically altered their body to reflect their true self.

Table 4.3. Terms in the Current LGBT+ Acronyms

L	lesbian	sexual orientation
G	gay	sexual orientation
B	bisexual	sexual orientation
T	transgender	gender identity
Q	queer	sexual orientation or gender identity
Q	questioning	sexual orientation or gender identity
I	intersex	biological sex
A	asexual	sexual attraction
A	aromantic	romantic attraction
+	plus	The + indicates inclusion of groups not noted in the written acronym, allowing users to be inclusive and concise. Thus, LGBT+ implies inclusion of LGBTQQIAA and others.
TGNC	transgender and gender nonconforming	gender identity; GNC has not (yet) been incorporated into the LGBT+ acronym and can be assumed to be represented by the +
SGM	sexual and gender minority	*sexual minority* refers to lesbian, gay, bisexual, queer, questioning, and asexual persons; *gender minority* refers to transgender, genderqueer, gender nonconforming, and intersex persons

Another surgical gender change represented by an acronym is intersex genital mutilation, often referred to simply as IGM. Briefly, these are surgeries performed upon infants whose genitals do not conform to the anticipated standard, the goal of which is to create bodies that appear to fit the expectation for either male or female. See chapter 5 for more about intersex variations.

Perhaps the simplest, most straightforward of the acronyms associated with gender identity are those indicating a gender change. When a biologically male person presents as female, hir gender change is *male to female*, represented by the acronym MTF or sometimes M2F. Similarly, the genetic female who presents as a male is called *female to male* (FTM, F2M). Throughout this book, readers will find both the MTF and FTM acronyms.

Finally, the "Resources" section at the end of this text includes acronyms after the names of many organizations. Acronyms are to phrases or organization names what instant messaging (yes, IMing) is to written communication. Those of us who still prize the postal letter find that occasions for using it continue to diminish under the reign of technology.

Phobias

While fears, large and small, can often be dispelled through education, fear itself often bars the way to education. *The New Shorter Oxford English Dictionary* defines *phobia* as "(a) fear, (a) horror, (an) aversion; especially an abnormal or irrational fear or dread aroused by a particular object or circumstance" and defines the suffix *-phobia* as "denoting (especially irrational) fear, dislike, [or] antipathy."[4] Note that both definitions hinge upon the use of the word *irrational*. Education is key to assuaging such deep-seated fears.

In *Families Like Mine*, author Abigail Garner takes the word *homophobia*, fear of homosexual people, to another level by identifying two levels of homophobia.[5] According to Garner, homophobes (people with homophobia) are either "homo-hesitant" or "homo-hostile," which is an important distinction. Homo-hesitant people are unsure where they stand on gay issues, probably because they are uninformed about them. When educated, these people could become allies for the LGBT+ community—or not. Homo-hesitant people may overcome their hesitancy when they learn more about gays, possibly by realizing just how many people they already know and accept are gay. On the other hand, homo-hostile people harbor a strong dislike for or even a revulsion toward gays. Homo-hostile people can be dangerous to persons they perceive to be gay—even if the target of their hostility is not actually gay. Homo-hostile people murdered the following individuals, and many others:

- Brandon Teena—a transman who lived to age twenty-one, and upon whose life and tragic death the 1999 movie *Boys Don't Cry* was based.
- Matthew Shepard—the twenty-one-year-old gay male University of Wyoming student whose ghastly murder, one of the worst anti-gay hate crimes in American history, became the basis for the stage play *The Laramie Project*.

- Gwen Arujo—the seventeen-year-old transgender girl who was beaten and strangled at a party after four intoxicated men determined that she was biologically male and upon whose life the 2006 television drama *A Girl Like Me: The Gwen Arujo Story* is based.

Homo-hostile people may feel justified in their disdain for people who are not "natural" or "normal," which includes LGBTQ people in their eyes. They seem to have no trouble using slurs or derogatory language to describe those whom they disdain.

Derogatory or Pejorative Words

Language used to hurt others, or derogatory language, twists the meaning of a word to make it pejorative. For example, when I refer to the gay community, meaning the LGBT+ community, the reference is positive, but someone who sneers and says, "That's so gay!" is slurring the meaning of the word. The speaker, when confronted, may deny intent to hurt homosexuals or those who care about them. Allowing even casually spoken slurs to go unchallenged sends a message of acceptance for such language and attitudes. While it may seem like a minor issue, voicing objections to such intolerant language is one step in the path toward reducing antigay or gender-based violence.

Speaking out against pejorative language need not be complicated. Simply informing the speaker that the negative or belittling language has been heard and is not appreciated conveys the message that "That's so gay!" might be a phrase the speaker should reconsider before using. Responses as plain as "Don't say that," "That's not cool," or "I don't appreciate it when you say that" alerts a speaker that such language is not acceptable.

Almost any word can be used pejoratively. Tone of voice conveys as much information as the word itself—sometimes more. Words that are meant to hurt, such as *faggot*, *queer*, and *dyke*, can be adopted by the group they were initially intended to hurt. When the targeted group takes ownership of and pride in the words, this is called "taking back the language." An excellent example of this appears in the title story on the young adult anthology *Am I Blue?* The story "Am I Blue?" features a character named Melvin, who was the victim of a fatal gay-bashing incident and now works as a fairy godfather. At one point Melvin explains how he landed his current job saying, "I didn't want to be anyone's guardian angel. . . . People had been calling me a fairy all my life, and now that I was dead, that was all I wanted to be."[6] Melvin does more than take back the language for a one-time use—he assumes it as his identity and employment.

> ⚠️ **Be Aware: *Use Another Word***
>
> ● The Safe Schools Coalition, an organization that works to make schools safe spaces for learning and teaching, has a brief document archived on its site about the Use Another Word campaign waged at Springfield High School in Springfield, Oregon, in 2006–2007. The study documents how a gentle use of positive reinforcement to "use another word" in place of slurs like *gay* and *fag* resulted in a campus where such slurs were heard less often. While the document isn't a manual, with a little research you could use this information to craft a similar campaign at your school.
>
> Get your copy at www.safeschoolscoalition.org/UseAnotherWord.pdf

Symbols

Symbols, or logos, use an image to represent an idea. Just as acronyms use letters to represent a phrase, visual symbols use images to convey a concept. Think of the Nike logo, that simple quasi-checkmark, or swoosh, that represents a huge company and its products, and even says something about the people who use them. The LGBT+ community also employs images to convey ideas. For example, it adopted the rainbow to represent the inclusion of diversity. Of course, other groups use the rainbow symbol. Indeed, in the story of Genesis, God sent a rainbow to Noah after the flood as a sign (or flag) of a covenant that another worldwide flood would not occur. In the late twentieth century, a movement that combined identity politics and economic struggle branded itself the Rainbow Coalition to signify its diverse nature.[7] The concept of accepting and celebrating diversity is embraced by a number of movements.

In 1978, Gilbert Baker stitched together the first gay pride flag in San Francisco.[8] Since the advent of the rainbow flag to represent the gay community, other groups within the gender and sexuality spectrum have developed flags. The transgender flag was created in 1999 by Monica Helms, a US Navy veteran who advocates for transgender rights and visibility, especially in the military. Helms created the transgender pride flag after she met Michael Page, who developed the bisexual pride flag the prior year.[9] All of the flags described herein use horizontal stripes of color. Whereas the gay pride flag displays the colors of the rainbow—and presently uses six bars of color, down from seven and eight in prior iterations—the transgender flag uses three colors in five bars as follows: two outer bars of pastel blue, two inner bars of pastel pink, with a white bar in the center. The bisexual pride flag was inspired by the bi-angles symbol popular in the 1990s, which showed two intersecting triangles, one pink and one blue. The resulting flag is topped with a double-wide band of a bold pink representing homosexuality, is anchored by a double-wide band of a bold blue representing heterosexuality, and has a central purple band representing the intersection of the two groups.[10]

The genderqueer and nonbinary pride flag was created in 2011 by a genderqueer activist named Marilyn Roxie, whose stated purpose was to help create visibility for the genderqueer community and related identities. This flag sports three equal bands of color. The top band is lavender, which blends the traditionally used colors for male and female of pastel blue and pink. The central white band represents agender gender identity and aligns with the gender-neutral white band on the transgender pride flag. The bottom band is a dark chartreuse green that is the inverse of lavender and represents those identities "outside of and without reference to the binary."[11]

A quick search of Google Images reveals a wide array of other flags representing others on the LGBTQIA+ spectrum. One intersex pride flag includes six equal bands of color arranged from top to bottom as follows: lavender, white, pastel blue, pastel pink, white, and lavender. Another version of the intersex pride flag displays a hollow purple circle, or an O, on a bold yellow background. Those who look will find pride flags representing those who are straight, asexual, LGBT+ allies, pansexual, and more. Indeed, searchers can even find country-specific gay pride flags.

Transgender woman holding transgender pride flag. © iStock / llewellyn_chin

During World War II in Nazi Germany, symbols were used to label undesirable people. In addition to tattooing numbers on their prisoners' forearms, the Nazis began by writing labels on their prisoners in concentration camps. At first, entering Jews were labeled *Juden* (Jew), while homosexuals had "Paragraph 175" (referring to the German penal code) written on their backs. Soon the Nazis realized that using symbols to label prisoners was much simpler. Jews were made to wear a yellow Star of David, and homosexuals were forced to wear pink triangles. Sometime after the war, the pink triangle was adopted as a symbol by the gay community. By the late twentieth century, the pink triangle had been co-opted by the gay community to communicate gay pride. It can be found on stickers, buttons, and jewelry for this reason.

Currently, icons signifying either gender identity or sexual orientation often stand alone, although those signifying LGBT+ may still be depicted inside a triangle. Figure 4.1 shows the most commonly used symbols, which are based on the internationally accepted symbols for male ♂ and female ♀. The transgender symbol depicted in the first edition of this book was developed by trans activist Nancy Nangeroni. Using the symbols for male and female, Nangeroni added a third, which combined the two to represent transgender, as shown in the bottom row of figure 4.1 (in the first edition, this symbol appeared within a triangular

Figure 4.1. Gender identity and sexual orientation icons. © iStock / tkacchuk

frame). Today, transgender may be represented by this symbol, or by the version in the top row of figure 4.1. Note the icon depicted for asexual identity, on the bottom row, retains the circle of the international male and female icons, but has no appendages.

Remember, figure 4.1 displays a sampling of possible configurations. A quick online image search will reveal others, most of which are straightforward enough that viewers can understand them easily.

Titles of Address

While visual symbols and logos symbolize concepts and acronyms represent words and phrases, how many of us give thought to the titles by which we ourselves are addressed? One frequently overlooked aspect of interpersonal communication is the title with which one person addresses another. You probably address your physician as *doctor* and a man with whom you are not on a first-name basis as *Mr.* Men do not encounter issues with titles quite as often as do women. Except for those who have earned some other title such as *doctor* or *reverend*, most women age twenty-something or beyond eventually encounter the issue of whether they wish to be addressed as *Miss*, *Ms.*, or *Mrs.*

Half a century ago, during the civil rights movement but before the women's liberation movement had taken hold, the choices were simpler. When the choices were simply *Miss* or *Mrs.*, one could size up the person being addressed (Was she wearing a wedding ring? Did she look old enough to be married?) and guess. Unmarried women would be addressed as *Miss*, while married women became *Mrs.*, a title generally followed by the husband's surname. Then women's liberation allowed women to protest the disparity between the sexes. Why were men always *Mr.*, a title that did not indicate marital status, but women were distinguished by marital status? When the neutral *Ms.* entered our vocabulary, women could choose to be addressed as *Ms.*, a title that acknowledges femininity without declaring marital status. With such a simple alternative, why don't we just address every female as *Ms.* and sidestep the whole issue of marital status? One reason is tradition.

Tradition is the usual, sometimes ritualistic, way we do things. (For example, it is traditional for stores to hold sales connected with holidays or certain times of the year. Can you imagine a July or August without a blizzard of back-to-school sales advertisements?) People hold onto traditions for all sorts of reasons. When a woman introduces herself as *Mrs.*, some people address her as such, while others may use *Ms.* or even *Miss*. The reasons for this may include ignorance, inattention, sloppiness, or even misguided flattery—such as when the speaker uses *Miss* to imply youthfulness on the part of the addressee. Similar mistakes might include addressing a young woman as *ma'am* or with the title *Mrs.* when the speaker wishes to imply maturity on the part of the addressee.

Another title of address is *Mx.*, which was coined in the 1970s but has yet to gain much traction with mainstream society in the United States. According to *Merriam-Webster*'s online dictionary, the title was originally intended for use by those who did not wish to reveal a gender through their title.[12] As such, *Mx.* provides a gender-neutral title well suited to those who identify as nonbinary. Remember, though, when seeing *Mx.* in use, do not assume the person using it is nonbinary. The user may employ *Mx.* to simply mask his, her, or their gender identity. *Merriam-Webster*'s Words We're Watching column indicates that the title is gaining traction in Britain where it appears on drivers licenses and banking documents, and points out that while *Ms.* was actually coined in 1901, it was not picked up by the *New York Times* until 1986.[13] Keep your eyes peeled for instances of *Mx.* in your world, and should you hear a title of address used that sounds like *mix* or *mux*, pat yourself on the back for knowing how to spell it!

The Wrap-Up

When all angles are considered, language is far more powerful than "just words." Changing the beginning of a word, or the tone with which a word is spoken, may change the entire message being conveyed. Most of us, myself included, fail to give language the credit it deserves. By neglecting to use care with our word choices, we risk not only degrading the language but also inadvertently hurting others with poorly chosen words.

My mother often said, "Think before you speak."

To that I now say, "Yes, Mom, that's good advice. I'll try harder."

BOY OR GIRL?

Delivery Room Decisions and Intersex Bodies

The New Arrival

When that long-awaited, much-anticipated event occurs in the delivery room, every parent wants to know immediately, "Is it a boy or a girl?" Imagine yourself as a new parent asking this question. It could be answered in one of three ways. First, you receive a direct answer—"It's a boy!" or "It's a girl!" This would likely elicit feelings of parental pride and joy. Second, your health-care practitioner answers the question directly, as above, but changes that answer later. Such contradictory responses may be initially anxiety provoking, but likely would result in the relief of having received a definitive answer. Third, the health care practitioner answers, "I'm not sure," perhaps continuing, "It could be either." Try wrapping your mind around this. How could the doctor be unsure? Certainly, you would have preferred a clear either-or response.

In most births, assigning a gender based on primary sex characteristics of an infant is as simple as checking for the presence of a penis or vagina. These primary sex characteristics—the external genitalia—are one of the distinct indicators of a person's sex. If the baby has a penis, then it is declared male; if it has a vagina, it is female. In the current jargon of gender politics, the infant has been assigned male (or female) at birth. In a minute number of cases, the delivery room staff may make the wrong determination. Unless the infant's legs are separated and the body carefully examined, an enlarged clitoris or an absent scrotum could be cause for an erroneous declaration made in haste.

The second scenario occurs across the United States, and around the world, when an infant is born with some sort of sexual ambiguity—what some may view as a deformity. As many as 1 percent of babies may be born with genitals that do not fit the standard male or female (see table 5.1 later in this chapter). Maybe the baby has an enlarged clitoris which the obstetrician identifies as a penis and announces, "It's a boy!" before the discovery of a vagina causes that proclamation to change. Maybe the baby has a micropenis, so small as to be mistaken for a clitoris, but after the announcement, "It's a girl!" no vagina is found. The medical personnel may explain the confusion as a minor problem requiring surgical intervention when the baby is a few months older to "correct" the so-called malformation.

When viewed as a deformity, intersex variations (defined on page 65) are treated as psychosocial emergencies—problems that affect the emotional and social well-being of the infant and the infant's family members. Health providers may believe parents need a definitive answer to the question of the child's sex, perhaps because they will interact differently with a boy baby than with a girl baby. This medicalization of the baby's natural state can result in what intersex advocates term *medical abuse* should the infant undergo surgical intervention before reaching an age of awareness, let alone consent. Indeed, such medical management of intersex conditions, which came into vogue in the mid-twentieth century, is more a response to cultural norms and societal values than a simply scientific endeavor.[1]

Hans Lindahl, an intersex activist who works with interACT Advocates for Intersex Youth, contributed her expertise to the language choices in this chapter. *Photographed by ER de Grey*

Terminology: Intersex versus Disorders of Sex Development

Language is tricky not only because the meanings of words (denotation) can change over time, but also because word choices carry subtler messages (connotation). What medical practitioners once inaccurately referred to as hermaphroditism, and later more accurately termed intersex conditions, are currently referred to as disorders of sex development by the medical community; however, the term *disorder* carries negative connotations, and even the word *condition*—when used to speak of intersex conditions—places a medical connotation upon what is simply a variation from typical development.

Hermaphrodite, as defined by *Merriam-Webster*, means "an animal or plant having both male and female reproductive organs."[a] Most people picture an animal having both a penis and a vagina.[b] Nature does not produce true hermaphrodites in human form. Additionally, the terms *hermaphrodite, true hermaphrodite*, and *pseudo-hermaphrodite* carry stigma in that they imply an identity (one *is* a hermaphrodite) and have negative connotations.

Indicating an intermediate condition between the sexes of male and female, *intersex* became the preferred term once the absence of true hermaphroditism in humans was recognized. The word denotes a state of being between male and female without implying (connoting) such a state is wrong. This term is preferred by intersex advocates; however, the medical community found the identity aspect—of *being* intersex—pejorative.

In 2006, the medical community agreed to use *disorders of sex development* (DSD) to describe such conditions. Indeed, *having* a disorder does not imply identity. To the medical community DSD may be an improvement, but some object to the label *disorder* because it implies something is wrong.[c] Some intersex supporters prefer to use *differences of sex development* as a descriptor.

Intersex advocates do not view intersex variations as being wrong and instead believe that visibility and acceptance of intersex people as whole individuals can combat forms of oppression such as intersex genital mutilation.[d]

Perhaps the adage "When in Rome, do as the Romans do" applies here. Consider the audience when choosing language, and then decide for yourself.

The third scenario is also possible. Some health-care practitioners in the delivery room may admit that the baby's sex is unclear. When the external genitalia are so atypical as to be not clearly and entirely either male or female, the ambiguity creates confusion. When delivery room staff are willing to admit confusion and be open to the infinite variabilities of nature, parents are given a voice. In geographic areas rich with medical professionals, such as cities with major teaching hospitals, gender assignment teams may be called in quickly for consultation. In communities without such luxuries, some children grow up with ambiguous genitals and without counseling. Some parents accept their baby as a child, rather than as a boy or a girl, and agree to an assignment of gender without allowing surgical intervention. The intersex child may receive a name common to either gender, such as Leslie or Taylor or Chris and then be given the room to grow.

Reactions to Ambiguity in Sex Determination

Present-day intersex advocacy organizations, like the Intersex Society of North America (ISNA), which operated between 1993 and 2008, advocate that no "corrective" action for ambiguous genitalia should be taken during infancy. Rather, the child should be allowed to grow up with no surgical intervention until after the onset of puberty—at which time the child can determine his or her gender. ISNA was formed by Cheryl Chase, who was distressed and angry at having been subjected to such surgery as an infant. She became an advocate for intersex people to inform the medical community that intersexual persons must navigate stigma and trauma, and that being intersex is not a problem of gender. Realizing that parents and health-care professionals are often traumatized by dealing with a situation as unfamiliar as intersex variations and that infant sex assignment is required on birth certificates, ISNA and subsequent intersex advocacy organizations promote assigning a gender without surgery at birth. Only after the patient is old enough to participate in the decision-making process should surgical intervention occur.[2] Beyond the identity issues, reasons for waiting include that genital surgeries can cause sterility and interfere with tactile sensation. Also, related complications could require additional surgery, hormone treatments, or other medical treatments.

Two research studies at Johns Hopkins Children's Center support ISNA's position. Both demonstrated that nature, not nurture, supplies the deciding element of gender identity.[3]

Today the American Academy of Pediatrics endorses the 2006 "Chicago Consensus," a set of guidelines created by a team of pediatric specialists. Among other things, these recommendations include involving an interdisciplinary team of doctors in intersex cases, shifting away from performing surgeries to "normalize" the appearance of an infant's genitals, and keeping the family informed and involved.[4]

Documentary: Intersexion (2012)

The award-winning documentary feature film *Intersexion: Gender Ambiguity Unveiled* was researched and presented by New Zealand's first out-and-proud intersex activist, Mani Bruce Mitchell, who uses female pronouns and sports a small goatee beard. The film addresses the fact that with at least one in two thousand babies being born with ambiguous genitalia, some three million people around the world are neither male nor female. Direct and powerful, the first-person stories allow viewers to put a face on the word *intersex* and to better understand why societies' gender choices must expand beyond Male and Female.

Search your favorite video streaming site for the title *Intersexion* to view the film.

Numbers

About one in every two thousand babies born each year—in hospitals with gender assignment teams—has genitals that are not clearly a penis or a vagina, but which appear ambiguous enough that the attending physicians consult specialists.[5] That works out to about five babies per day in the United States.[6] The baby could grow up to identify with any gender. Consider also, some people with genitalia that are clearly penises or vaginas have chromosomal (genetic) anomalies and/or hormonal imbalances that create ambiguity. These may not become evident until much later in life, perhaps when a young woman does not menstruate, a person is tested for infertility, or a world-class athlete's sex is called into question. Indeed, genetic testing was instituted at the international level for single-sex competitions midway through the twentieth century, when athletes competing as female so outperformed their counterparts that questions arose about their true sex. (See chapter 10, "Whole Person Health," for more about gender identity in athletics.) When counted together, persons born with ambiguous genitalia and persons with clearly male or female anatomy but with chromosomal anomalies and/or hormonal imbalances, the occurrence of intersex conditions may be as high as 2 percent.[7] But intersex variations are far more common than those numbers would lead one to believe. The Accord Alliance website states that if you are in a superstore, or at a packed football stadium, or even in a large school, then there are probably intersex people nearby because these conditions affect "our families, neighbors, coworkers, and friends."[8]

The term *intersex* is used to describe more variations than simply ambiguous genitalia; read the section on chromosomes and fetal development to better understand. This book uses *intersex* over *disorders of sex development* because the word *disorder* carries negative connotations I prefer to avoid. Furthermore, all individuals are unique and deserve to be celebrated as such. (See chapter 4, "Terminology: What Do All Those Words Mean?" for more about shades of meaning in language.) No matter the response to the question "What [sex] is it?" all new parents have a precious baby, ready to be loved.

Nature versus Nurture

As previously mentioned, the appearance of ambiguous genitalia may trigger one of two very divergent responses: The practice of assigning a sex, surgically intervening to make the child's genitals conform to that sex, and then raising the child in that gender was the standard medical practice for years. Yet, intersex allies have long advocated for accepting the child as delivered, taking no immediate "corrective" action, and leaving the possibility of any surgical intervention to be decided by the child itself later in life.

Beyond the premise that only two sexes exist, the question central to each of these responses is that of nature versus nurture. The nature contingent believe a child's gender identity is inborn and develops independently of outside forces, while the nurture contingent believe a child's gender identity can be molded by its environment. While boiling down the complexities of human sexual development to just these two forces is a massive oversimplification, doing so facilitates our discussion.

Currently the United States, like most countries, only recognizes *male* and *female* categories of sex and gender, forcing a selection of one or the other before issuing a birth certificate; however, in a historic ruling in June 2016, an Oregon circuit court recognized the first person in the United States to be classified as having a nonbinary gender.[9] (See chapter 8, "Legal Issues," for more about the legalities of recognizing a third gender.) As of this writing, babies with clearly ambiguous genitalia must still be fit, legally, into one of the standard binary categories. Although the practice of gender-"normalizing" surgeries has declined in the past decade, parents may still opt to have surgery performed. Teams of gender specialists who evaluate and treat the child and its family are not often found outside of urban areas. Such teams are equipped to help families live with ambiguity until a child is old enough to consent. Furthermore, gender-normalizing surgeries are considered by some intersex advocates to be intersex genital mutilation because they are nonconsensual, medically unnecessary, and permanently alter the infant's body. Indeed in late 2017, the Physicians for Human Rights published a press release calling for an immediate moratorium on unnecessary surgeries on intersex children.[10] Such surgeries have the potential to result in a body that is sterile or unable to experience the sexual pleasure afforded by the presence of a clitoris or penis. Parents and physicians who can accept living with ambiguity allow nature and the child to reveal what is "right" for that person, in time.

Nature Includes Variation

Keep in mind that the presence of unambiguous genitalia, where an infant's sex assigned at birth is clearly determined by the presence of a penis or a vagina, provides no guarantee that the newborn, once grown, will continue to identify with the assigned sex. As we will see later in this chapter, some intersex differences remain undetected until puberty, or later. Not only that, this book exists because gender identity does not always match biological sex. Variations from the standard male-female dichotomy are not unique to human beings and can be found in both the plant and animal kingdoms, where sex changes in species occur for a variety of reasons. Worms, snails, and slugs are naturally hermaphroditic, meaning they have two complete sets of reproductive organs—both male and female—in one body. Intersex differences have been observed in myriad mammals, including black bears, spotted hyenas, and leopard geckos—similar to the chromosomal and hormonal conditions discussed later in this chapter. Finally, fish are fascinating creatures. Some species, such as clownfish, can undergo protandry, meaning they can change sex from male to female. Other species can undergo protogyny and change sex from female to male, and others can change sex bidirectionally.[11]

Nurture's Epic Fail

One case in human history illustrates how the nurture side of the debate might not be wholly correct. Dr. John Money, a medical psychologist who was known in the mid-to-late twentieth century as "the world's undisputed authority on the psychological ramifications of ambiguous genitalia,"[12] advocated the practice of unequivocally assigning a sex to a baby whose sex was unclear, and then raising the child as the assigned sex. In cases of intersex children, his research team completed male-to-female sexual reassignment surgeries and then helped the patients feel comfortable with the new sex assignment. Dr. Money was certain that boys having the surgery within the first two and a half years of life could successfully be raised as girls. He reported positive experiences doing this for several infants who had been born with at least partially formed genitals of both sexes.

In the late 1960s a young Canadian couple, Ron and Janet Reimer, brought a case to Dr. Money's attention that seemed tailor-made to prove or disprove his hypothesis. The Reimers' identical twin sons—Bruce and Brian—were hospitalized for routine circumcisions at eight months of age; however, the first surgery went awry, destroying and essentially removing Bruce's penis. Brian's surgery was canceled. When Bruce went home, his bladder drained through a tube exiting his body below the belly button. His parents hesitated to pursue phallic reconstruction (the rebuilding of Bruce's penis), which would result in a penis that looked strange and lacked sensation. When they saw Dr. Money on a television talk show, discussing his work with intersex children and gender identity, they contacted him.

For the research team at Johns Hopkins, the opportunity to reassign the sex of a baby born a boy, who had an identical twin on whom no surgery would be performed, was enormously exciting and could confirm the team's conclusions. The Reimers understood that the surgery recommended for Bruce had been performed before, but not that the procedure would be experimental in Bruce's case. The Johns Hopkins team had previously performed sex reassignment surgeries only on intersex children.[13] Bruce would be the first child with what doctors considered a penis within normal range, given a vaginoplasty.

Once the parents were convinced that a surgical sex change was appropriate, the toddler underwent physical castration at the Johns Hopkins Hospital. At home again, he was raised as Brenda, with longer hair, frilly dresses, and positive reinforcement for female behaviors. Brenda still gravitated toward "boy toys" and mannerisms; however, his mother only reported the instances of feminine behavior to the psychologist. When the child visited Johns Hopkins for annual psychological tests and interviews, Dr. Money failed to notice Brenda's masculine tendencies. At school, teachers were confused by her boyish behavior until the parents disclosed the child's history.

In 1972, when Brenda was six years old, Dr. Money published his landmark text *Man & Woman, Boy & Girl* wherein he reported Brenda's transformation to be a total success.[14] When the child was eight years old, Dr. Money wanted to complete his work by surgically constructing a vagina for Brenda, but she adamantly refused. Her childhood continued to be difficult; she did not fit in with her female peers. Upon reaching puberty, she was started on estrogen therapy—the female hormone—to guide her body's development into womanhood. After her hips and waist became more rounded and her breasts developed, Brenda indulged in eating binges to disguise her body in fat. When the twins were fourteen years old, the Reimers disclosed the truth to Brenda and Brian.

Relieved to understand the basis of her conflicting feelings, Brenda knew what she wanted: she would live life as a man. After choosing the name David—a strong biblical name representing the triumph of good over evil, like David who

Explore Further: David Reimer's Life Story

To read more about the baby Bruce who became Brenda and finally asserted himself as David, check out *As Nature Made Him: The Boy Who Was Raised as a Girl* by John Colapinto (2000).

A condensed version of David Reimer's story was made into a documentary produced for the BBC television show *Horizon*. Find it online through Documentary Storm. The title is *Dr. Money and the Boy with No Penis*. Visit documentary storm.com/dr-money-and-the-boy-with-no-penis/.

slew the giant Goliath—the estrogen therapy was replaced by testosterone injections. A double mastectomy removed Brenda's breasts, but the surgery was so traumatic and painful that David postponed further surgeries.

The twins eventually matured and led independent lives. Brian married and fathered two children, and David realized that marriage and fatherhood were the future he wanted also. When Jane, a single mother of three, entered his life, he was able to enjoy family and fatherhood. Eventually, David chose to make his story public in hopes of saving other children from a similar plight.

Ultimately Dr. Money did change his opinion about the nature-versus-nurture argument and came to stand firmly behind biology as being the stronger force.

Before exploring some of the more frequent variations resulting in intersex persons, a review of the basics is in order.

Chromosomes and Fetal Development

In general, humans have forty-six chromosomes in each of the cells in our bodies, twenty-three pairs. Twenty-two chromosomes and a sex chromosome (X) come from the mother, while twenty-two chromosomes and either an X or a Y chromosome come from the father. A blood test called a *karyotype* is used to analyze chromosomal makeup. Most people's karyotype is either 46,XX (female) or 46,XY (male). When anomalies occur, the resulting baby is different from most people. A well-known genetic anomaly unrelated to gender identity is Down syndrome, where one of the two initial cells (either the egg or the sperm) has an extra twenty-first chromosome, resulting in the baby having forty-seven, instead of forty-six, chromosomes in each of its cells. Although some intersex variations are just as common as Down syndrome, they remain nearly invisible in our society for cultural reasons.

At conception, the egg cell provides an X chromosome, and the sperm cell provides either a female-determining X chromosome or a male-determining Y chromosome. Nevertheless, intersex variations may occur, and a fertilized egg cell containing a Y chromosome can develop into a female or an intersex child. A specific gene on the Y chromosome has been identified as the sex-determining region of the Y chromosome (or SRY). If the Y chromosome is missing this SRY gene, the egg will develop into a female.[15] A developed male infant has a penis; gonads (reproductive glands) that have developed into testes; a Wolffian duct, which has developed into the duct system leaving the testes and includes the epididymis, vas deferens, seminal vesicle, and ejaculatory ducts; and XY sex chromosomes. A developed female infant has a clitoris, which has developed from the erectile tissue; the Mullerian duct, which has differentiated into the vagina, uterus, ovaries, and fallopian tubes; and XX sex chromosomes.

Irregularities may develop while chromosomes, gonads, or genitals are taking shape. When these three critical elements are not all aligned as male or female, the child is intersex. Usually, though, only ambiguities in genital appearance trigger concern about an intersex variation in the delivery room. A few of the possible intersex differences are described next.

Klinefelter Syndrome

One of the most common chromosomal variations in humans is Klinefelter syndrome (KS), which involves an extra X chromosome in males and creates a hormonal imbalance in the body. Named for Dr. Harry Klinefelter, one of the authors of a 1942 paper published about the condition, the syndrome occurs about once in every five hundred to seven hundred live-born male infants. KS is not a genetic condition; it cannot be inherited from parents or passed on to children. Many males with the syndrome go undiagnosed, likely because they exhibit no symptom that provides reason for testing. The most common characteristics of KS include infertility, breast development, decreased facial and body hair, and problems either socially or with school and learning. In males who have low hormone levels, treatment with testosterone is best started in the teenage years and generally enlarges testes, increases sex drive and muscular build, and promotes hair growth. Research into treatments for infertility is ongoing, and while unlikely today, it is possible for men with KS to father children, usually when assisted reproductive technologies are employed.[16]

Explore Further: Klinefelter Syndrome

As with any topic, many Klinefelter syndrome–related videos of various quality are available on YouTube and range from general educational to medical reviews for health-care professionals to personal, self-revelatory narratives. Here are two of the general educational variety:

- "What Is Klinefelter's Syndrome" runs under four minutes and features a discussion of the general features and reproductive aspects of KS. Visit www .youtube.com/watch?v=c9ne4Cwy9T4&list=RDKw_RIjUKilM&index=2.
- "Klinefelter's Syndrome by Daniel Richmond," a silent PowerPoint presentation running five-and-a-half minutes, was created as a project for the producer's grade 11 biology class, and offers a straightforward, detailed overview of KS and its affects. Forewarning: Richmond refers to persons with KS as "victims." Visit www.youtube.com/watch?v=lyRUryBShTo&index=13&list=RDKw_RIjUKilM.

In addition, the "Resources" section at the back of the book lists several organizations dedicated to providing information and support around Klinefelter syndrome. You might also check out an article by Teens Health at kidshealth. org/en/teens/klinefelter.html.

Turner Syndrome

A chromosomal condition affecting babies with X chromosomes only, Turner syndrome occurs when one of the two X chromosomes normally found in females is absent or incomplete. Named for Dr. Henry Turner, who first described the condition's features in the late 1930s, Turner syndrome is characterized most commonly by limited height and deficient ovarian development. Caused by the partly or completely missing X chromosome, Turner syndrome seems to occur randomly in about one in two thousand live female births. Now diagnosable by

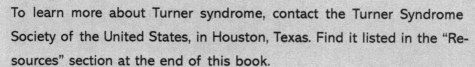

Explore Further: Turner Syndrome

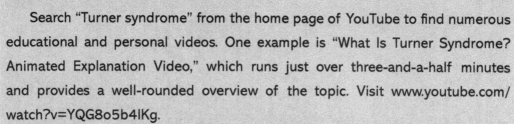

To learn more about Turner syndrome, contact the Turner Syndrome Society of the United States, in Houston, Texas. Find it listed in the "Resources" section at the end of this book.

Search "Turner syndrome" from the home page of YouTube to find numerous educational and personal videos. One example is "What Is Turner Syndrome? Animated Explanation Video," which runs just over three-and-a-half minutes and provides a well-rounded overview of the topic. Visit www.youtube.com/watch?v=YQG8o5b4lKg.

a simple blood test, Turner syndrome has no known cure, but those affected can live complete and fulfilling lives. Treatments may include the introduction of growth hormone to help patients achieve "normal" height and estrogen replacement therapy to aid in the development of secondary sexual characteristics. Modern reproductive technologies assist with achieving pregnancy. Other problems, including conditions of the heart, thyroid, or kidneys, may require that the Turner syndrome patient receive good medical care throughout life.[17]

Mayer Rokitansky Kuster Hauser Syndrome

Mayer Rokitansky Kuster Hauser syndrome (abbreviated as MRKH or MRKHauser syndrome) is named for all the doctors who discovered it; it is also known as Müllerian agenesis or vaginal agenesis. A congenital disorder of the female reproductive tract, MRKH includes a total or partial absence of the uterus or vagina. Affecting about one in every five thousand female births, MRKH babies are typical XX females who are born with normal ovaries and fallopian tubes and who display typical external genitalia, but whose vagina and uterus are undersized, incomplete, or missing. Often these girls are born with the lower portion of the vagina intact, which means that MRKH can easily go undetected until puberty when the absence of menstruation may alert the young woman and her medical practitioners to an irregularity.[18]

Jaclyn Schultz, who has MRKH, won the first beauty pageant she entered and was crowned Miss Michigan 2013. Following this, she read a comment on

Explore Further: Mayer Rokitansky Kuster Hauser Syndrome

More information about MRKH syndrome is available online. Start your research with the following sites:

- The Center for Young Women's Health of Boston Children's Hospital has extensive guides for MRKH young women (youngwomenshealth .org/2013/10/02/mrkh) and for their parents and medical providers (youngwomenshealth.org/?orderby=relevance&s=mrkh).
- MRKH.org offers links, articles, and support groups, www.mrkh.org.
- The Beautiful You MRKH Foundation, www.beautifulyoumrkh.org. The "Resources" section has more information on this organization.

If you prefer your information to be more up close and in person, check out the annual MRKH Conference, sponsored by the Boston Children's Hospital Division of Gynecology and the Center for Young Women's Health. It is held for women ages fourteen to twenty-five who have been diagnosed with MRKH. Send questions about upcoming conferences to cywh@childrens.harvard.edu.

Facebook claiming her new job was to "just be pretty" for the year. Wanting to do more with her title, she chose to raise awareness for MRKH by coming out publicly as having the syndrome. During her bid for the Miss USA crown later that year, she became known as "the Pageant Queen without a Uterus" because she made MRKH awareness part of her Miss USA platform. The following year she participated on the television show *Survivor*, where she placed as the first runner-up; in a 2015 *Cosmopolitan.com* interview she revealed that the $100,000 prize money would go toward freezing her eggs for future parenthood.[19] As a spokesperson for the Beautiful You MRKH Foundation, Schultz reaches women around the world by sharing information about this supportive community that partners with health-care professionals to increase awareness and to empower women of all ages with MRKH to feel beautiful, just as they are.

Androgen Insensitivity Syndrome

Androgen insensitivity syndrome (AIS), androgen receptor deficiency, and androgen resistance syndrome are different terms for the same condition. Those with AIS have XY chromosomes, which are typically associated with the male path of sexual development, but their bodies cannot respond to androgens (certain male sex hormones). Affecting sexual development in utero and during puberty, complete and partial AIS each occur in approximately two to five babies out of one hundred thousand with XY chromosomes; the mild form is less common. The three descriptors for AIS are complete androgen insensitivity syndrome (CAIS), partial androgen insensitivity syndrome (PAIS), and mild androgen insensitivity syndrome (MAIS).

Those with CAIS cannot react to androgens at all, and typically have a vulva but no uterus; a short, or partial, vagina may be present. They are socially read female, develop breasts, and many identify as female although they cannot menstruate or give birth. Testes are generally present internally but are either undescended or only partially descended; they may pose a slight risk for cancer later in life if not removed. The conundrum of being infertile females with XY chromosomes and testes instead of ovaries can lead to an emotional strain and feelings of difference. (This challenge is beautifully illustrated in I. W. Gregorio's young adult novel *None of the Above*; see page 77.)

PAIS babies can present one of three observable anatomies (phenotypes): have a clitoris within what doctors might consider a normal range, have a penis within that similar "normal" range, or have ambiguous genitalia somewhere between.[20] Those with PAIS may identify as, and be raised as, either male or female. They, too, are generally born without a uterus but with testes, which are often internal.

MAIS babies are clearly male at birth but may experience breast development (gynecomastia) at puberty.[21]

Congenital Adrenal Hyperplasia

Congenital adrenal hyperplasia (CAH), a group of inherited disorders affecting the adrenal glands, affects XX and XY infants equally. Classical CAH, the severe form, is detected in infants through newborn screenings. Newborn XX infants with classical CAH may display genital anomalies including enlarged clitoris and fused labia that resemble a scrotal sac; where the anomaly is significant, the labia may be identified as a scrotum. Such observable genital variations are only on the outside; ovaries are typically present. Three-fourths of infants with classical CAH also have aldosterone insufficiency, which can result in salt wasting,[22] a condition where the body is unable to retain sufficient salt to function properly. If the salt-

Explore Further: Androgen Insensitivity Syndrome

To learn more about androgen insensitivity syndrome, explore the website of the Androgen Insensitivity Syndrome—Differences of Sex Development (AIS-DSD) Support Group, listed in the "Resources" section of this book. In addition, search for "androgen insensitivity syndrome" on YouTube, and you'll find an upbeat, engaging series of short videos about intersex topics by Emily Quinn, whose "Intersexperiences" show is about the intersex experiences of Emily and her friends. One episode titled "Intersex: Complete Androgen Insensitivity—Explained!" runs just over six minutes. Visit www.youtube.com/watch?v=5vDVUPjBJiM&t=12s.

Finally, reading I. W. Gregorio's young adult novel *None of the Above* (2015) will help you experience what it might be like to have AIS. You will feel the confusion and dismay of high school junior and first-person narrator Kristin Lattimer when she learns from her gynecologist that she has testicles, and no ovaries, cervix, or uterus.

wasting variety of CAH is present, the condition can be life-threatening unless treated soon after birth; undiagnosed infants with this variety of classical CAH may show symptoms such as vomiting or life-threatening shock.

The nonclassical form of CAH, sometimes called late-onset CAH, is not immediately life-threatening. Although it may be identified through newborn screening tests, no treatment will generally be required. Symptoms, which may be mistaken for early puberty, generally appear anywhere from early childhood to early adulthood and vary from person to person. Only those experiencing troublesome symptoms require treatment.[23]

Progestin-Induced Virilization

An XX fetus exposed to androgens—such as progestin, which was used in the 1950s and 1960s to prevent miscarriage—can be born with observable sexual characteristics ranging from female with larger clitoris to male with no testes. Ovaries and a uterus do develop, although in some extreme cases the vagina and cervix may be absent. Occasionally, such children are assigned male identities and raised as boys. Today progestin virilization may occur when a woman takes a drug to treat severe endometriosis without realizing she is pregnant at the time.[24] Intersex advocates would have parents delay any cosmetic surgery until the child is of an age to understand the condition and consent to any surgical intervention.

5-Alpha Reductase Deficiency

5-alpha reductase (5-AR) is the enzyme that helps convert testosterone into dihydrotestosterone (DHT), which is critical to typical male development. When a fetus lacks the 5-AR enzyme, the proto-gonads develop into testes but the testosterone cannot be converted into DHT, and the result is a child with 5-alpha reductase deficiency (5-ARD) whose genitals have developed more like a typical

Memoir and Contemporary Literature: Born Both (2017) versus Middlesex (2002)

Born Both: An Intersex Life is a combination personal and political memoir, written by intersex activist Hida Viloria, a child of South American immigrants. (See chapter 4, "Terminology: What Do All Those Words Mean?" for more about language and pronouns.) Viloria is the founding director of the Unites States affiliate of the Organisation Intersex International (OII), initially known as OII-USA, and now called Intersex Campaign for Equality (IC4E). Honest and engaging, Viloria's fascinating narrative is an unflinching account of one raised female who came to realize her intersex status in her early twenties.

The narrator of Jeffrey Eugenides's Pulitzer Prize–winning novel *Middlesex* (2002) introduces himself from page 1 as the subject of a published medical study titled "Gender Identity in 5-Alpha-Reductase Pseudohermaphrodites" and then proceeds to enthrall readers with an intergenerational family saga about Cal Stephanides, who was born and raised as "Calliope" until as a teenager he was discovered to be something more than female—a hermaphrodite.[e] *Middlesex* is a work of fiction loosely based upon the nineteenth-century memoir of hermaphrodite Herculine Barbin—available in translation as *Herculine Barbin: Being the Recently Discovered Memoirs of a Nineteenth-Century French Hermaphrodite* (1978).

female's; however, come puberty, the 5-AR enzyme is unnecessary and the surge in testosterone causes the boy's body to develop in a male-typical fashion. The penis grows, the voice deepens, and other male-typical characteristics develop including some facial and body hair, and male-typical musculature.[25]

Hypospadias and Epispadias

Hypospadias and epispadias are birth differences that are consequences of atypical penile development while the embryo is forming. Normally the urethra runs the length of the penis, to form an opening at its tip, but sometimes the urethra fails to reach the tip of the penis. In hypospadias, the urethra forms an opening on the underside of the penis. In epispadias the urethra exits on the penis's upper side. Surgery can be performed to extend the urethra to the tip of the penis. If the original opening is very close to the base of the penis, such that sperm are not deposited far enough into the vagina, surgery may be necessary to facilitate natural reproduction (without requiring the assistance of reproductive technologies). Unless the urethra is actually blocked, surgery to extend the urethra to the tip of the penis is rarely medically necessary; a risk-versus-benefit analysis should always be made before performing cosmetic surgery. Surgery for hypospadias, often considered cosmetic by the intersex community, is risky in that complications may require additional surgeries, and sexual function may be irreversibly damaged.[26]

Differences Make Us Special

Several more classifications of intersex differences exist, all of them as complex and life changing as those we've already examined. The frequency of these is not well documented, which may help to explain the broad variation in statistics offered by differing sources. Based on the work of Dr. Anna Fausto-Sterling and her colleagues, ISNA reports the numbers shown in table 5.1.

Overall, though, some 1 to 2 percent of the population is intersex. That means that intersex variations occur in humans about as frequently as does red hair in the United States. Have you ever met anyone with red hair? (Can you imagine having not ever met anyone with red hair?) To extrapolate, it is safe to say that you also know people who are intersex; however, unlike red hair, the condition is not readily apparent.

Every human body is unique. Like snowflakes, we appear generally the same from a distance; however, when one stops to examine closely, every human is different, just as every snowflake is unique. Physical variances between people are part of what make each person special, adding to our inherent individuality.

Table 5.1. Frequency of Intersex Variations

classical congenital adrenal hyperplasia	1 in 13,000 births
late onset adrenal hyperplasia	1 in 66 people
vaginal agenesis	1 in 6,000 births
ovotestes	1 in 83,000 births
not XX and not XY	1 in 1,666 births
androgen insensitivity syndrome	1 in 13,000 births
partial androgen insensitivity syndrome	1 in 130,000 births
Klinefelter (XXY)	1 in 1,000 births
hypospadias (urethral opening along the penile shaft)	1 in 2,000 births
hypospadias (urethral opening between the corona and the tip)	1 in 770 births
total number of people whose bodies differ from the standard male or female	1 in 100 births
total number of people receiving surgery to "normalize" genital appearance	1 in 1,000 births

Source: Intersex Society of North America, "How Common Is Intersex?" www.isna.org/faq/frequency.html

TEDx on Intersex

At a TEDx conference in Boulder, Colorado, Cecelia McDonald told the audience how at age seventeen she went to the doctor because she had not entered puberty. She went on to explain what intersex means, what it meant for her, how this was "the first time in a medical setting that I felt like a thing that needed to be fixed," and how her story turned out. Her presentation was lighthearted, but her point is serious: intersex persons need visibility in order to end the life-altering, nonconsensual treatments.

If you can spare ten minutes, check out her TEDxBoulder talk on YouTube: www.youtube.com/watch?v=CKEGaSJi3bk&t=331s.

Circumcision: Who, What, When, Why?

Circumcision in males is a surgical procedure where the foreskin is re-moved from the penis. The procedure deprives the organ of its protec-tive shroud and provides a cleaner environment less prone to infection. In some religions, male circumcision is a traditional rite of passage. Male Jewish infants characteristically have circumcision performed on the eighth day after birth in a ritual ceremony called the Brit (or Bris) Milah. Muslim males undergo the circumcision or *tahara* (purification) anywhere from the seventh day after birth up to the onset of puberty. For other infants, circumcision is performed at their parents' request.

In the United States, medical male circumcision of infants continues to be practiced routinely in many hospitals, whereas female circumcision, also called female genital mutilation (FGM), has been outlawed since 1996. FGM refers to any surgery that removes all or part of the female genitalia and is understood to be detrimental to a woman's physical, psychological, and sexual health.

Times Are Changing

A good part of this section is the stories; recast to focus on the stories that have come out in the news. Although sexual variations have been in existence for likely as long as humans have peopled the earth, public discussion of intersex persons was uncommon up through the twentieth century. By the summer of 2004, articles about intersex people were appearing prominently in some mainstream newspapers in the United States. Not buried deep within a section, intersex variations and the people they affect landed on the front pages of the sections in which they were placed, including the news section of the *Record* of northern New Jersey, the Sunday Styles section of the *New York Times*, and the Children First section of the *Detroit Free Press*.

Medical writer Patricia Anstett of Detroit's *Free Press* attributed the attention to the publicity around Jeffrey Eugenides's 2002 novel *Middlesex* and to nationwide reports about David Reimer's death in 2004. Anstett's article about a Michigan State University professor's activism on behalf of intersex children appeared on the front page of the *Free Press*'s Children First section.[27]

Staff writer Ruth Padawer of New Jersey's *Record* credited the front-page placement of her stories to the fact that "the condition is little known by the general public and the editors [believe the topic is] of high interest, particularly because of the nuanced and emotional issues associated with it."[28] Her articles described the experiences of various intersex people, some of whom were subjected to sex assignment surgery as infants. Betsy, one person profiled in the series, now in her fifties, is an intersex activist. She was born with a long phallus, which doctors determined was a penis and therefore classified the infant as male. When doctors later found a uterus and ovaries, the baby's penis was renamed an enlarged clitoris and the child was assigned female. Her surgery, the removal of most of the enlarged clitoris, left her unable to experience sexual pleasure. She likens herself to a survivor of child sexual abuse—abuse presented as medical treatment.

Another person, Deborah, was also born with an enlarged clitoris; it was larger than normal by one-fifth of an inch. When she reached eighteen months, doctors discovered testes and Deborah was renamed Thomas. With such a different anatomy, Thomas became an unhappy boy who did not fit in with other boys and, as a child, never used a public restroom. Although he knew he had an endocrine disorder, Thomas had not been told that most people with his syndrome were identified as female. When his breasts began to grow at age twelve, he was most distressed; a doctor recommended a double mastectomy and Thomas underwent the surgery at thirteen. However, his voice never deepened, his shoulders failed to broaden, and the hair on his cheeks stayed soft. Although he never did fit in as a boy, Thomas was not offered a chance to be a girl. As an adult, Thomas resumed life as Deborah and had breast reconstruction surgery. When Deborah's physical masculinity reappeared in the form of testicular cancer, she let her colleagues assume she had "female trouble."

Another story in Padawer's article described a woman who found out she had XY chromosomes when she went to get her premarital blood test. Her female-appearing body lacked a cervix and a uterus, but it was clear to both her and her fiancé that she was definitely female. Happily married now, the couple has an adopted son who has not been informed of his mother's condition.

Ten years after Padawer's article was published, interACT Advocates led their first-ever youth retreat—and they are planning more. In 2017, they published a youth marketing brochure, giving a loud-and-proud voice to intersex youth seeking to spread the word. You can learn more about interACT Advocates in the "Resources" section.

Intersex Youth Voices

To hear from intersex youth, start by reading the interACT youth marketing brochure, which will put a face to the word *intersex* for you. Find it at interactadvocates.org/wp-content/uploads/2017/05/interACTYouthMarketingBrochure.pdf.

To actually hear their voices, try the YouTube channels of intersex advocacy organizations such as interACT and IGLYO:

- On the interACT channel, check out the BuzzFeed video from March 28, 2015, wherein four intersex young people from the United States talk about "What It's Like to Be Intersex." Visit www.youtube.com/watch?v=AxOKAnY_j3k.
- On the IGLYO channel, check out "We Are Here: Intersex Youth," a video commissioned by IGLYO—The International Lesbian, Gay, Bisexual, Transgender, Queer & Intersex (LGBTQI) Youth & Student Organisation based in Belgium—and produced in cooperation with interACT Advocates and OII Europe. In the video, five young intersex people share their stories on Intersex Awareness Day 2016, to increase visibility and combat isolation. Visit www.youtube.com/watch?v=16gQDXxsnjM&t=106s.

A Brighter Future

Since the 2006 Chicago Consensus statement was released, the treatment of intersex infants in the United States has moved toward the ideal of postponing any surgical intervention until the individual is of an age to understand and consent. Even so, such "corrective" surgeries continue—if less frequently. In October 2017, Physicians for Human Rights, a New York–based patient advocacy organization, issued a strongly worded call to halt genital surgeries on infants with atypical genitalia "before they are able to give meaningful consent to such surgeries."[29] The rest of the organization's statement unambiguously identifies the nonconsensual treatment of intersex infants as a human rights issue, something

Spread the Word: Intersex Awareness Day

On October 26, 1996, intersex activists from ISNA—Morgan Holmes and Max Beck—and their allies from Transsexual Menace held the first public intersex demonstration in Boston, Massachusetts, where the American Academy of Pediatrics was holding its annual conference. Their aim was to make it difficult for the medical community to overlook the growing intersex rights movement. Then in 2004, intersex activists Betsy Driver and Emi Koyama, established October 26 as Intersex Awareness Day (IAD) to raise issues around intersex, selecting the date of that first public protest. Now recognized around the globe, this day is an opportunity to raise awareness of the existence of intersex persons and the myriad issues they face.[f]

On the interACT Advocates for Intersex Youth website, find ready-made images you can share through social media or your school community, putting a face to intersex issues while proclaiming IAD is October 26. The IGLYO video "We Are Here: Intersex Youth," created for IAD 2016 is there, too. Visit interactadvocates.org/intersex-awareness-day/.

Also, be sure to view the resolution released in 2016 for the twentieth anniversary of IAD. Signed by individuals representing over seventy organizations worldwide, the straightforward, three-item resolution asks that intersex persons be treated with the same dignity and respect as all human beings. Find it from the page cited earlier, or view it directly at docs.google.com/document/u/1/d/16skW1o_ISP5pjdq9WUVcttJNgndO88W5cMZw3YwB3qc/pub?embedded=true.

for which intersex organizations have long advocated. Now, medical associations need to answer this call to action.

Beyond the medical community, though, the general public may become more aware of intersex issues thanks to the work of such organizations as interACT Advocates for Intersex Youth. This advocacy organization is helping intersex youth give voice to themselves as proud individuals—not as medical specimens. One high-profile advocate who has teamed up with interACT is Belgian super-model Hanne Gaby Odiele. Although she has been modeling since 2005, Odiele chose to make her intersex status public in 2017, going so far as to make a video to accompany her appearance in *Teen Vogue*.

Now that you are aware of how human bodies exist beyond the binary, you will doubtlessly notice similar stories as they unfold in the media. May the movement in favor of individual rights continue to gain traction as the old ways designed to hide or even obliterate differences fall by the wayside.

GENDER CONVERSATIONS

....

Exploring Gender

Exploring gender with a group—whether in a youth group, a classroom, or a Gay-Straight Alliance (GSA)—can be an enlightening experience. Becoming aware of our own deeply held gender expectations and beliefs is often surprising, especially to those of us who like to think of ourselves as open-minded and accepting. In this chapter, you'll find a few exercises to help unearth those preoccupations you harbor and some activities, films, and readings focused on gender roles. Try some out in a group of people with whom you feel safe, and you may broaden your own horizons.

Keeping a journal throughout this series of exercises will provide you a document to review at the end. Set aside a notebook or digital file to use as a journal as you work through each of the following exercises. Journal as many of your reactions to the questions posed as possible before sharing them with a group; where that is not possible, always journal at the end of each group meeting.

Advertising Imagery

The members of your GSA, class, or youth group may not be sure where to begin a discussion about gender. Images encountered frequently in daily life may provide a place to start. Look around. What messages about gender are implicit in the images encountered?

Savvy consumers understand that advertising is designed to encourage us to purchase a product or service, but how often do we look beneath the surface of the ads? Here's an exercise to try with a group.

Have each participant bring in several full-page advertisements featuring people as models. Or bring an assortment of magazines to the group and spend a few minutes together flipping through them. Tear out advertisements that catch your eye without regard to why you think they snagged your attention. Next, line the walls with the print advertisements. (Use masking tape or sticky tack with care. You'll want to leave the walls looking as good as they did before you started.) Stand back. Consider the images in silence for a couple of minutes and then regroup for the discussion phase.

Together, go around the group once to elicit people's initial reactions to the collection or to specific images. Allot each speaker a limited time, perhaps one minute, and then move promptly to the next person.

- What do the images and words say to the viewers about gender or gender roles?
- What unstated "promises" do the ads appear to make?
- What gender-based messages do the images convey?
- How many of them use sex as a selling tool?
- Which ones are blatant, and which are subtle? How?
- What else do you find remarkable about the images?

After working your way through this list of questions, and any your group has chosen to add, what general conclusions can your group draw—both about advertising and about gender in advertising—based on this exercise? Lastly, allot a minute for each speaker to report on his or her experience with this exercise. What surprised the participants? What did participants learn from the exercise?

There's No Place like Home

Pull up a chair to watch a video. Have your group consider these four videos over several sessions, and discuss questions about what makes a family, what roles family members have—being true to themselves and to their relatives—and how gender influences us as individuals and within these roles.

First, have a group member borrow a copy of *That's a Family* (2000), an award-winning film that features children speaking about their family experiences. (Try public and school libraries before renting or buying the DVD.) Although the thirty-five-minute film is geared for younger audiences (ages kindergarten through eighth grade), it is also used with adult groups. The images it provides can facilitate conversation about how the face of the American family has changed over the last sixty years.

After viewing the film, discuss what you've seen using the following questions:

- What did people find surprising, informative, or thought provoking?
- How do families in the documentary compare to participants' family experiences?

- What can be said about gender roles after viewing the film?
- Is this a film you would want to share with younger siblings, relatives, or a student group? Why or why not?

A second film to consider is the 1997 *Ma Vie en Rose* (*My Life in Pink*), a ninety-minute rated-R film about a little boy who feels he's a girl. Although the soundtrack is in French, the film has English subtitles. *Ma Vie en Rose* deftly captures one child's struggle for acceptance in a world rife with gender role expectations that don't fit his personal identity. Viewers will want to watch for the reactions of the child's family members, neighbors, and "friends," and the father's employer.

The discussion questions following this film focus around cultural and societal expectations:

- What are the varied reactions you see in the film?
- With what characters do you identify?
- What reasons do you attribute to each character's behavior?
- How does the film challenge your preconceptions of family relations, of employer-family relations, and of neighborhood expectations?

Next, have a member locate and borrow a copy of the made-for-cable movie *Normal* (2003), which we discussed in chapter 2 on brain sex. This feature-length family drama is set in America's heartland, in a conservative, rural town, and focuses on a transsexual adult. After twenty-five years of marriage, Roy tells his family and community that he wishes to become "Ruth." Watch how this community reacts, and who ultimately comes forward to support Roy's transition. His family—an adolescent daughter, an adult son, and wife—his pastor and religious community, and his employer and coworkers all play significant roles in Roy's life.

Following the film, begin the group discussion by considering the same questions used for *Ma Vie en Rose*. Talk over the role of each family member and the responses of each group member. Then consider the following:

- How would each of you react to such a pronouncement by your own parent or significant adult role model?
- What gender role does each of your adult role models play now?
- How would the sex change of one of these adults impact each group member and that person's place in society?

To conclude the video portion of the group's gender exploration, pull up the MTV documentary *Transformation* that was live-streamed on November 17, 2016. This forty-five-minute documentary follows nonbinary Madin Lopez as they provide their hair styling services to the Los Angeles LGBT Center's Lifeworks Makeover Event. Here, six transgender teens and new adults are affirmed in their gender identities. Lopez is the founder of Project Q through which they routinely volunteer their services to transgender and gender-nonconforming young people at shelters serving LGBT youth. The Lifeworks Mentoring Coordinator, Nia Clark, a transgender woman, says the Makeover is more of an affirmation of who the six really are than an actual makeover. *Transformation* follows the six young people, ages fifteen to twenty-two, through hair, makeup, and wardrobe before their photo shoots and runway session.

Unlike the previous films, not all in *Transformation* have homes or families; makeover winner Jessica-Jean is homeless, and both Lopez and Clark speak about their experiences with homelessness as teens. Have participants share their thoughts about the participants interviewed, and then consider the following questions:

- How did your group members feel to see the individuals as they saw themselves with their gender identities affirmed?
- Which person struck viewers the most and why?
- Considering the earlier films viewed, how did it feel to watch the families celebrating their affirmed family member?
- What impact did the facilitators' statements have on viewers as Lopez and Clark recounted their reasons for doing this work?
- How did members feel the 1950s-style, black-and-white sections with the voiceover impacted the film's message?

Now, take the discussion further. *Transformation* discussed how the rate of attempted suicide for transgender and gender-nonconforming (TGNC) persons is 45 percent. Practically half of the TGNC population attempts suicide. Ask participants how they can be allies when they encounter someone else experiencing harassment or bullying for their gender, gender identity, or gender expression.

Finally, take a moment to reconsider the entire series of videos. What have the four films added to your understanding of gender roles? Overall, how has this video exercise helped you feel more likely or more able to be an ally?

Gender Roles and Memories

This exercise involves reading, writing, and sharing. First, list what you remember about gender messages you received growing up:

- Did your household insist that boys take out the trash, while girls worked in the kitchen?
- For what behaviors did you receive positive gender messages like "That-taboy!" or "Such a little lady!" and how did such comments make you feel?
- Can you remember a time when you were explicitly taught to behave as a girl or a boy? How did you feel about the message? Did you welcome the instruction and eagerly seek to please your instructor, or did you chafe against being forced to behave like one gender or the other?

Next, ask yourself what you expect of a boy and a girl. Consider the list of potentially gendered roles below. Half a century ago, many of these were very clearly gendered roles in most American households. Which, if any, does your household treat with gender bias? Regardless of practices in your own home, which roles, if any, do you view with gender bias? That is, which roles do you imagine would be best performed by persons of a specific gender, and why?

Potentially Gendered Roles

- Taking out the trash
- Kitchen chores: cooking, washing dishes, cleaning up
- Laundry: sorting, washing, folding, putting away
- Car care: checking oil and fluids, airing up the tires
- Sewing or mending
- Team sports: football, tennis, baseball, softball, volleyball, soccer, lacrosse
- Performing as a dancer
- House cleaning: vacuuming, dusting, straightening
- Yard work: mowing a lawn, raking leaves, trimming shrubs, sawing limbs
- Building maintenance: exterior painting, cleaning gutters, changing light bulbs, fixing leaky faucets
- Child care: caring for younger children, feeding and changing infants
- Shopping: for groceries, clothing, sports equipment, power tools, household supplies
- Money management: paying bills, filing tax returns, creating savings, financial investments

Read Loki Leigh's "What Is My Gender?" (see below) aloud together. Discuss the concept of being transmasculine—having a woman's body and wanting facial hair but not a penis. Consider why this choice is preferable for Loki.

Imagine yourself in the future: What is your body like? Can you imagine yourself in the future, but without a body? Or can you imagine yourself with a body of the opposite sex? Try it. What did you discover? Imagine your best friend or a close sibling going through the struggle for self that Loki has experienced. How would you react? Consider both how you would like to imagine yourself reacting and how you think you would actually react.

Consider, also, that the preceding questions assume a gender binary. If your group has the time, visit chapter 5 about intersex persons, and view the documentary *Intersexion* described on page 67. What might your life be like if your experience crossed the gender binary by having a body that did not easily fit into either the *male* or *female* categories alone?

Personal Experience: "What Is My Gender?" by Loki Leigh, age 29, Southern California

I'd like to talk about gender identity and queerness as it relates to my sense of self and my own life.

This has proven to be more difficult than I had expected.

I have always known that I didn't quite fit in with those around me. Though I was assigned female at birth (AFAB), I have always been more masculine in the Western tradition than I am feminine. I hate pink, hate dresses, hate makeup, and I despise heels. Even when I was a child I wanted my hair to be really short, but I was told by my parents that "girls don't have short hair." I did play sports, though. I played softball, soccer, and water polo, I did swimming and I took karate. I often hung out with more boys than I did girls, and I enjoyed more stereotypically boy interests than I did girl interests. I was always a "tomboy" or "one of the guys." I was that girl who likes roughhousing and doesn't really understand the point of dresses or tea parties or princesses.

Once I got into middle school, this became a big issue. I was still very much a tomboy while the other girls were discovering makeup, fancy hairstyles, and pretty dresses. I still wanted to play sports and play fight, even though it had become increasingly difficult to find others willing to do this with me. The girls didn't like me because I was more comfortable around boys, and the boys didn't like me because I was stronger and tougher than they. I had a few friends in both groups who seemed to like me, but I still never really felt like I quite fit in properly.

When I hit puberty, I discovered that I was attracted to both girls and boys. While my girl friends were discussing boys, my boy friends were discussing girls, and no one was discussing feelings for both. I thought I was alone, and while the late 90s and early 2000s in Southern California were a better time and place to grow up queer than others, it was still not quite accepted. While I was realizing that I was bisexual, I was hearing from others that it was a negative thing, it meant that there is something wrong with that person.

When I finally came out to my friends as bisexual, they were all very accepting. They said it was a part of me, and they liked who I am, and it just didn't affect their opinion of me. But I still didn't have anyone in my life who was like me; anyone in my life with whom I could really relate. I was picked on all throughout high school for "looking like a dyke," and I heard from the adults in my life that same-sex attraction was disgusting and wrong. The world seemed to be telling me that being queer was a negative thing.

Flash forward to about 23 or 25 years old. I reclaimed the word "dyke" for myself, and used it as a personal descriptor. It felt powerful to reclaim a word that was used so often to hurt me when I was younger, but it just didn't feel like it fit properly. I tried putting other words around it to make it fit better, but nothing really seemed to help. It was like a piece of clothing that is just a little bit too small or too big. It almost fits, but is still slightly uncomfortable. In this same time frame, I learned about the existence of other genders than the standard binary I had grown up with, and realized that I am attracted to people of all gender identities, expressions, and sexes. I had completely accepted my sexuality as pansexual, and wore it proudly, and through learning about gender on a spectrum, I started thinking more about myself as a queer individual.

At 26, I went to University and joined the queer social sorority, Gamma Rho Lambda. I hadn't been very active in the queer community in my life. I wanted to change that and this fresh start in a new place was a very good opportunity for that. While I was an active member of GRL, I learned a lot more about gender identities and different experiences of gender. I started identifying as genderqueer and genderfluid, because I knew that I didn't really fit into either category of male or female.

As I'm nearing 30, I'm regularly using a chest binder, and I am finding that I feel much more comfortable with myself. I stopped shaving a few years ago, and have realized that I feel more comfortable with myself when I don't shave. It feels much more like me than I ever did while I was shaving. I keep my hair short, generally getting what would be described as a men's haircut. This fits me much better than my long hair ever did.

On June 8, 2016, I had a moment where I looked in the mirror and saw the man I'm going to be. It was . . . shocking; I almost took a step back from the sink because I didn't quite recognize myself. But it was also very affirming. It was a moment of clarity and realness. I saw the sharper facial structure I want; I saw the broad shoulders and strong arms. I had my arm across my chest adjusting my shirt, so I couldn't see my breasts, and I could imagine my flat chest. My hair was a little messy from bedhead, but looked definitively masculine.

It was only a moment. I could have blinked and missed it. But it was there. It gave me hope for the future when I was close to losing that. It had been a more difficult year than most; each week seemed to be getting more difficult. It was a nice moment to experience, and it came exactly when it was needed. I wish I could have grabbed a picture of that moment, to keep for when things get tough again.

I used to think that I just didn't believe in gender roles, and that there are no such things as masculine interests or personality traits. And while it is true that gender roles and the idea of gendered interests are pretty bullshit, I know that I am actually transmasculine and not butch feminine. I realize that my ambivalence and discomfort with my breasts is gender dysphoria, as is my disgust with my menstrual cycle. I realize the real terror I experience at the thought of being pregnant is also a form of dysphoria, instead of simply evidence that I don't want children. I don't really feel like I want a penis, but I do want facial hair, and for my face to have a more masculine sculpt to it. I want my voice to have a more masculine tone to it, and my body to have a more masculine form. I look forward to seeing my chest, masculine and flat without any aid.

While the world is still a very scary place for queer people, I know that I am going to be fine. Things will work themselves out, one way or the other. I may lose my blood family, but I have a chosen family who supports me fully. I have my partners, I have my sorority siblings, and I have my friends. Whenever the world gets scary, I can turn to them for help. Though things may be difficult, it is possible to find those who will see you through the rough times. I am scared for what my future holds, but I still know that it will be bright. I will become the man that I am, inside and out, and I will have the love and support of those closest to me in the process.[a]

Loki's narrative allows us to better understand some of the complexities of living across gender lines. Every personal story provides some insight into a world beyond our own realm of experience. In the next section, your group will consider the stories of a handful of teens whose experiences cross the gender spectrum.

Gender Roles

Next, have the group obtain copies of Susan Kuklin's book *Beyond Magenta: Transgender Teens Speak Out* (2014). Kuklin shares the stories of six transgender teens she interviewed. Have your group pick one or two stories to consider for each meeting; as the author notes, the stories need not be considered in the order she presents them.

For each person's story that your group discusses, consider how the following questions apply to each:

- What was the person's experience of gender as a young child?
- When did he, she, or they decide that society's gender classifications or rules did not apply to them?
- How was their difference treated in the home, at school, and in the community?
- How did each of you feel about the end of the story being discussed?

In addition to these questions, what struck you most about each person's story? How did this collection affect your identity as a potential ally or advocate?

Photographs

Now that you have read stories in *Beyond Magenta* and Loki Leigh's story, consider the series of photographs provided by social documentary photographer Zoe Perry-Wood. For more than a decade, she has attended and photographed participants at the prom hosted by the Boston Alliance of LGBTQ+ Youth (BAGLY), an organization founded in 1980 as the Boston Alliance for Gay and Lesbian Youth (hence the acronym, which has not changed even as the organization has grown). Perry-Wood's series "Hanging in the Balance: Portraits from the BAGLY Prom" documents lesbian, gay, bisexual, transgender, queer, questioning, and nonbinary youth at their prom—the prom where they may come as they are to celebrate and be celebrated. To see more of these photos, watch for the book she plans to publish featuring a selection of these portraits.

Consider each of the photographs included on pages 96–99. Each photo documents an individual in transition, on the road to becoming his, her, or their true self—which may differ from the self each presents to society every day. We have little information about the persons depicted. The photographer did not ask attendees to document gender identity when posing for photos. In your group, consider the following questions:

- What do you imagine about each person?
- Do you think you can see a bit of how society perhaps views each, as well as how they wish to be viewed?

This is Karma dancing in a blue chiffon dress while attending the 2015 BAGLY Prom in Boston, Massachusetts. *Photographed by Zoe Perry-Wood*

This is Hunter attending the 2017 BAGLY Prom in Boston, Massachusetts. Note the trans flag Hunter wears as a cape. *Photographed by Zoe Perry-Wood*

This is Eleonore attending the 2016 BAGLY Prom in Boston, Massachusetts. *Photographed by Zoe Perry-Wood*

These are friends (from left to right) Declan, Brandon, and Andre attending the 2015 BAGLY Prom in Boston, Massachusetts. *Photographed by Zoe Perry-Wood*

Here are Brandon (left) and their brother, Dan, attending the 2015 BAGLY Prom in Boston, Massachusetts. *Photographed by Zoe Perry-Wood*

This is Rae attending the 2016 BAGLY Prom in Boston, Massachusetts. *Photographed by Zoe Perry-Wood*

Try to imagine each person as a part of your circle of peers.

- How do you imagine yourself interacting with him, her, or them?
- How do you imagine yourself responding to comments by others about each person's gender expression?

Contemporary Literature: Parrotfish *by Ellen Whittlinger (2007)*

Told by the oldest of three children, a high school sophomore who has just changed his name from Angela to Grady, *Parrotfish* documents one young man's transition amid confusion at home and the ridicule of classmates.

Contemporary Literature: Luna *by Julie Ann Peters* (2004)

Luna is told by Regan, the younger sister of Liam—a boy who says he's a girl. As Liam slowly transitions into life as Luna, Regan watches—but with whom can she talk about it?

Note that in one of the photos, Brandon's brother Dan attended the prom with them. Would you have done this for your sibling? Why or why not? Lastly, what has this brief exercise taught you about yourself—your own fears, biases, and limitations?

Gender Roles in Young Adult Literature

Next, read some young adult literature. This can be done alone or with a group. Two suggestions of novels with transgender characters are included here. More can be found scattered throughout this book. If you work alone, keep a journal and imagine yourself in the narrator's place. If you're working with a group, hold discussions both midway through each book and at the end:

- How do others' views differ from your own?
- Does hearing others' thoughts change how you think about an issue?

Imagine Grady's family in *Parrotfish* or Regan's family in *Luna* as your next-door neighbor.

- Would the close proximity in any way change how you feel? Why do you imagine that could be?

Finally, after completing the other exercises in this chapter, and after reading both *Parrotfish* and *Luna*, ask yourself if you feel any different about persons choosing a gender expression other than that of the gender assigned to them at birth. What do you think prompted any change?

How Many Transgender People Are There?

Now that your group has considered the concept of gender and some of the aspects of transgender life, consider the numbers. What proportion of society is transgender? While studies have produced widely varying numbers over the years, no one has a good answer to the question. All agree the number is exceedingly small. There are numerous barriers to obtaining accurate numbers. Not only do most studies fail to directly ask questions about a person's gender identity, but also participants may decline to answer honestly. Indeed, the United States Decennial Census, taken every ten years since 1790, has yet to collect data on respondents' sexual orientation let alone include questions about gender identity. A 2016 study estimated the number of transgender persons in the United States at 0.58 percent, with North Dakota being the state estimated to have the lowest number of transgender residents at 0.3 percent, Hawaii the state estimated to have the highest transgender population at 0.78 percent, and the District of Columbia estimated to have 2.77 percent adult residents identifying as transgender. (The District of Columbia's urban geography and demographics make it unique.)[1]

As public acceptance for transgender persons increases, and as LGBTQ+ populations become more recognized by those who collect data, one might expect that the population estimate would also increase. In 2017, the Gay and Lesbian Alliance Against Defamation (now simply known as GLAAD)[2] noted that 6.4 percent of characters on broadcast television programs are LBGTQ. Many Americans see television as representative of the world at large and, thus, become more accepting of the unfamiliar after it has been normalized on television. I am hopeful that transgender visibility will continue to increase in society at large.

It's a Wrap

These conversations about gender have most likely impacted your perception of gender. To close your discussion, have the group consider how these photos, readings, films, and discussions have colored the ways you now see the world around you:

- In what ways do you think you will see the world differently now?
- In what ways do you think it may impact your interactions with very young children, with androgynous persons, or with people whose gender expression somehow conflicts with your expectation of their gender role?

Answer these questions in the journal you have maintained, and then look back over your growth over the course of these weeks.

Continuing the Conversation

After pursuing the suggestions in this chapter, you and your group will be equipped to consider gender more fully than before your discussions—and likely more fully than those persons around you who have not delved so deeply into the question. Some of you may wish to continue the journey. Visit the "Resources" section at the end of this book to find organizations and a wealth of information that will allow your group to design its own gender conversations.

TRANSFORMATIONS

Choosing to Change

At some point, any one of us may decide the time is right to make a change. Meeting the expectations of society may be comfortable in some respects, but sometimes the need to be ourselves overrides the aim to please. When the issue is a deep-seated need within a person, she or he can either continue with the status quo or make the change that feels right.

Some of these changes are more drastic than others. The middle-aged man who buys a new sports car and drives about with the top down may turn a few heads or incite gossip, but for the most part the worst he will face is some ribbing from his buddies. Today, even the closeted homosexual can come out as a lesbian or gay man in most parts of the United States without her or his world grinding to a halt—although loss of employment, family, and/or community supports may occur. For most, a degree of social discomfort can be expected, and some families may experience irreparable rifts, but as more and more people come out, and LBGT+ life gains visibility and acceptance in the media, gay life becomes more commonplace in the eyes of those who did not accept it previously.

For transgender and gender-nonconforming persons, full acceptance is farther away. Transgender storylines are increasing on television, in movies, and in books, and the short-lived 2017 courtroom drama *Doubt* featured Laverne Cox playing a strong trans woman attorney. However, transgender characters in crime dramas such as *Law & Order*, *NCIS*, and *Criminal Minds* are frequently depicted as victims of violence, including homicide.

> **❗ Even Shakespeare Knew**
>
> In William Shakespeare's *Hamlet*, a famous line occurs in act 1, scene 3, when Polonius advises his son Laertes, "This above all: to thine own self be true, and it must follow as the night the day, thou cans't not then be false to any man."[a]

Despite the risks, many people experience a driving need to reshape their lives around their true selves. For the transgender person, there is no one right or wrong way to make such a change. One must change to the extent he, she, or ze feels comfortable—until one feels at home in his, her, or hir body. Some persons will be satisfied by simply dressing and acting in the manner of their true sex, expressing their gender identity, and have no desire or need to change their physical bodies through the use of hormones or surgery. Some may make temporary cosmetic or wardrobe changes, much the way shapewear (what your grandmother knew as a *girdle*) controls a midriff bulge, lasting only as long as the garment is worn. Others may use hormones to cause the body to appear more feminine or masculine. Those who choose to make surgical changes have a far greater need to inhabit a body that brings their sex in line with their gender identity; surgery is invasive, permanent, and very expensive.

Changing genders is a life-altering process. The enormity of the process the trans person undergoes is unfathomable to the majority of us. While any outcome of transitioning is acceptable if it helps a person feel more whole or real, the public nature of the process itself often puts a trans person at risk. The seemingly simple choice of which restroom to use can become fraught with anxiety or even danger. A male transitioning to female may have difficulty locating an appropriate restroom until ze can successfully pass most of the time. Imagine someone who appears to be a man, wearing a dress and entering into a large public restroom; think for a minute about how other patrons might react. While a person who appears to be a woman dressed as a man—wearing pants, or a suit and tie—is more likely to be accepted in a women's restroom or to pass in the men's room (a discussion of standing to urinate is located later in this chapter), ze still risks disdain or ridicule, at the least. But more goes into a gender transition than clothing. Not only are males and females built differently, but they also tend to move (walk, sit, stand, or gesture) and speak differently. A trans person must be an excellent student, observing nuances in tone and mannerisms, then molding his or her own speech and movement to fit society's expectations of the gender role he or she is presenting.

World's First Transsexual

In 1952 Christine Jorgensen garnered worldwide attention by becoming the world's first public male-to-female transsexual. Stepping into the limelight following her surgery, Christine became a media magnet who intrigued the public for years. Much attention was given to her appearance, for her actions directly contradicted the notion that sex and gender were unchangeable. Jorgenson, formerly a private in the US Army, was a beautiful, charismatic, and successful woman.

Reactions of Family and Colleagues

Major transitions result in permanent changes in a person's life. When coming out to one's family, whether as transgender or homosexual, a person cannot be sure of unconditional support. Many families do not survive such announcements and may sever ties. The numbers of homeless gay, lesbian, and transgender teens

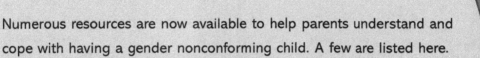

Helping Parents Understand

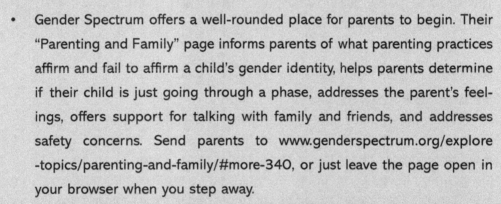

Numerous resources are now available to help parents understand and cope with having a gender nonconforming child. A few are listed here.

- Gender Spectrum offers a well-rounded place for parents to begin. Their "Parenting and Family" page informs parents of what parenting practices affirm and fail to affirm a child's gender identity, helps parents determine if their child is just going through a phase, addresses the parent's feelings, offers support for talking with family and friends, and addresses safety concerns. Send parents to www.genderspectrum.org/explore -topics/parenting-and-family/#more-340, or just leave the page open in your browser when you step away.
- The Trans Youth Equality Foundation's website parent resource page offers more than a half-dozen videos recommended for parents, and offers a glossary, and links to school and legal resources. The videos include a homemade video by a young transman, a couple of short documentaries, a commentary by the medical director of the Transyouth Center for Health and Development, and various TEDx talks. Recommend this site to parents: www.transyouthequality.org/for-parents/.
- For those wanting to start with a general parenting site, not one specific to gender issues, try FamilyEducation.com. Their "6 Tips for Understanding and Raising a Transgender Child" article is informative and affirming, and includes links to other resources. Send parents to www.familyeducation.com/life/gender-differences/6-tips-understanding -raising-transgender-child.

continue to rise in the United States as youth become increasingly bold about asserting individual identities. Indeed, a 2012 study determined that LGBT youth represent about 7 percent of the general population but comprise 40 percent of the population of homeless youth.[1] Some teens are subjected to violence in their homes, and they may choose to leave a bad situation or may find themselves put out onto the street. As open-minded as many parents perceive themselves to be, the news that a child wishes to change their gender or to love a person of the same sex can be devastating to the parent's perception of the child and the child's future. Even if the child is an adult living independently from the family of origin, to parents the child is still their baby.

Transitioning while at school or working in an office creates its own set of challenges. Some people will doubtless be supportive and eager to understand, but others may be uncomfortable, distrustful, or even afraid. If you are preparing to transition, make arrangements with your school or place of employment to have safe havens. Some restrooms might become off-limits—to either the person in transition or to his or her colleagues—in order to provide comfortable facilities for all. Prepare peers and colleagues before making a complete transition, and prepare yourself for potential rejection or even violent backlash.

Making the Change

Understand that some of the changes described herein are permanent. Not everyone who transitions chooses to remain in the new gender. For a myriad of reasons, some people choose to revert to the sex they were assigned at birth, months or years after making a transition. No matter when the detransition occurs, one cannot undo the infertility or sterility caused by the long-term use of sex hormones or the surgical removal of sex organs. Additionally, persons wanting the option of having biological children one day, and who have reached sexual maturity in the bodies into which they were born, should discuss the possibility of banking sperm or harvesting and freezing eggs prior to undergoing irreversible changes.

As stated previously, people change along a continuum, hopefully to whatever degree each person is comfortable, but this may be limited to the change a person can afford financially. Hairstyle, wardrobe, and makeup changes can start the process. At the same time, anyone attempting such a transition must of necessity become a student of human behavior, observing the ways in which people speak (tone of voice, volume, word choices, even how they cough or clear their throat), how they move (body carriage, the purposefulness of each step, even hand gestures), and how they interact. People act differently around persons of the opposite sex than with their own gender. Tutors and coaches are available, for a fee, to help one learn new behaviors.

Beyond the expense of a new wardrobe (provided that one has even felt comfortable enough to shop for new clothes), how does a person fit a body of one sex into the clothing of the other? A female seeking to pass as a male may find mammary tissue poses an obstacle, but breasts can be bound close-to-flat using binders sold specifically for female-to-male transitions or using firm sports bras. To enhance the appearance of maleness, a suggestive bulge can be created near the crotch of tight-fitting pants using something as simple as a rolled pair of tube socks; this is called *packing*. A male seeking to pass as a female must reverse the process. To create a semblance of breasts, a bra can be padded with wadded tissue or cloth, or gel inserts might be used. To create a smoother panty line, males can tuck the external genitals into tightly fitted briefs. These, of course, are temporary measures. For a more complete effect, one can take hormones or have surgery—but both require prior medical approval.

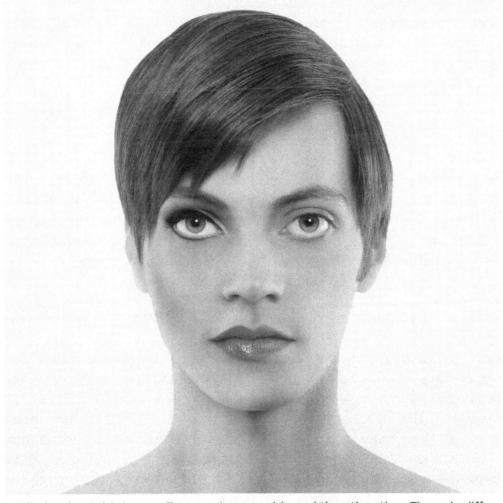

Look closely at this image. Try covering one side and then the other. The only differences between each side are the haircut and makeup. Is the subject male or female?
© iStock / Visivasnc

Haircuts

Women with short hair who are not taking testosterone generally look different from men with short hair. A good barber can create a convincing haircut, but sideburns must grow in (or be applied with makeup) to complete the male appearance. Men may find wigs useful during transition since growing out one's own hair takes time.

Hair Removal

Male-to-female trans persons must deal with the male body's tendency to produce excessive hair. Although female hormone treatments reduce the amount of body hair, facial hair is less affected. Shaving can provide a temporary fix, but electrolysis actually destroys hair at the root. The authors of *True Selves: Understanding Transsexualism* estimate that an average male has at least thirty thousand thick facial hairs, which may require three hundred to five hundred hours of treatment. Not only is the process tedious and painful, but it may cost as much as sexual reassignment surgery itself.[2]

Voice

Although estrogen does not affect the pitch of a man's voice, testosterone lowers the register of a woman's voice by thickening the vocal chords. Male-to-female (MTF) trans persons, then, may need to search out voice coaches more often than will their female-to-male (FTM) counterparts. To start the process, one can use free vocal coaching resources available on the GenderLife website.[3]

Chests and Breasts—Nonsurgical Techniques

Pretestosterone FTMs likely will have greater breast development than desired. Chest binding can provide a convincing male silhouette, but it requires that upper-body clothing be worn throughout the day—even on hot summer days when other males may wear just an undershirt, if that. Chest binders should be used sparingly, no more than eight to ten hours a day at most. Continual binding breaks down tissue and can cause breathing problems, skin irritation, and even back pain. Never bind with an elastic bandage, as this can restrict proper breathing and movement. Whereas firm sports bras are designed to move with a person during a workout, chest binders are not. Listen to your body: if it hurts, stop.

Resources for MTF trans persons can be found through outlets for the trans community or for female post-mastectomy patients. Well before considering breast augmentation surgery, options include padding a bra or wearing false breasts inserted into a bra. Never inject silicone under the skin, as the results can be disastrous. (See the later section on silicone.)

Packing and Restroom Survival

In order to pass successfully in public, FTM trans persons may choose to "pack" their pants with stuffing to create a bulge suggestive of a penis. (In the opening scene of *Boys Don't Cry*, Hilary Swank's character is preparing to become Brandon. She is seen packing a rolled pair of sweat socks into the front of the jeans she's wearing that night.) Those who seek greater realism can find any number of imitations available in adult stores, up to and including prosthetic penises.

Those wanting to both pack and urinate from a standing position might investigate "pack and pee" devices such as the Mango (not a fruit, but *man* + *go*; get it?), which is designed specifically for preoperative transmen. A combination packing and urinary device, the Mango is designed to be worn all day and enable those with female genital anatomy to stand and urinate in public with confidence. Resources for FTM trans people can be found online and through advertisements and stores of various transgender organizations. Also, devices marketed to women for use when camping or traveling (for standing urination) can be found online and through some sporting goods stores.

Silicone

People seeking to enhance their bodily curves, whether the goal is fuller cheeks or the development of breast tissue, may consider silicone injections; however, Google "silicone for cheeks and breasts" and you will get more results for why silicone should never be injected into the body, and horror stories to illustrate the point. Injecting silicone into the body, while it may produce quick and pleasing results, can be exceedingly problematic, even life-threatening. In the United States, physicians are prohibited by law from injecting medical-grade silicone into the human body.

Those eager for quick results may resort to using an underground network of nonmedical personnel who pump industrial-grade silicone (such as that used in caulking compounds found in hardware and auto parts stores) under the skin for a sizable fee. One single treatment may cost a few hundred dollars, and multiple treatments are often required to achieve the desired result. Providers who skip

This transgender man's well-developed facial hair doubtlessly serves to aid his easily being "read" by others as male. © iStock / Monsterstock1

With her curvy figure and feminine carriage, this young transgender woman should be easily "read" by others as female. © iStock / Ranta images

into and out of town quickly enough to avoid detection by authorities leave their clients without support should complications ensue—and some complications may not arise for years.

One hazard with silicone injections is acute respiratory distress,[4] which can occur several years following the injection. Another hazard is that silicone may soften and move within the body, causing unsightly lumps and bumps in undesirable locations.[5] Once silicone is introduced into the body, it can be difficult to remove; people who have had silicone injected to enlarge breast tissue sometimes require a mastectomy (removal of the entire breast) to remove it later. Anyone seeking to make permanent changes to his or her appearance is urged to carefully research both the procedure and the provider before acting.

Puberty Blockers

Puberty generally begins around age ten in female-bodied persons and age eleven in male-bodied persons, when the pituitary gland releases the hormones LH (luteinizing hormone) and FSH (follicle-stimulating hormone). In female-bodied persons, these hormones stimulate the ovaries to produce the sex hormone estrogen; in male-bodied persons they stimulate the testes to produce the sex hormone testosterone. (The effects of the sex hormones are detailed later.) Gender-dysphoric young persons who have not yet entered the second stage of puberty can consult with a pediatric endocrinologist who may prescribe puberty blockers—medicines that essentially pause the body's biological drive to develop fully into adulthood by suppressing the release of FSH and LH into the body.

Adolescents who use puberty blockers followed by cross-gender hormone treatments will never develop reproductive function in their birth sex. This means any opportunity for producing biological offspring will be lost, so consider the ramifications before you take this step.[6]

Puberty blockers are available either in an injectable form or as an under-the-skin implant. The injections are administered either once a month or once every three months, and can be done at home. The implant is designed to last for a year and must be placed by a surgeon using local anesthesia. When the use of puberty blockers is discontinued, the body is able to continue with puberty.

These same medicines may be used to suppress the body's hormone production during medical transition in adult patients, to increase the effectiveness of cross-hormone therapy.[7]

Hormone Treatments

After working with a gender therapist for some months, a trans person may be deemed ready to undertake hormone treatments.[8] The introduction of male or female hormones to the body causes distinct changes. According to the World Professional Association for Transgender Health (WPATH) *Standards of Care*, hormones should be used with supervision and with parental consent in the case of adolescents.[9] In some countries adolescents may make their own medical decisions as early as age sixteen, but in the United States one must be eighteen to do so.

Hormone treatments carry risks and side effects, including increased blood pressure, heart or liver disease, and blood clots. Once hormone treatments have been started, they need to be continued throughout a person's life.

Testosterone

For the FTM trans person, testosterone injections cause a number of changes. Those listed in the WPATH *Standards of Care* include the following:

- Deepened voice
- Clitoral enlargement (varies)
- Growth of facial and body hair
- Cessation of menstruation and ovulation
- Atrophy (shrinking) of breast tissue
- Increased libido
- Decreased body fat in relation to muscle mass[10]

Additionally, the *Standards of Care* suggest other medications that can be used briefly at the start of hormone therapy in patients who have begun menstruating, to encourage the body to stop menstruation.

Estrogen

For the MTF trans person, estrogen can be taken by injections, pills, or skin patches. It generally causes a number of changes. Those listed in the WPATH *Standards of Care* include the following:

- Breast growth
- Decreased libido and erections
- Decreased testicular size
- Increase of body fat compared to muscle mass[11]

Additionally, the WPATH *Standards of Care* lists androgen-reducing medications, also called antiandrogens or testosterone blockers, which are often used in conjunction with estrogen. These antiandrogens reduce the body's testosterone levels or activity, enabling MTF trans persons to rely on lower doses of estrogen.

Surgeries

Several nongenital cosmetic surgical procedures are available. For the MTF trans person, these may include the following:

- Breast augmentation mammoplasty
- Facial feminization surgery
- Liposuction
- Lipofilling
- Voice surgery
- Thyroid cartilage reduction
- Gluteal augmentation
- Hair reconstruction
- Various aesthetic procedures[12]

For the FTM trans person, the nongenital cosmetic surgeries may include the following:

- Mastectomy to create a male chest
- Voice surgery (although this is rare)
- Liposuction
- Lipofilling
- Pectoral implants
- Various aesthetic procedures[13]

Sexual reassignment surgery (SRS) is major surgery, and it may include a number of operations. According to the WPATH *Standards of Care*, prerequisites include achieving the legal age of majority for medical decision making (which is eighteen years old in the United States), and living full time in the desired gender for at least one full year. Further, one letter of support from a qualified mental health professional is required as a prerequisite to breast or chest surgery, also referred to as "top" surgery, and two such letters are required before "bottom" surgery.[14]

See figure 7.1 for a timeline of the transition from female to male, and see figure 7.2 for a timeline of the transition from male to female.

SRS may also be referred to as GRS (gender reassignment surgery) or GCS (gender confirmation surgery). Whichever name is used, "top" surgery refers

Female to Male Timeline

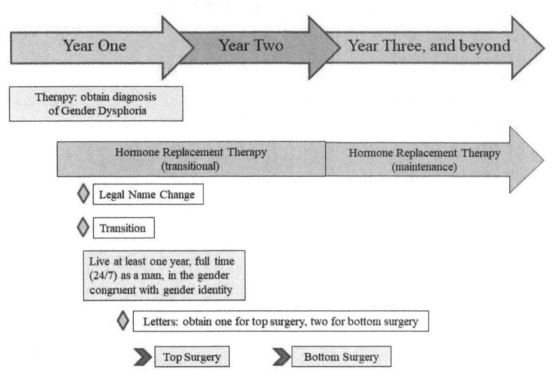

Figure 7.1. Timeline for transition from female to male. Prerequisites for gender reassignment surgery include therapy and a diagnosis of gender dysphoria from a qualified mental health professional; hormone replacement therapy; living full time in the gender congruent with one's gender identity; and obtaining letters of support from professionals in the field. *Slide adapted from one provided in 2006 by Mary Ann Horton, PhD, of Red Ace Consulting Services using the WPATH Standards of Care version 7.*

to mammoplasty, which may include mastectomy (breast removal), chest reconstruction, or breast augmentation. Although hormone therapy is not a prerequisite for top surgery in FTM patients, it is recommended that MTF trans persons undergo at least a full year of feminizing hormone therapy before surgery. "Bottom" surgery refers to the removal of the sex organs and the creation of genitals through plastic surgery. Bottom operations could include hysterectomy, vaginectomy, urethroplasty, and phalloplasty for the FTM trans person, and vaginoplasty and labiaplasty for the MTF trans person. Although such surgeries do not create internal organs, they can create structures that are similar in appearance to genetic female or male genitalia. Election to undergo SRS is an extremely personal choice. A full year of hormone replacement therapy and a full year of living full time in the gender role that is congruent with the person's gender identity are prerequisites to undergoing bottom surgery.

Surgery can be prohibitively expensive. Prior to surgery, costs include counseling, hormone therapy, and—of course—that new wardrobe. After surgery, costs include follow-up medical care and counseling, and hormone therapy for life.

Male to Female Timeline

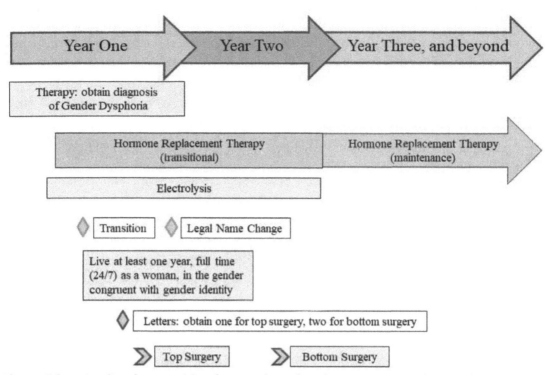

Figure 7.2. Timeline for transition from male to female. Prerequisites for gender reassignment surgery include therapy, and a diagnosis of gender dysphoria from a qualified mental health professional; hormone replacement therapy; living full time in the gender congruent with one's gender identity; and obtaining letters of support from professionals in the field. *Slide adapted from one provided in 2006 by Mary Ann Horton, PhD, of Red Ace Consulting Services using the WPATH Standards of Care version 7.*

Surgery, including all the prerequisite costs, can cost anywhere from tens of thousands of dollars to more than $100,000. Plastic surgery performed for cosmetic reasons is generally not covered by an insurance plan; however, if it is viewed as medically necessary to alleviate gender dysphoria, surgery is more likely to be covered by insurance. In 2014, Medicare, which provides insurance coverage for older Americans and persons with disabilities, removed its categorical exclusion of transsexual surgery and now considers such surgeries on a case-by-case basis.[15] The Human Rights Campaign website's State Map of Laws and Policies regarding transgender health care identifies four states that ban insurance exclusions for transgender health care, and twelve states that both ban such insurance exclusions and provide transgender-inclusive health benefits for state employees.[16] Although insurance coverage for transgender care is gaining ground, many people are without such coverage. Some people choose to seek treatment overseas. Even with the expense of travel, treatment in some other countries may be thousands of dollars less expensive than in the United States.

Beyond the financial cost, persons considering GCS must weigh the risks and benefits. Any surgical procedure carries with it a measure of medical risk. Internal bleeding or postoperative infection can be a life-threatening complication. No one undergoes GCS without first undertaking extensive and time-consuming preparations.

Additionally, a very few persons who have undergone GCS later opt to de-transition; such "reversal" surgeries are extraordinarily rare, but are possible. In Belgrade, Serbia, one specialist in genital reconstruction has been performing gender reversal surgeries for five years now and has completed a few more than a dozen to date.[17]

Legal Changes

At the beginning of the experience of living full time in the gender role congruent with one's gender identity, various legal hurdles present themselves. Most people assume a new name in addition to the new gender, and these changes require revisions to existing legal documents. While younger people may be able to postpone making legal changes, those driving cars, voting, or in the workforce cannot. A multitude of documents require changes, including one's driver's license, social security card, credit cards and bank accounts, employment and school records, titles and deeds to property, professional licenses and credentials, patents, will, stocks or bonds, and passport. Laws regarding changes to birth certificates and driver's licenses vary from state to state. Since 2010, passport gender markers "may be changed from 'M' to 'F' or vice versa with a letter from a doctor rather than requiring sex reassignment surgery."[18] Some states, including all of those on the West Coast, now also allow nonbinary gender markers on various forms of government identification.[19] Accomplishing all of these changes is a daunting task that is both time-consuming and often frustrating. During the process, transgender persons must use care to not obliterate all past records, as sometimes they might need to prove their prior identities.[20]

Needless to say, each of the steps involved in a gender transition require emotional strength and fortitude. In obtaining a diagnosis of gender dysphoria, a person becomes a mental health patient, a fact that may prove troublesome in the future. No one undertakes such an all-encompassing change lightly.

The WPATH *Standards of Care*

The World Professional Association for Transgender Health was originally named the Harry Benjamin International Gender Dysphoria Association (HBIGDA), after one of the first physicians to work with gender dysphoric persons, Harry

> ## WPATH Identity Recognition Statement
>
> In November 2017, WPATH updated its Identity Recognition Statement to state, "WPATH recognizes that, for optimal physical and mental health, persons must be able to freely express their gender identity, whether or not that identity conforms to the expectations of others." (To read the full WPATH Identity Recognition Statement, see Appendix A.)

Benjamin (1885–1986). HBIGDA established standards of care in 1977, which have been regularly updated since 1977. Now in its seventh revision, the WPATH *Standards of Care for the Health of Transsexual, Transgender, and Gender Nonconforming People* provides prerequisites to hormone treatments or sex reassignment surgery. For surgical gonad removal—hysterectomy and ovariectomy (removal of uterus and ovaries) for FTM persons or orchiectomy (removal of testicles) for MTF persons—for the purpose of treating gender dysphoria, the prerequisites include the following:

- Persistent, well-documented gender dysphoria
- Ability to make one's own decisions and give fully informed consent
- Being of the age of majority (legal adult)
- Being without significant medical or mental health concerns (or with such issues well controlled)
- A full year of continuous hormone therapy appropriate to the person's gender goals

For surgical construction of new genitals (penis or vagina), the *Standards of Care* specify the preceding prerequisites and add twelve continuous months of living in the gender role congruent with one's gender identity.[21]

Although some persons find the twelve months of living in the gender role congruent with one's gender identity to be cumbersome, the standards help ensure that only appropriate individuals are approved for such treatments.

LEGAL ISSUES

I f you look around—in school, at the mall, or in a park—you may be aware of varied gender expressions: the girl with the buzz cut, the boy who is more effeminate than macho. But for the most part, everyone (including the two aforementioned individuals) will look relatively normal to you. Why is that? For one thing, we're living in the twenty-first century, where diversity is often expressed and even celebrated. Today's women, men, and gender-nonconforming persons have far more socially accepted ways of expressing themselves and their gender than did our forebears. Think about it. Can you imagine life before blue jeans? Can you imagine being female before women wore pants?

Although today's women wear pants, run for public office and vote, and enter careers as a matter of course, legal protections for sexual minorities and gender-variant individuals have much room for improvement. The laws concerning gender issues have evolved over recent years, and they continue to change today. Whether the laws are about school climate, gender markers, bathroom use, employment, military service, marriage, or foster parenting and adoption, the lives of LGBTQIA persons among us are greatly impacted by legislation.

Having guidelines for acceptable behavior enshrined in law is helpful. Take, for example, the continuing evolution of bathroom laws in the country (see chapter 9). Although having laws is not the same as having a wholly like-minded

! Arrested for Wearing Pants

Cross-dressing was once illegal. In November 1852, the *New York Daily Times* reported that Emma Snodgrass, age seventeen, had been arrested in Boston, for a second time, for wearing pants. Her unusual attire garnered publicity from New York to California. In June 1863, the *Democrat Banner* of Davenport, Iowa, reported that Snodgrass had been arrested in Cleveland, Ohio, but the following month the *Grant County Herald* of Lancaster, Wisconsin, reported, "Emma Snodgrass has repented, gone home, taken off her breeches, and sworn eternal attachment to petticoats and propriety. This is to her credit."[a]

citizenry, once a law is in place, life within that law's confines becomes easier. To get a picture of laws and policies affecting gender and sexual minority persons in the United States in general, and in your state specifically, the Movement Advancement Project (MAP) offers a website chock-full of up-to-date graphic images. Several appear in this chapter. Visit lgbtmap.org/ to see what MAP offers.

School Climate

What rights do you feel that gender-variant individuals should have? Should "all men are created equal" really mean that all people are created equal—and deserve equal protection in the eyes of the law? Think about it. Each time a minority or an oppressed class of persons is granted an equal right, then the majority or ruling class effectively loses some special treatment previously accorded them. When *Brown v. Board of Education*[1] decided that racial segregation of schools was unconstitutional and black students should be allowed to attend white schools, the privileged white students lost their right to have racially separate schools. While we all gained something by having culturally diverse learning environments, those formerly at the top also lost their exclusive privilege to have the best education that could be offered in a culturally homogenous learning environment.

One aspect of educational equality involves students' right to protection from harm while at school. Gender-variant (LGBT and gender-nonconforming) students need to have their rights stated in the law so that they can realize protections equal to those of their peers while in school. Long before the bathroom battles began, Safe Schools laws were enacted to ensure LGBT youth could learn in supportive environments. In 1993, Massachusetts became the first state to enact a Safe Schools law. Laws like this give all students, including those who are gender-variant, the right to feel safe in their educational environment and make it illegal to harass and intimidate those who are perceived as being different with regard to sex, sexual orientation, or gender identity. Without these laws, intimidating someone by scrawling "queer" across his or her locker might be perceived by some as morally wrong, but it would not be illegal. Even with Safe Schools laws in place and a supportive faculty and staff, LGBTQIA students, who often face teasing and harassment in schools, must advocate for themselves.

Even before the advent of Safe Schools laws, New York City's consideration of school safety for LGBTQ youth became clear with the opening of the Harvey Milk High School in 1985. Named for San Francisco's openly gay city supervisor Harvey Milk, who was slain at City Hall in 1978, Milk High School began as a two-room alternative program designed to provide a haven for the most at-risk gay students who had been harassed in other school settings. The world's first gay school program within an existing high school quietly helped students for

> ## Safe Schools Law
>
> In response to a 1993 education report and extensive personal testimony by gay and lesbian adolescents before the state legislature, Massachusetts governor William Weld signed a law deeming that schools must be kept safe for LGBT youth.[b]
>
> Today, policy models are available online. By providing the resources, you can assist your school or district craft effective policies of their own. Here are links to two places where models can be found:
>
> - GLSEN provides resource downloads for state, district, and school model policies. Visit www.glsen.org/article/model-laws-policies.
> - The Safe Schools Coalition has a page devoted to model and sample school and district policies and procedures sourced from myriad states and districts. The district policy from Vancouver, British Columbia, is offered in eight languages. Visit safeschoolscoalition.org/lawpolicy-models.html.

nearly twenty years. But when the school opened as a distinctly separate building in 2003, it quickly became controversial. Although the school is technically open to all students, opponents argue that federal and state tax dollars should not be "used to fund a segregated high school for homosexual students."[2] When it was targeted as a segregationist school providing special services to LGBT youth, Milk High School was defended by advocates for LGBT youth, including New York City mayor Michael Bloomberg. Since the school's inception in 1985, other programs have been modeled after Harvey Milk High.

Federal and state laws mandate that schools provide safe spaces for students to learn. Some state policies specifically address sexual orientation or gender identity. The Movement Advancement Project provides an array of maps like those in figures 8.1 and 8.2 that depict state-level laws and policies and are updated in real time as policy changes occur. As of this writing, nineteen states and the District of Columbia have laws that expressly prohibit bullying in schools on the basis of sexual orientation and gender identity, while twenty-four states have no law protecting LGBT students in school. (See sidebar "Safe Schools Law" above for guidelines about Safe Schools policies, and models of effective policies.) Feeling unsafe at school can be a frightening, isolating experience. Even with student and faculty support, every time homo- and transphobic taunts are aired, the cli-

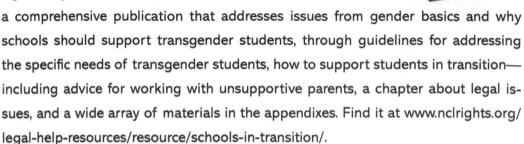

Resource Booklet: Schools in Transition (2015)

Schools in Transition: A Guide for Supporting Transgender Students in K–12 Schools is a comprehensive publication that addresses issues from gender basics and why schools should support transgender students, through guidelines for addressing the specific needs of transgender students, how to support students in transition—including advice for working with unsupportive parents, a chapter about legal issues, and a wide array of materials in the appendixes. Find it at www.nclrights.org/legal-help-resources/resource/schools-in-transition/.

mate of safety is weakened. If you feel unsafe in your school, find out what the law requires in your location, what policy the school has in place, and then seek moral support from a trusted adult. Try visiting the Safe Schools Coalition website and follow the pink triangle beside "Resources by Location" to find an extensive listing of community-based LGBTQ support groups and Safe Schools coalitions across the United States and around the globe. What do you think? Should every student be protected from bullying while at school?

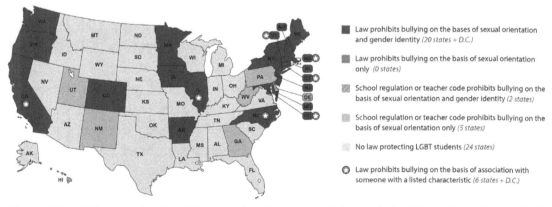

Safe School Anti-Bullying Laws

- Law prohibits bullying on the bases of sexual orientation and gender identity *(20 states + D.C.)*
- Law prohibits bullying on the basis of sexual orientation only *(0 states)*
- School regulation or teacher code prohibits bullying on the basis of sexual orientation and gender identity *(2 states)*
- School regulation or teacher code prohibits bullying on the basis of sexual orientation only *(5 states)*
- No law protecting LGBT students *(24 states)*
- Law prohibits bullying on the basis of association with someone with a listed characteristic *(6 states + D.C.)*

Figure 8.1. This map by the Movement Advancement Project depicts ratings for antibullying laws and statewide regulations protecting LGBT students from bullying by other students, teachers, and school staff on the basis of sexual orientation and gender identity by state and is current to September 17, 2018. The updated map and links to the state-by-state statutes are available at www.lgbtmap.org/equality-maps/safe_school_laws. *Courtesy of the Movement Advancement Project*

Identity Document Laws and Policies

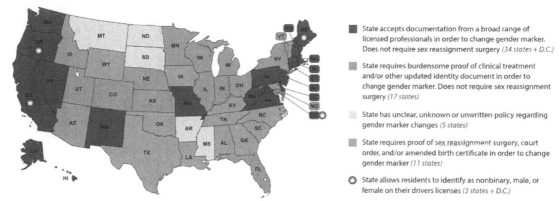

Figure 8.2. This map by the Movement Advancement Project depicts ratings for laws and policies governing identity documents by state and is current to September 17, 2018. Updated maps are available at http://www.lgbtmap.org/equality-maps. *Courtesy of the Movement Advancement Project*

Changing Name and/or Gender Markers on Identity Documents

In today's United States cross-gender dressing can be greeted less-than-enthusiastically. Having names and gender markers on legal documents that match a person's gender identity is important. In order to open a bank account, enroll in school, start a new job, or travel, accurate and consistent identity documents are necessary.

Name Changes

Changing one's name can be an entirely free and informal process—up to a point. Nicknames are an example of this. You can call friends by whatever name they ask you to, even if it is not their legal name, because informally, no legal documentation is required. Yet, formal arrangements (such as enrolling in school, applying for a job, or traveling) require legal documentation. When one is ready to travel, for example, airline tickets must be issued in the name matching the legal documentation shown at the airport, whether that's a passport, driver's license, or school ID.

Birth certificates are the first legal document bearing a person's name and gender marker and become the basis for issuance of future documents such as Social Security cards, driver's licenses, passports, and school records—including academic transcripts and degrees. Just because a person chooses to change his or her name does not automatically necessitate a change to previous documents. For example, I am a cisgender female who now carries a third name. The first was issued at birth. The second came about due to marriage. The third was obtained by directly petitioning the court. Now, when applying for licensure or federal employment, at some point in the process I will provide each name and the years during which each was used. Previously issued documents—including Social Security card, driver's license, and passport—needed modifications; no changes to birth certificate or school records were made. Yet, for transgender persons, especially if the names being changed clearly indicate gender, a more thorough approach to earlier documents would be in order.

Name changes generally require court approval, and requirements for changing one's legal name vary from state to state. The "Identity Documents Center" section of the National Center for Transgender Equality (NCTE) website can help you navigate the process for changing any government-issued identity documents in your state, district, or territory. (Visit transequality.org/documents.)

The cost for changing one's name varies widely. According to one article, the cost generally ranges between $150 and $500 for court and filing fees. The documentation varies by state and the filing fees vary by county. After the court orders the name change, you will need to obtain official copies of the court document, which may run you fifteen or twenty dollars per copy. With this document in hand, you can then begin the process of changing your name elsewhere, including any of the following that apply to your case: driver's license or state ID, passport, birth certificate, credit cards and rewards programs, bank accounts, mortgages or loans, Social Security card, insurance policies, voter registration, and investment and retirement accounts. Some of the aforementioned will require fees, although many do not.[3]

Gender Marker Changes

Having the correct gender marker on a person's identity documents allows one to function more effectively in society. The transgender person who is living authentically but showing documents that do not match is open for being questioned or ridiculed; being denied employment, housing, or public benefits; and being targeted with physical violence. Changing one's name and gender on identity documents can be complicated and very expensive. As such, only about one-fifth of transgender people who have transitioned have been able to update all their IDs and records.[4]

Nonbinary

In June 2016, Jamie Shupe became the first person in the United States to be granted a nonbinary gender by the courts.[5] Jamie Shupe was assigned male at birth. After serving the US Army as a sergeant, Shupe was discharged as a female.

Video: "Movie Theater"

To get a quick feel for why matching identity documents are important in everyday life, watch "Movie Theater," a brief video advertisement by MAP. In it a transgender man goes to the movies with friends, but then breaks off from his group to purchase an adult beverage. When he shows his ID, the gender marker does not match his gender identity and presentation. Not only does he face ridicule from the server, but also the server intercedes when the man attempts to use the restroom. The one-minute segment closes as the transgender man is being escorted from the business.

Watch the video on the MAP website at www.lgbtmap.org/movie-theater-ad. Or find it on YouTube at www.youtube.com/watch?v=GSbg-zc2aV4.

Yet, neither classification fits this person, who uses the pronoun *they*. Shupe, who lived for nearly fifty years as male and, as of 2016, had lived three years wholly as female, wrote in an op-ed for the *Guardian*: "As a transgender person with male biology and distinctly feminine traits, I believe myself to be a unique variation of nature. I am not ashamed of who I am. I was not born into the wrong body. My genitals are not a birth defect. And I am not to be sterilized by psychiatry and a medical establishment that has run amok. After a historic court ruling, I am free."[6] Shupe wanted the nonbinary classification not only for themself, but also for all those who follow. And follow they have.

Kelly Keenan, who is intersex and uses the pronoun *she*, was granted a nonbinary gender classification in the Superior Court of Santa Cruz, California, in September 2016. Five other petitions for nonbinary gender classifications were scheduled to be heard in four additional Northern California counties that fall. Keenan planned to seek change within the California Department of Motor Vehicles (DMV) so that she might obtain an updated license, and the New York Bureau of Vital Statistics so that she might amend her birth certificate. (California's DMV will begin issuing gender-neutral licenses in early 2019.) In an article about her petition, Keenan said, "Creating a legal nonbinary designation is just the government and society catching up to reality. To believe no blending ever occurs between male and female is like believing the flat earth theory."[7]

In October 2017, California governor Jerry Brown signed SB 179, the Gender Recognition Act, making California the first state to legally recognize a third gender. Brown also signed legislation allowing transgender inmates to change their name while in prison, which could be useful when they reintegrate into society

---

In Their Own Words: Jamie Shupe

In an opinion piece for the *Guardian*, Jamie Shupe, the first person in the United States to be granted a nonbinary gender classification, wrote powerfully,

> In the face of adversity, I have declared my right to define my existence and won that right. As a transgender person, I can no longer be accused of appropriating the identity of a cisgender female, because I have created my own, and been awarded the right to exist as that identity. But most importantly, my court victory has opened the door for all those like myself to also taste freedom from the gender binary.[c]

---

after being released.[8] Other states and countries have also changed policy. As of July 2017, Oregon allowed an X gender classification on state-issued IDs and in June 2017, Washington, DC, issued gender-neutral driver's licenses. Other countries that allow gender-neutral designations on legal documents include the United Kingdom, Australia, New Zealand, Pakistan, Nepal, and Canada; many of these use the "X" classification.[9]

What do you think? Is the United States ready for a third gender classification? Would having a nonbinary designation make people bearing such IDs targets for discrimination and harassment?

Birth Certificates

The regulations for updating gender markers on birth certificates vary widely. Here are four examples from the NCTE's Identity Documents Center: In Washington State, birth certificates for adults or emancipated minors will be changed to M, F, or X with no documentation beyond the application form required; for minors, the form must be signed by a parent or legal guardian and a medical or mental health professional. In the District of Columbia, an application form accompanied by a written statement by a licensed health-care provider that appropriate treatment for a gender transition has been completed will suffice. In Alabama, one must show proof of having had sex reassignment surgery to have the birth certificate changed. At least one state, Tennessee, has an explicit law stating, "The sex of an individual will not be changed on the original certificate of birth as a result of sex change surgery."[10] Please refer to the NCTE's Identity Documents Center for guidance about the requirements within your state, district, or territory as each has its own requirements.

Driver's Licenses

As of June 2018, driver's licenses can be obtained with gender-neutral designations in two states and the District of Columbia; California will add a gender-neutral option effective January 2019. These locales and two other states offer easy-to-understand application forms and allow gender marker changes on licenses without requiring provider certification. Each state has guidelines for updating name and gender on driver licenses. Refer to the NCTE Identity Documents Center for the requirements in your state.

HOW TRANS-FRIENDLY IS THE DRIVER'S LICENSE GENDER CHANGE POLICY IN YOUR STATE?

National Center for **TRANSGENDER EQUALITY**

A+	Easy-to understand form, gender-neutral option available, no provider certification required (2 states + DC)	Oregon (2017), District of Columbia (2017), California (starting Jan 2019)
A	Easy-to-understand form, no gender neutral option, no provider certification required (2 states)	Massachusetts (2018), Nevada (2018)
A-	Easy-to-understand form, gender-neutral option available, provider certification required (1 state)	Maine (2018)
B+	Easy-to-understand form, certification from a range of licensed professionals (13 states + 1 territory)	Alaska* (2012), Connecticut (2013)*, Delaware* (2011), Hawai'i (2012), Missouri (2016), New Hampshire (2015), New Jersey* (2009), New Mexico* (2010), Pennsylvania* (2010), Puerto Rico (2016), Rhode Island (2012), Virginia (2012), Washington State (2009)
B	Easy-to-understand form, certification by a limited range of licensed professionals (1 states)	Ohio (2009)
B-	Easy-to-understand form but must be certified by physician only (4 states)	Colorado (2006), Indiana (2014), Nebraska (2010), West Virginia (2015)
C+	No form, no requirement of proof of surgery or court order; certification from medical/mental health professional (9)	Arizona (1995), Florida (2011), Idaho (2013) Illinois (2013), Kansas (2011), Minnesota (2013), New York (1987), Vermont, Wisconsin
C	No form, and burdensome process requirements, but does not require proof of surgery, court order, or amended birth certificate (3 states)	Maryland (requires medical and mental health provider letters), Michigan (requires updated passport), Utah (must provide other updated ID, such as a passport)
D	Unclear, unknown or unwritten policy (5 states + 4 territories)	Arkansas, Mississippi, Montana, North Dakota, South Dakota, American Samoa, Guam, Northern Marianas Island, U.S. Virgin Islands
F	Proof of surgery, court order, or amended birth certificate required (11 states)	Alabama, Georgia, Iowa, Kentucky, Louisiana, North Carolina, Oklahoma, South Carolina, Tennessee, Texas, Wyoming

* In these states, licensed professionals must certify that their practice includes the treatment and counseling of individuals with gender identity issues.

For more information, please contact:
Arli Christian, State Policy Counsel, National Center for Transgender Equality
achristian@transequality.org; (202) 804-6044

How trans-friendly is the driver's license gender change policy in your state? Visit https://transequality.org/documents to find a one-stop hub for name and gender change information. *Courtesy of the National Center for Transgender Equality*

Social Security Administration—Social Security Cards

In 2013, the Social Security Administration (SSA) unveiled a new policy for updating gender on Social Security records: a transgender person no longer needs to submit documentation of sexual reassignment surgery. Now it's enough to submit with doctor certification of appropriate clinical treatment or government-issued documentation such as US passport or birth certificate showing the correct gender.[11] While a Social Security card only lists a name and social security number, the SSA maintains computer records of additional demographic data—including gender—for statistical and research purposes.[12] For more information about how changing your gender with SSA may impact you, visit the NCTE Identity Documents Center and enter "Social Security Records" in the Federal IDs and Records drop-down field.

Department of State—Passports

US passports are issued with male or female designations only, at present. Persons with an impending name or gender change, as well as those whose naturalization certificates are pending, can be issued a two-year, limited validity passport. (Regular passports are issued for ten years for persons ages sixteen and above, and five years for children under sixteen.) Once transition is complete (through clinical treatment *or* surgery), a passport valid for the full term of either five or ten years can be issued.

In 2014, intersex activist Dayna Zzyym, who uses the pronoun *they*, needed to travel abroad for work and applied for a US passport; however, they were unable to select a sex, faced only with the options of male and female. Even though their birth certificate lists their sex as "unknown" and the US Department of Veterans Affairs confirmed they are intersex, their passport application was denied. Lambda Legal filed suit on their behalf,[13] and on September 20, 2018, a judge ruled Zzyym could not be denied a U.S passport "for refusing to specify a sex."[14]

Selective Service

The Selective Service System was established in 1917 to administer the draft and maintain a database of eligible potential draftees. Although designed as a simple system that registered men only because women were exempt, it fails to account for transgender persons. American citizens and resident aliens, ages eighteen to twenty-five, who were assigned male at birth (regardless of their transition status) are required to register with the Selective Service System within thirty days following their eighteenth birthday. Those assigned female at birth are exempt. Applications for federal financial aid for higher education, federal employment, US citizenship, and other government benefits are contingent upon Selective Service registration. For more information about Selective Service registration and transgender persons, visit the NCTE Identity Documents Center and enter "Selective Service" in the Federal IDs and Records drop-down field.

Although changing the name and/or gender marker on legal documents may be a laborious and often prohibitively expensive process, the result is worthwhile. Having identification that matches who you are makes navigating society much simpler. It also potentially lessens the possibility of being harassed for not having an ID with a name and gender that matches your gender presentation—32 percent of respondents to the 2015 *US Transgender Survey* said they have been so harassed. Yet, that same survey found only 11 percent of respondents had all their identity documents in their preferred name and gender, and 68 percent had no ID that reflected these items. The cost of changing the documents was cited as the reason the updates were not completed.[15]

Employment

Many transgender people, especially those who do not pass as cisgender, have difficulty obtaining steady work. As a result, many have resorted to sex work over the years—which is illegal throughout the United States, except for specifically licensed brothels in Nevada.[16] In her memoir *Redefining Realness: My Path to Womanhood, Identity, Love & So Much More* (2014), transgender rights activist Janet Mock writes eloquently about her experiences growing up as a poor, transgender person of color in Hawaii; she also talks candidly about her work in the sex industry and about transgender sex workers in general. Mock's second memoir, *Surpassing Certainty: What My Twenties Taught Me* (2017), speaks to the next phase of her life: working in the world of publishing.

Would that all LGBTQ persons could obtain and maintain legal employment. Many do and are highly successful, yet hurdles abound. On the Lambda Legal website, in the "Know Your Rights" area, you can find information about your state's workplace protections.[17]

According to NCTE's *Report of the 2015 U.S. Transgender Survey (USTS)*, nearly one-third of respondents (29 percent) were living in poverty. The overall poverty rate in this country is 12 percent. The poverty rate was attributed to the high unemployment rate of transgender persons—15 percent of respondents were unemployed, although the US unemployment rate was only 5 percent at that time. As a result, only 16 percent of respondents owned a home; although the rate of home ownership in the United States was then 63 percent. Despite these bleak numbers, a positive finding was the vast increase in respondents, nearly four-fold, over the 2008–2009 National Transgender Discrimination Survey.[18]

Video: "Transform California Stories: Dana"

For a positive take on employment while transgender, watch the video titled "Transform California Stories: Dana." In it, Dana Hargrave, a twenty-eight-year US Navy veteran and a transgender woman, speaks with her aerospace industry coworkers.

"Dana—Transform California Stories" can be found at www.youtube.com/watch?v=tazJnGdnSIO. Or watch it on the MAP website at www.lgbtmap.org/transform-california-dana.

The "Know Your Rights" section of the NCTE's website provides links to pages about employment within the federal government as well as general employment. Although the list of rights enumerated on the federal employment page is more extensive, in all cases you have the right to be treated with respect and not harassed. Sex-based harassment that is severe or widespread is unlawful. You have the right to safe and adequate restrooms and other facilities consistent with your gender identity. Despite comments by the Trump administration that might cause confusion, "trans people are still protected at work."[19]

Should you encounter employment discrimination at work, the NCTE encourages you to try to resolve it at work and provides suggestions as to how this might be done.

Know your rights and do your best to exercise them without alienating those who do not understand. Your actions as an LGBTQ person on the job and in society can be construed as being representative of the entire LGBTQ community. Help those around you learn to respect and appreciate LGBTQ people.

Military Service

During both the Revolutionary and Civil Wars, many women masqueraded as men to get around the ban against women serving in the military. They likely believed they had skills to offer and felt it worth the risk—not only to their lives for serving in battle, but to their reputations and those of their families should they be unmasked. While the numbers will never be known, some four hundred women are thought to have served during the Civil War, many without ever being discovered.

Regulations regarding military service by LGBTQ persons date back to colonial times. Here are a few key dates gleaned from an extensive list in a post written on the *Naval History Blog*:[20]

- In 1778, Lieutenant Gotthold Frederick Enslin was the first documented person to be discharged from the US military for homosexuality.
- In 1976, Technical Sergeant Leonard Matlovich admitted to being homosexual and challenged the military's antigay policy on constitutional grounds; he eventually accepted an honorable discharge.
- In 1993, President Clinton signed into law the policy known as "Don't Ask, Don't Tell" under which gay servicemembers could serve provided they remained closeted.
- In 2010, President Obama repealed "Don't Ask, Don't Tell," which took effect the following year.
- In 2016, Secretary of Defense Ash Carter removed the ban on transgender individuals serving openly in the military.
- In March 2018, the White House released "a memo stating that individuals with a history of gender dysphoria will be disqualified from military service except under certain limited circumstances."[21]
- In June 2018, a federal court in Seattle denied the Trump administration's renewed attempt to implement its transgender military ban.[22] The case is expected to go to trial in April 2019.

According to the 2015 *USTS*, 18 percent of the survey respondents have served in the military and 15 percent were veterans—nearly twice the rate in the US population. That bears repeating: even though transgender persons were barred from military service at the time of the survey, they were serving at nearly twice the rate of the US population.

What do you think? Should all able-bodied and otherwise qualified to serve persons be allowed to serve in the US military—despite sexual orientation, gender identity, and gender expression?

Housing

Anti-LGBT housing discrimination is illegal in eighteen states, the District of Columbia, and Puerto Rico. Transgender people are also protected by federal fair housing laws under the category of sex discrimination. The law also prohibits discrimination because of race, color, national origin, religion, familial status, or disability (including if you are, or are perceived as, a person living with HIV/AIDS). In addition, discrimination because of sexual orientation or marital status is prohibited in all federally funded housing. According to the NCTE resource

"Know Your Rights: Fair Housing and Transgender People," many providers of housing "are not aware that it is illegal for them to turn someone away because they are LGBT or do not conform to gender stereotypes."[23] The NCTE suggests that making providers aware of the law may help resolve a problem. Beyond that, should you experience discrimination, you do have recourse. Your best defense is to know your rights. To learn more, visit transequality.org/know-your-rights/housing-and-homeless-shelters.

Marriage Equality

Marriage equality is an area of law that has been evolving. Long before the issue of same-sex marriage was raised, the issue of interracial marriage existed. Beginning during slavery, laws existed prohibiting interracial relationships and marriages. Starting with California in 1948, all fifty states have struck down laws against interracial marriage; the last was removed in 2000. Same-sex marriage rights faced a similar uphill battle.

Surprisingly, same-sex unions are not a modern-day occurrence. Charity Bryant and Sylvia Drake met in the early 1800s and established a household together in 1809 in Weybridge, Vermont. The couple, highly respected in their community and church, successfully maintained a same-sex domestic household for forty-four years. Theirs was a marriage in all eyes but those of the law.[24]

The 1970s brought legal challenges to same-sex marriage bans. In 1970, University of Minnesota students Richard Baker and James Michael McConnell applied for a marriage license in Minneapolis, but were turned away because they were a same-sex couple. The couple challenged County Clerk Gerald Nelson in court, but in 1971 the Minnesota Supreme Court determined that the denial of marriage licenses to same-sex couples does not violate the Constitution of the United States.[25] Baker and McConnell appealed, but the US Supreme Court declined to hear their case. This decision set federal precedent that held until same-sex marriage was legalized in 2015.[26]

Before 2015, individual states weighed in on the issue—through ballot initiatives and through the courts. In 1999, the Vermont Supreme Court established civil unions, which ruled that same-sex couples be allowed the rights and benefits of marriage. By establishing civil unions, the legislature continued to maintain that marriage can occur only between a man and a woman, but created a parallel set of rights and benefits for same-sex couples. Connecticut became the second state to approve same-sex civil unions in 2005. Massachusetts became the first state in the union to grant full marriage rights to same-sex couples. State-by-state challenges and changes continued annually until 2015.

Although same-sex marriage has been legal throughout the country since 2015, LGBT+ persons—married or single—face legal and illegal discrimination every day.

IN JUNE 2015, THOUSANDS OF LGBT PEOPLE ACROSS AMERICA COULD GAIN THE FREEDOM TO MARRY . . .

...BUT IN JULY...

 52% OF LGBT PEOPLE WOULD BE AT RISK OF BEING:
- FIRED FROM THEIR JOBS
- KICKED OUT OF THEIR HOMES
- DENIED ACCESS TO DOCTOR'S OFFICES AND RESTAURANTS

 57% PERCENT OF LGBT PEOPLE WOULD LIVE IN STATES WHERE LGBT CHILDREN ARE NOT PROTECTED FROM DISCRIMINATION IN SCHOOL AND **86%** IN STATES WHERE THEIR CHILD IS NOT PROTECTED FROM DISCRIMINATION IN SCHOOL FOR HAVING LGBT PARENTS.

 29% OF LGBT PEOPLE WOULD LIVE IN STATES WITHOUT PROTECTIONS FROM HATE CRIMES FOR LESBIAN, GAY, OR BISEXUAL PEOPLE.

 72% OF LGBT PEOPLE WOULD LIVE IN STATES THAT CREATE BURDENSOME OBSTACLES FOR TRANSGENDER PEOPLE SEEKING TO CHANGE A GENDER MARKER ON A BIRTH CERTIFICATE.

 81% OF LGBT PEOPLE WOULD LIVE IN STATES THAT PERMIT HARMFUL "CONVERSION THERAPY" FOR LGBT YOUTH.

 74% OF LGBT PEOPLE WOULD LIVE IN STATES THAT CRIMINALIZE EXPOSURE OR TRANSMISSION OF HIV.

This postmarriage equality infographic by MAP depicts challenges faced by LGBT people as of July 2015, despite the June 2015 Supreme Court decision to overturn the Defense of Marriage Act, making same-sex marriages legal across the country. *Courtesy of the Movement Advancement Project*

Language: Gay Marriage versus Marriage Equality

Since this book is sensitive to the power of language and word choice, the distinctions between the terms *gay marriage* and *marriage equality* bear mentioning. *Gay marriage* is another way of saying *same-sex marriage*. The words *marriage equality*, although often used interchangeably with the first two terms (as they are in this chapter), actually have a much broader meaning. *Marriage equality* refers to the rights and benefits of marriage being available to all who are married without actually identifying a type of marriage, such as that between a man and a woman, between persons of different races, or between persons of the same sex. For an in-depth discussion of the distinction, see writer Murray Lipp's articulate *Huffington Post* piece "'Gay Marriage' and 'Marriage Equality'—Both Terms Matter."[d]

Explore Further: Transgender Family Law

Transgender persons, whether in same- or different-sex relationships, may legally marry; however, given the multitude of legal hurdles facing them, transgender couples would do well to take questions about transgender family law to experts. Start by visiting the websites for the National Center for Lesbian Rights at www.nclrights.org or the Transgender Law Center at www.transgenderlawcenter.org.

Parenting, Adoption, and Foster Parenting

According to MAP, all fifty states and the District of Columbia have laws that create legal ties to both parents for children born to same-sex parents in a legally recognized relationship. As such, both members of a married, same-sex couple must be listed on the birth certificate of a child born into such a marriage.[27] The National Center for Lesbian Rights (NCLR), in the "Family and Relationship

Contemporary Literature: Ashes to Asheville by Sarah Dooley (2017)

Ashes to Asheville beautifully addresses one of the issues of LGBT families: the members' legal rights to be a "family." Although geared toward readers in grades five through eight, the writing is beautiful, and the story is both tragic and hilarious, making it a good read for all ages. Narrated by twelve-year-old Fella who was sent to live with her maternal grandmother, Mrs. Madison, after Mama Lacy—her biological mother died—the story reveals the heartbreak of a family torn apart because of the lack of legal ties. For a few hours of good story, augmented by your own laughter and potential tears, give this novel a try; it puts faces to the issues you've read about in this chapter.

Resources" section of its website, has many downloadable documents with information on parenting and marriage, with both categories including national and state-specific resources. NCLR is an excellent resource for learning about documentation families may need to retain their full rights to adopted children. When a family constellation is formed without the traditional two-parent, heterosexual base, being prepared for unforeseen circumstances in advance is wise.[28]

Thousands of children around the United States have transgender parents; some parents transitioned before the child was born, while others may not transition until much later. A child may know a transgender parent by a gendered name that does not fit with how the world at large perceives the parent's gender. Transgender parents are parents—period. As part of its *Transgender Rights Toolkit: A Legal Guide for Trans People and Their Advocates* (2016), Lambda Legal includes a chapter about transgender parents, which can be downloaded as a separate, four-page document.

According to the Adoption Network Law Center, in 2015, over 670,000 children spent time in the US foster care system. Some children in foster care are reunited with their original families. Some are adopted into other families. Some simply age out of the foster care system. About 140,000 children are adopted by American families each year; however, thousands of these are international adoptions.[29]

Even with so many children in need of homes, foster care and adoption laws vary by state, and some states allow agencies to legally discriminate against LGBTQ families. (Find the MAP Project's Foster and Adoption Laws Map at www.lgbtmap.org/equality-maps/foster_and_adoption_laws.) Foster care non-

Transmasculine Births

What do you suppose the phrase *transmasculine births* means? Look at it. The phrase means exactly what it says: births by transmen. But wait, how can a man give birth? Remember, being a transman does not necessarily mean a person has undergone sex reassignment surgery. Also, provided the female-to-male trans person's fertility is intact, transmasculine pregnancy can occur—followed by a transmasculine birth.

One transman, Trevor MacDonald, wrote about his experience with pregnancy and delivery as a transman in an opinion piece for the *Guardian*. In it he explains that he stopped taking testosterone after a few years with the aim to conceive. Of breastfeeding he writes, "A baby doesn't know what your pronouns are."[e] Although medical checks by his midwives triggered the gender dysphoria he had feared, Trevor ultimately chose to conceive a second child—which he birthed at home, without a midwife.

The 2005 feature film *Transparent* documents the stories of nineteen female-to-male trans parents in the United States. The sixty-minute film received acclaim and awards both in the US and internationally.[f]

Transgender parenting may challenge long-held gender assumptions, but at its core—it's just parenting.

discrimination laws are supposed to protect LGBT foster parents from discrimination by foster care agencies and officials. However, some states permit state-licensed child welfare agencies to refuse to place children with certain families, including LGBT people and same-sex couples, if doing so conflicts with the agencies' religious beliefs.[30]

Survivors of Violence

Sexual minorities, especially transgender people, are subject to violence at a greater rate than the general population. Transgender women of color are at exceptionally high risk for being assaulted. Of the victims in the United States, 86 percent were trans people of color and/or Native American.[31]

TGIJP Videos

The Transgender, Gender Variant, and Intersex Justice Project (TGIJP) website has a section devoted to informational videos about the experiences of transgender, gender variant, and intersex people in jails, prisons, and detention centers. Be forewarned: prisons are not pretty places—nor are they meant to be; the information included in the videos is provided from the point of view of persons who have been imprisoned, many of whom speak candidly about being abused and assaulted.

- "Bustin' Out: From Solitary to Re-Entry," www.youtube.com/watch?v=T9Qo6koD5dw
- "Prison Industrial Complex—Trans Views," www.youtube.com/watch?time_continue=463&v=S5qw2kViAaM
- "Make It Happen!" vimeo.com/16952110

Find all the TGIJP videos here: www.tgijp.org/videos.html.

According to the 2015 *USTS*, 13 percent of respondents reported being physically attacked in the prior year for any reason, with 9 percent reporting being physically attacked because they were transgender. Five percent of the overall respondents reported being physically attacked in public by strangers because they were transgender—of these, 19 percent were Native American, 12 percent Middle Eastern, 11 percent multiracial, 9 percent Asian, 9 percent black, 8 percent Latina, and 6 percent white. Persons who were confined to prisons, jails, or detention centers also reported being victims of violence, whether physical or sexual.[32]

It's a Wrap

When legal protections for LGBTQ persons—or any minority group—are in place, the environment for all citizens is improved. Just having laws and policies in place does not necessarily mean they are enforced. People who are aware of the laws and policies in their areas and work to see that they are enforced do much for their communities. Students can ask about school, district, and campus policies. Those

Legal Resources

Several agencies provide legal resources for LGBTQ persons. A couple are listed here. Refer to the "Resources" section at the end of this book for the contact information for other agencies involved with LGBTQ law.

- *Transgender Rights Toolkit: A Legal Guide for Trans People and Their Advocates* (2016) is Lamba Legal's sixty-page resource covering thirteen subject areas. Download your copy from www.lambdalegal.org/publications/toolkits.
- *Protected and Served?* is Lambda Legal's national survey that explores discrimination by police, courts, prisons, and school security against LGBT people and people living with HIV in the United States. Download your copy from www.lambdalegal.org/sites/default/files/publications/downloads/ps_executive-summary.pdf. Or visit the full report online, where you can navigate to various sections using the hyperlinks provided. Go to www.lambdalegal.org/protected-and-served.

of legal age who register to vote, inform themselves of the issues, and vote are influential. To make yourself aware of the issues in your community, start with local news outlets—city, county, and regional newspapers are good places to start.

Remember, if you do not like the laws and policies in place around you, then you can work to change them. As the Reverend Dr. Martin Luther King Jr. said when paraphrasing nineteenth-century clergyman Theodore Parker, "The arc of the moral universe is long, but it bends toward justice." Of course, it only bends toward justice when communities work for justice. Advocating for justice today will make the world a better place to live tomorrow.

RESTROOM WARS

While other cultures have long viewed the United States as being uptight and repressive about issues of sexuality in general—beginning in the days of Puritan settlers in New England, and reflected more currently by an intricate system of movie and television ratings degrees of nudity or intimacy depicted—American citizens like to think of ourselves as forward-thinking and evolved. Yet, when it comes to issues of gender identity and expression, and same- and opposite-sex attractions, America continues to struggle—even amid huge social gains and landmark decisions. (See table 9.1 for an overview of the restroom wars in the United States through early 2018. This timeline may help you navigate some of the political influences that shape this chapter.)

Table 9.1. Timeline of the Restroom Wars in the United States

1887	Massachusetts passes a law requiring businesses employing women to provide gender-segregated restrooms.
2003	While likely not the first to do so, the University of Vermont changes signage on men's and women's restrooms to unisex.
April 29, 2014	US Department of Education Office for Civil Rights, under President Obama, issues a document stating Title IX's sex discrimination provision includes gender identity.
March 23, 2016	North Carolina passes HB2, the notorious "bathroom bill of Charlotte" also known as the Public Facilities Privacy and Security Act, requiring persons to use restrooms that match the gender on their birth certificate.

(continued)

Table 9.1. *Continued*

May 13, 2016	US Departments of Education and Justice, under President Obama, issue a joint letter of guidance interpreting Title IX to extend to gender identity.
February 22, 2017	US Departments of Education and Justice, under President Trump, rescind the 2016 joint letter of guidance concerning gender identity, deferring to states to decide individually.
March 30, 2017	North Carolina's legislature passes House Bill 142, partially repealing the HB2 bathroom bill, allowing persons to use the restroom that matches their gender identity while in state government buildings.
October 18, 2017	North Carolina governor Roy Cooper issues Executive Order 24 decreeing that the state will not discriminate against employees for sexual orientation and gender identity and that state departments and agencies must provide equal access to state services and services funded by the state.
March 13, 2018	The US District Court for the District of Maryland rules that both Title IX and the Equal Protection Clause of the Fourteenth Amendment of the Constitution require states to treat people equally under the law; thus a transgender student must be allowed to use the restroom and locker room matching his or her gender identity.
May 22, 2018	The US District Court for the Eastern District of Virginia denies a motion by the Gloucester County School Board to dismiss the lawsuit brought by student Gavin Grimm, with Judge Wright Allen writing that Mr. Grimm's transgender status constituted a claim of sex discrimination and the bathroom policy excluding him from using boys' rooms violated the law.

The History through Title IX Guidance Letter of 2016

Transgender people who "pass" as cisgender and successfully present to society in their true gender identity, have been sharing public restrooms with cisgender folks without incident for who knows how long. We cannot know because that is the nature of passing.

What we do know is that until the late nineteenth century, public restrooms, also known as public accommodations, were for anyone to use. With the advent of indoor plumbing—bathrooms located indoors that could be flushed to outside— the single-stall unisex outhouse was replaced by multi-stall indoor "water closets." While millworkers in factories, both male and female, often shared the same single- user accommodations, this offended Victorian sensibilities. University of Utah law professor Terry Kogan explains how political motivations of the day combined with advances in sanitation, dangerous conditions in increasingly mechanized factories, and Victorian values to push the idea that women, the "weaker sex," needed to be protected—or, at least, their virtue needed protecting. Yet, according to science writer Stephanie Pappas, during Victorian times public restrooms out- side of the workplace were almost exclusively reserved for men. This reflected an attitude that women belonged at home. In 1887, Massachusetts was the first state to enact a law requiring single-sex restrooms in businesses that employed women.[1] Protections for Victorian women soon included single-sex public restrooms, sepa- rate ladies' reading rooms in libraries, ladies' cars on railroad trains—for women and their male escorts—and women-only parlor spaces in various businesses. "By 1920," Kogan writes, "over forty states had adopted similar legislation requiring that public restrooms be separated by sex."[2]

Fast forward to the twenty-first century, when society is accustomed to sex- segregated restrooms—and when an increasing number of transgender students are asserting their gender identities within school, community, and athletic set- tings and are beginning to effect change. In 2003, the University of Vermont be- gan retrofitting the men's and women's restrooms in administrative and classroom buildings into unisex spaces, simply by changing the door signage to indicate unisex restrooms. In 2007, the university built a new student center that included four single-occupancy gender-neutral bathrooms, each of which had not only a toilet, sink, and locking door, but also a shower. By this time, at least seventeen colleges and universities had incorporated gender-neutral restrooms onto their campuses.[3] The restrooms and bathrooms designed for single-occupants allow us- ers, especially transgender users, to feel comfortable, without having to navigate judgment they could face using multi-stall single-gender facilities.

The movement to install gender-neutral restrooms on college and university campuses has grown. During 2012 and 2013, 150 campuses added gender-neutral

Title IX and Sex Discrimination

Title IX states, "No person in the United States shall, on the basis of sex, be excluded from participation in, be denied the benefits of, or be subjected to discrimination under any education program or activity receiving Federal financial assistance."

The scope of Title IX extends to all institutions—schools, museums, libraries, and so on—that receive federal financial assistance from the United States Department of Education.[a]

facilities, as did some high schools. During 2013 and 2014, a handful of major cities passed laws requiring gender-neutral signage on restrooms for single occupants.[4] This groundswell of change around the issue of restrooms and restroom use caused conservative citizens and lawmakers to focus their anti-LGBTQIA energies upon the use of gender-appropriate restrooms.

Title IX of the Education Amendments of 1972 protects people from discrimination based on sex in education programs or activities that receive federal financial assistance. Interpretations of Title IX under President Barack Obama provided assistance to transgender students. In April 2014, the United States Department of Education Office for Civil Rights (OCR) issued a document that protects transgender and gender-nonconforming students from discrimination in schools that receive Title IX funds.[5]

In May 2016, the US Departments of Education and Justice issued a letter to school districts around the country, indicating that gender identity was included in the sex protections afforded by Title IX.[6]

Faces of the Restroom Wars

Four of the faces of these restroom wars belong to transgender teen trailblazers Nicole Maines, Jazz Jennings, Gavin Grimm, and Max Brennan. Nicole and her twin brother, Jonas, dealt with these issues in Maine, Jazz's experience was centered in Florida, Gavin's in Virginia, and Max's in Maryland. Each teen's experience was similar, despite the geographical separation, because each had to battle for access to gender-appropriate facilities.

Nicole Maines

Wyatt and Jonas were identical twin boys born in upstate New York in 1997 to Sarah, a young, single mother. Sarah's cousin, Kelly Maines, and her husband, Wayne, adopted the twins in 1998, making them officially Jonas and Wyatt Maines.

Early in life, Wyatt gravitated toward "girl" things. Although Kelly was quicker to adjust to the idea of having a transgender child than was Wayne, both parents were strong supporters of both children when legal and political challenges became part of their lives.

In September 2007, when the twins entered fifth grade, Wyatt transitioned publicly and started the schoolyear as Nicole. Most of her classmates had been referring to Wyatt as a "boy-girl" for a couple of school years already, and had no problem with the change. For parents, though, this was a first. One classmate's grandfather and guardian had actively advocated against LGBT rights for over a decade and was outraged when he heard about Nicole. Paul Melanson approached both the principal and school administrator, but when neither would hear his complaint, he took matters into his own hands.

Melanson told his grandson to start stalking Nicole, even entering the girls' bathroom to urinate when she was there. Nicole was upset, humiliated in front of her friends, and for the first time, made to feel "freakish."[7] The bullying continued, and the administration finally recommended that Nicole use a staff bathroom. But that wasn't enough. By the end of the year a staff person was following Nicole around to offer "eyes-on" protection from harassment.

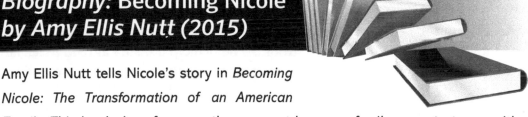

Biography: Becoming Nicole by Amy Ellis Nutt (2015)

Amy Ellis Nutt tells Nicole's story in *Becoming Nicole: The Transformation of an American Family*. This book does far more than recount how one family came to terms with having a transgender daughter. As a science writer, Nutt thoroughly explores the science and politics that impact Nicole and her family. Watch the family grow and develop together, into vocal advocates for the LGBTQ+ community. Available in print, electronic, and audio versions, *Becoming Nicole* makes a complex topic manageable and fascinating.

In September 2008, the twins entered sixth grade, with the same principal who oversaw the elementary school. The eyes-on policy continued, as did the instruction that Nicole use a gender-neutral bathroom. One night when Nicole attended an after-hours event in the high school building, where no gender-neutral bathroom was available, Nicole was accosted by other girls when she tried to use the girls' room. When her parents complained, the administration found Nicole to be at fault because she had been told to use a gender-neutral restroom. By the end of that year, the Maines family decided that it was time to move.

The Maines family chose to move to Portland, Maine, and to have Nicole go "stealth" at her new school; in other words, they pretended that Nicole had always been known as a girl. Think about what it would mean to start a new school, try to make new friends, all the while pretending that two years of your recent life had not happened. Could you do it?

Nicole's story encompasses far more than bathroom politics, as does the story of every transgender, gender variant, or genderqueer person. By the time she was to graduate high school, both Nicole and her father had become passionate public speakers and advocates for the LGBTQ community. That they not only survived adversity, but thrived as a result, speaks to the entire family's strength.

Jazz Jennings

When Jazz Jennings entered kindergarten, she still went by the name Jaron. Her parents tried to meet with the principal to discuss enrolling their daughter as a girl, but Mrs. Reynolds kept putting them off. Jazz's parents finally wrote to the local paper, leaving out the specifics; then the principal agreed to meet. Although Mrs. Reynolds allowed Jaron to enroll as a girl, she insisted on adherence to the school dress code—only pants or shorts were allowed for boys—and she would not allow Jaron to use the girls' restroom. The principal finally agreed to let Jaron wear skorts, which are skirts with shorts underneath, but these presented their own set of difficulties since they aren't made for boy bodies.[8] For bathrooms, the school offered two options: Jaron could use a unisex bathroom in the classroom that had no lock or a restroom in the nurse's office that "was used for sick kids to puke in more than anything else."[9] Neither option was appealing.

Throughout elementary school, Jaron was not allowed to use the girls' restroom. Sometimes she wet her pants rather than use the options provided her. Middle school changed things. A progressive charter school welcomed her as a transgender girl, let her use the girls' restroom, and accepted her as Jazz, which the elementary school never did. When Jaron tried to change her name in elementary school, the principal had deemed the change unacceptable. Middle school was a welcome change.

Memoir: Being Jazz *by Jazz Jennings (2016)*

Jazz Jennings, young transgender activist, tells her story in *Being Jazz: My Life as a (Transgender) Teen*. This plain-spoken autobiography is available as a book, e-book, and audiobook, which Jazz herself reads.

Jazz because an advocate for transgender rights at six years old. After her parents wrote the local paper about not getting a meeting with the principal, the story attracted nationwide attention and Barbara Walters invited the family to be on the news show *20/20*. Jazz's parents finally agreed because they wanted other families with transgender children to know they were not alone. For protection, the whole family took the new last name Jennings, and Jaron chose a new name—Jazz.

Since then, Jazz has written a memoir and a children's book. She has also appeared in a documentary on her life, and as of 2018, her reality show *I Am Jazz* is in its fourth season.

Gavin Grimm

Gavin Grimm is another transgender student whose battle to be treated fairly within his gender identity centered on the issue of restrooms and reached a nationwide audience. A resident of Gloucester, Virginia, Gavin came out to his friends as transgender at the end of middle school. Over the summer break, he legally changed his name, and ensured that his school records listed him as male. In October 2014, during Gavin's sophomore year and with the approval of his principal, he first used the boys' restroom at school. Although he had been using men's restrooms in public already, the citizens of Gloucester took exception to his using the boys' restroom in school, and soon Gavin's case was at the center of a heated public discussion. Gavin had received such negative attention from the adults in the community that he decided to address the school board (you can view Gavin's speech on YouTube at www.youtube.com/watch?v=My0GYq_Wydw&feature=youtu.be). In just a few weeks, Gavin went from being a quiet, shy teen to becoming a national symbol of the transgender bathroom controversy. In 2015, Gavin filed a federal civil rights lawsuit against his school district, and in August 2016, the school board asked the United States Supreme Court to hear the case.[10]

On April, 2, 2016, crowds rallied in Asheville, North Carolina, to protest the passage of the Public Facilities Privacy and Security Act, better known as HB2, the North Carolina law that requires persons to use restrooms that match the gender on their birth certificates. Other signs seen at this rally included "Say No to HB2," "Genitalia ≠ Gender," and "Trans Lives Matter." © iStock / AwakenedEye

Gavin's case was bounced between courts from March 2017 to May 2018, when Judge Arenda L. Wright Allen of the US District Court for the Eastern District of Virginia sided with Gavin and denied the Gloucester County School Board's motion to dismiss Gavin Grimm's lawsuit. Gavin expressed relief at the decision and said, "After fighting this policy since I was fifteen years old, I finally have a court decision saying that what the Gloucester County School Board did to me was wrong and it was against the law."[11]

Max Brennan

While Gavin was fighting his own battle, in March 2018, fifteen-year-old Max Brennan won a victory in the US District Court against Maryland's Talbot County Public Schools. Max, who acknowledged he was transgender in sixth grade, was told by St. Michaels Middle High School that he could not use boys' restrooms or locker rooms. Instead, the school directed him to use any of three single-stall, gender-neutral restrooms to change clothes or use the bathroom. The court ruled "a transgender student must be permitted to use both the restroom and locker room that is 'in alignment with their gender identity.'"[12] Thus, Max was entitled to use facilities designated for males.

North Carolina: A Study on Bathroom Bills

On March 23, 2016, the North Carolina legislature passed House Bill 2 (HB2), officially known as the Public Facilities Privacy and Security Act. The passage of HB2 meant that students attending public schools were now required to use the school's toilet facilities and locker rooms that aligned with the sex on their birth certificate.

Soon, retaliation against North Carolina's new law began. In April 2016, PayPal cancelled plans to expand in Charlotte, costing the state four hundred new jobs. The cancellation of some entertainment events followed—including Bruce Springsteen, Itzhak Perlman, and Pearl Jam—and then then NBA announced it would move the All-Star game out of Charlotte starting in 2017, a move estimated to cost the city $100 million dollars. In September, the National Collegiate Athletic Association moved seven championship games scheduled for the 2016–2017 academic year, citing HB2 as the cause. Next, the Atlantic Coast Conference (ACC), which is headquartered in the state, declared it would move the December ACC football championship, scheduled to be held in Charlotte, out of state.

The following spring, on March 30, 2017, the North Carolina legislature repealed House Bill 2 by passing House Bill 142, a compromise that allows transgender and gender nonconforming persons to use the restroom consistent with their gender identity.[13] Many LGBT rights activists say the new bill doesn't go far enough to protect transgender rights.

Bathroom Ban Laws Compromise Safety

When using a restroom, both privacy and safety are important. Opponents of laws that would allow transgender and gender-nonconforming (TGNC) persons to use the restrooms congruent with their gender identity often claim that such laws pose safety issues. Since laws already on the books protect persons from harassment and assault in public spaces, including restrooms, nondiscrimination laws do not open persons to new threats. According to a 2016 report by the Movement Advancement Project, it is the bathroom ban laws that compromise safety—particularly the safety of TGNC persons. Further, proper enforcement of bathroom ban laws would violate privacy. After all, how can an enforcement official know if a person's genitals match the sex on their birth certificate without checking both the person's birth certificate and genitalia?

All-gender restroom beside single-sex restroom options. Such facilities cater to parents with growing children, caregivers with charges of a different gender, and transgender and gender-nonconforming persons. © iStock / ciud

As the state of North Carolina discovered, bathroom ban laws have other repercussions. They hurt businesses, employment, and the economy. They also make it very difficult for TGNC persons to go about their lives in public spaces. Imagine spending an entire day—every day you are out—trying to avoid using any restroom. Most public spaces still only provide single-gender facilities, although family restrooms are becoming more common as well. Family restrooms beside single-gender facilities provide spaces where parents or caregivers caring for persons of a different gender can use facilities comfortably; yet, the implication is that persons will enter together. The all-gender restroom, while it may serve the same purpose as a family restroom, is an improvement because of the implication that individuals may enter alone.

All-gender or gender-neutral multi-occupant facilities, when they are not accompanied by single-gender multi-occupant facilities, also have drawbacks. These drawbacks have little to do with privacy or safety, and everything to do with the manner in which different genders are socialized to restroom use. Ask anyone who cleans restrooms in public buildings, where only single-gender facilities are available, if one is generally cleaner than the other. I strongly suspected that the women's rooms are generally cleaner and posed the question to career custodian Lester Lyle of Nashville, Tennessee. Lyle, with over four decades of experience cleaning government, hospital, and church facilities, concurred. Chuckling, he said, "There's no question that the women's [facilities] are cleaner."[14] I believe the difference may lie in the way women are socialized to interact with one another over the sinks and mirrors.

Single-occupancy facilities for all provide both privacy and safety; however, retrofitting multi-user facilities into individual restrooms would be cost prohibitive. As you read in the stories of Nicole Maines, Jazz Jennings, and Gavin Grimm, schools that relegate TGNC students to single-occupancy restrooms when other students are allowed to use multi-occupancy facilities fail to provide "reasonable accommodations" to the TGNC students. Students relegated to single-occupancy restrooms not only are treated as "other"; they also lose valuable educational time trekking across sometimes-vast campuses to reach those separate facilities.

In 2016, at Montclair High School in Montclair, New Jersey, students petitioned for an all-gender restroom. In response, a first-floor boys' bathroom with urinals and a stall was designated "all-gender." Some parents took issue with the change. In a May 2018 article, one parent was quoted as having directed her son to refrain from entering the facility because it was shared by both boys and girls. The article reports a suspected sexual crime that occurred when a male student allegedly touched a female student inappropriately in the all-gender facility. Despite the location of the alleged crime, gay-rights groups were quick to point out that the issue was not the location of the assault but merely the fact that an assault occurred. Socially conservative groups countered that the incident highlights the risks such policies can create.[15] In your opinion, what is the issue here? Is it the alleged assault, which could have happened anywhere, or the existence of the all-gender restroom in which the alleged assault occurred?

Think about all that you have read in this chapter. How should public buildings—schools, libraries, businesses—best "fix" the issue of bathrooms for all? What does the landscape look like in your city with regard to this issue? What would you like to see done in your school and town? Finally, what are you going to do now that you have this knowledge?

WHOLE-PERSON HEALTH

Familial, Physical, and Spiritual

Whole-person health encompasses familial, physical, and spiritual dimensions. A person may have excellent physical health but have an unhealthy home environment. Or a person might have a good home and top-notch physical health but lack a welcoming spiritual or religious community. Feeling accepted and appreciated in all areas of life is crucial to achieving whole-person health. Attaining balance in all three areas is ideal; yet, this goal can be elusive.

Home and Family

Ideally, our homes should be a safe space, a sanctuary to which we can retreat after a busy or disappointing day—a place to rest, regroup, and reenergize. When the cares of the world wear us down, we should be able to go home, close the door, breathe a sigh of relief, and feel better. Unfortunately, the idea of home as sanctuary is simply an idea for persons who are homeless or for those who have homes but whose families are unsupportive or rejecting. Anyone who lives with other persons will experience discord on occasion. Disharmony can be the result of issues as simple as disagreeing about meal or entertainment choices; thankfully, such issues are short-lived. Squabbles among persons who hold differing opinions come and go, but outright rejection of someone because of an integral aspect of one's personhood—such as gender identity or sexual orientation—can be devastating.

When families learn that a child's sexual orientation or gender identity is inconsistent with their perceptions, it interferes with their plans and dreams for that

Contemporary Literature: Aristotle and Dante Discover the Secrets of the Universe *by Benjamin Alire Sáenz (2012)*

Benjamin Alire Sáenz's young adult novel *Aristotle and Dante Discover the Secrets of the Universe* received twenty-seven literary honors and awards for its portrayal of the Latino cultural experience. The novel is a coming-of-age story about two Mexican American teen boys and the two families who love their gay children without reservation.

Be forewarned: an antitransgender hate crime is briefly mentioned late in the book; the inclusion of that incident may be difficult for some readers.

---

child—and it may go against generations of family ideals. Everyone needs time to adjust, and some need longer than others. Even families who are wholly accepting of LGBTQ+ persons outside the family nucleus may need time to adjust. Although having cisgender, heterosexual children does not guarantee any parent future weddings or grandchildren, parents often have dreams they may feel are threatened by this new announcement. That LGBTQ+ persons marry and have children—by the same various means that cisgender, straight couples do—may be overlooked at first by a distraught parent.

Conversion Therapy

Families who are greatly distressed by a child's revelation of a sexual orientation, gender identity, or gender expression different from the family's expectations have been known to resort to conversion therapy. This practice purports to change a person's sexual orientation or gender identity. Although being LGBTQ does not constitute a mental disorder, being part of a sexual or gender minority is "associated with increased risk of psychosocial issues such as psychological distress, mistreatment, and discrimination."[1] Families can learn to support their LGBTQ children, and they "do so more quickly when guidance and services are provided in ways that resonate for them, including education presented in the

Contemporary Literature: The Miseducation of Cameron Post by Emily M. Danforth (2012)

The Miseducation of Cameron Post is a young adult novel about one teen's experience with Christian gay conversion therapy. Some readers might find the 470-page length to be a challenge, but the book was named to several best-of-the-year lists for 2012. It was developed into a feature-length film that debuted in theaters in August 2018.

context of cultural and deeply held values."[2] Unfortunately, sometimes the very persons families turn to for support believe that sexual orientation or gender identity can be changed.

Conversion therapy has been practiced since the late nineteenth century in the United States.[3] Some licensed professionals use it to provide health care, while some faith leaders use it as part of a religious practice. As of January 2018, nine states, the District of Columbia, and thirty-two localities had "banned health care professionals from using conversion therapy on youth."[4] One group estimates that 698,000 adults in the United States have received conversion therapy, including 350,000 who received it during adolescence.[5] Some medical associations have issued statements opposing the use of conversion therapy because it is harmful and ineffective.[6]

The Family Acceptance Project at San Francisco State University is developing a new family model to increase family support, decrease risk, and promote the well-being of LGBT children and youth. This model is based on accepting families' deeply held cultural values and viewing them as strengths. The ultimate goal is helping families accept and support their LGBTQ child rather than rejecting their child or subjecting her or him to conversion therapy.[7] The project "found that families from all ethnic groups were shocked to learn that reactions they thought would help or would protect their children from being gay or transgender—instead put their children at very high risk for health and mental health problems."[8] Through education and support of the parents, the project helps parents to support their LGBTQ child. See the "Resources" section for more information on the Family Acceptance Project and its educational publications and videos.

Personal Essay: "Family Rejection," by Clare K., age 21

I am a twenty-one-year-old transgender woman.

I was forced out of my home at fourteen when my parents stalked me via informants and learned about my sexuality and gender. I was beaten, called a faggot, blamed for my parents' failing marriage, called a poison to my family, threatened with castration, and forced to read Bible verses aloud until 2:00 a.m. before I was allowed to go to sleep. My parents were much more concerned with their social standing as a result of my inconvenient existence. My sister, no more than eight at the time, woke up to all of this, but my parents forced her to go to bed because she wouldn't leave my side. They forced me to stay awake, recounting what a mistake I was, and how I was not their child, yelling at me for hours while I sobbed. My parents threatened to kill me, and I cried out with, "I want to kill myself." The night had been long and painful. My mother simply said, "You're not going to do anything. If you wanted to kill yourself, you would have done it already."

All of my clothing was thrown out onto the lawn because it was too feminine, aside from one T-shirt and two pairs of baggy jeans. My father and mother told me about how the night that they were married, my mother held my father in her arms while he cried about latent homoerotic feelings that he had, and that he "had changed." After I had been allowed to go to bed, my dad burst in the door to my room not ten minutes later, put me in a hold, punching my back while yelling, "Not my son," and picked me up while I was in nothing but a blanket (it's December 21st by the way, so there's snow everywhere) and tossed me outside only to lock the door behind me. I sat on a picnic table listening to my mom cry and my dad yell and hit things while I watched the snow fall all over my clothing in the security lights, naked and crying. I was, eventually, let back in by my mother (albeit much later and very reluctantly), and I was forced to agree to conversion therapy in order to be given the reprieve of sleep that I desperately needed.

My parents pulled me out of public school and tried to force me into religious institutions. Conversion therapy was held in a dark church basement, where an old "ex-gay" pastor dredged up many horrific images and traumatic mental torture, advising my parents with what can only be described as "prescriptions" to modify my behavior, such as cutting my hair as short as possible, making me wear masculine clothing, saying that my friends had taken the place of God and that they had to be removed from my life. Constant monitoring and videos on a screen during the therapy listed and showed diseases, death rates, fear-mongering, sexist stereotypes, and delusions. Sometimes the pastor would lock the door with my parents outside, forcing me to endure what he would say on my own, with no verbal defense for myself.

To make everything stop, I learned to lie. I claimed that I had lied about everything and that I wasn't really myself. I effectively went back into the closet at home while my peers and I knew the truth. Lies, however, are never eternal. Through informants, my parents found out that I had lied. The cycle continued until I was basically living out of my car and working sixteen-hour days on my feet to survive at seventeen years old. I got good enough grades and worked hard enough to get myself into the university of my choice.

The moment I had the opportunity, I left and never looked back. It's important to remember though, that coming out is by no means inherently a good fortune, nor can it always make someone more comfortable. The absolute carnage of my young adult life still has traumatic ripple effects in my psyche today.[a]

Family acceptance and support are critical to a young person's well-being as these help build resilience and self-acceptance.[9] Using resources such as those offered by the Family Acceptance Project can help families build resilient LGBT youth. Youth who experience family rejection are at risk. Some may seek to injure themselves. Some may choose to run away from home. Others may find their families evict them from the home.

Homelessness

Everyone experiences difficult family dynamics at one time or another, especially during the adolescent and young adult years. These are years when we try on new selves, not necessarily in line with how we were raised. Whether the changes involve dying one's hair screaming pink, adding facial jewelry or body art, or coming to terms with one's sexual orientation or gender identity, each represents a milestone in self-development. Having family who not only tolerate these changes but wholly embrace and accept you as the changed individual *and* a member of the family unit is enormously important. Rejection by family can be catastrophic, especially when the family member is ejected from the family unit and from his or her home.

Individual homelessness is felt by LGBT youth at alarming rates. A 2017 report declared that LGBT youth are at more than twice the risk for homelessness than other youth.[10]

Gender and sexual-minority youth may become homeless because they leave their homes in search of more accepting spaces; however, many become homeless when rejected by their families. Clare's harrowing account of her experience (see page 154) begins at age fourteen when her parents kicked her out into the snow in the middle of a December night. While they allowed her to return the same night, she had to agree to undergo conversion therapy. Clare lived in an extremely unhappy home situation until age seventeen, when she chose to live in her car rather than with her family.

Those gender- and sexual-minority youth who reside in families who accept them unconditionally will find their families face unique challenges. Parents, guardians, and siblings may worry about their LGBTQ members. Families who are wholly supportive of their LGBTQIA members can face difficulties when their neighbors, acquaintances, and colleagues are less accepting. Families need not navigate unfamiliar waters alone. Explore the resources presented in this chapter and at the end of this book to find support. If you live near a major

Resource: "On Our Own"

Far too many youth are forced from their homes because they are LGBTQ+ and are unable to depend on parents or guardians financially. To help these young people, the Human Rights Campaign—in conjunction with the True Colors Fund and the Time Out Youth Center of Charlotte, North Carolina—produced a downloadable resource titled "On Our Own: A Survival Guide for Independent LGBTQ Youth." In four sections, it covers a wealth of necessary information for the newly independent young person. Visit assets2.hrc.org/files/assets/resources/HRC-OnOurOwn-LGBTQYouth.pdf.

metropolitan area, the likelihood of finding in-person support resources is good—and increases each year.

Physical/Athletic

Another aspect of whole-person health is the physical or athletic. Sports competitions are frequently segregated by sex—males and females compete separately from each other. For years, women were discouraged from participating in athletic competitions. Athletes push their physical limits—straining, gasping, sweating, and otherwise behaving in ways deemed unfeminine by societal mores of the time. As recently as the early to mid-twentieth century, women's athleticism was considered potentially injurious to reproductive health, and women were cautioned to avoid athletic pursuits. Today we understand that the extreme training of high-performance athletics can lead to menstrual irregularities and possibly infertility;[11] however, such outcomes only impact those regularly engaging in very intense physical exertion.

LGBT athletes face their own challenges—in the locker room, on the field, and in public. Cyd Zeigler is a gay athlete and author. When he and Jim Buzinski started the online newsmagazine *Outsports* in 1999, gay athletes were disenfranchised not only by those in sports, but also by the gay community. Zeigler recalls being called "butch" by other gay men for liking sports and feeling that other gay men would have preferred that he embrace Broadway music instead. Today, he writes, "those two disparate worlds have merged,"[12] and cites attendance at a 2015 LGBT Pride Night event hosted by the Los Angeles Dodgers.

LGBT athletes face antigay slurs as a matter of routine, whether closeted or out. Such language may be a matter of course in locker rooms, but those hurling the insults fail to consider how upsetting their words may be to teammates—ones they have no intention of hurting. Derrick Gordon, a basketball player for the University of Massachusetts, chose to be alone rather than socialize with those who said hurtful things. Indeed, he reached such a low point that he considered giving up the game. Yet, when he came out to teammates in 2014, those who had been the worst offenders were deeply moved; they had not realized how they had been hurting Gordon. While they had no problem with Gordon being gay, his teammates had concerns about what they might face should he come out publicly; basically, "the team wanted him to stay quiet."[13] The next academic year, Gordon transferred to Seton Hall, where he continued to play Division I basketball; however, in 2016, after being passed over in the NBA draft, Gordon opted to leave basketball to pursue a career as a firefighter. "The NBA has had one openly gay player to date—Jason Collins, who signed with the Brooklyn Nets in 2014 after coming out."[14]

Transgender Athletes

Transgender and intersex athletes face unique hurdles. Should transgender athletes be allowed to participate in gender-segregated sports congruent with their gender identities? Or does this give players an unfair advantage? At issue is the male-to-female athlete. The male hormone testosterone aids strength and muscular development; this is the basis for the generality that men are stronger than women and for the argument that male-to-female transgender athletes might have an unfair advantage due to male hormone levels. The counter-argument is that transgender women taking female hormones and drugs to suppress testosterone generally have even lower levels of testosterone in their bodies than do cisgender females. Since a woman's ovaries produce a small amount of testosterone, a female with ovaries will have an advantage—in terms of testosterone levels—over the transgender female who has been taking male hormone suppressants for a year.

That said, the physiology of the human pelvis does not change even when its owner's gender identity does. Because of skeletal differences, some say the advantage remains even after transition, since the male body stride cannot be adjusted with hormones. While it's true that a person assigned male at birth who is a transgender female can learn to move in a more feminine manner, will that learning be carried into athletic competitions?

Over forty years ago, a professional tennis player underwent gender reassignment surgery; she is now an accomplished eye surgeon known as Dr. Renée Richards. She was the first out professional transgender athlete.

In 2016, Chris Mosier made history as the first known transgender athlete to compete in an International Triathlon Union (ITU) championship. This was his first competition as part of Team USA. He ran and cycled in the world duathlon championship. Among the field of over 400 competitors, he finished 144th; among his age group (thirty-five to thirty-nine), he finished twenty-sixth; among men competing from the United States in his age group, he finished second. The ITU uses the same rules for trans athletes as the International Olympic Committee (IOC).[15] The IOC Consensus meeting in 2015 allows transgender athletes to compete without requiring any gender confirmation surgery. In 2013, Mosier founded TransAthlete.com as a resource for transgender athletes; you can learn more about his organization in the "Resources" section.

On the K–12 level, trans activist Jazz Jennings has experience with trying to participate in sports as a girl. (Read more about Jazz in chapter 9, "Restroom Wars.") In her early elementary years, Jazz wanted to play on a girls' soccer team. When registering Jazz, her parents obscured her gender marker—first with "an 'accidental' coffee ring over the little box with an 'M' in it,"[16] and then with her dad's thumb over that box when he presented the paper. But, when trying to register her for a travel soccer team in third grade, Jazz's parents came clean—

Explore Further: Skeletal Differences

The physiology of the human pelvis does not change even when its owner's gender identity does. The addition or suppression of sex hormones does not alter a person's skeletal structure. While I do not fully understand the implications of these differences, I report them here because a nonbinary person with an interest in sports physiology emphasized their importance.

The male pelvis is narrower than the female's and creates a different stride when a person walks or runs. This is evident when viewed in video grid presentations. The following list contains links to a few examples—two three-dimensional presentations and two grid presentations. Watch each brief video clip and then play with the animation that you can adjust for various attributes—sex, weight, attitude/nervousness, and mood—by Ontario's Bio Motion Lab. These clips will help you begin to formulate your own conclusions.

- "Female Standard Walk—3ds Max Animation," www.youtube.com/watch?v=mAlblUhu-fQ
- "Animation Reference—Female Standard Walk—Grid Overlay," www.youtube.com/watch?v=G8Veye-N0A4
- "Athletic Male Standard Walk—3ds Max Animation," www.youtube.com/watch?v=hFJDON7VQhM
- "Animation Reference—Athletic Male Standard Walk," www.youtube.com/watch?v=vq9A5FD8G5w
- The Body Motion Lab walker demo, www.biomotionlab.ca/Demos/BMLwalker.html

offering a clean copy of her birth certificate and letters from her physician and therapist about her being transgender. The honesty resulted in Jazz being denied a female soccer player card by the state soccer association; however, her coach chose to keep Jazz on the team as an unregistered guest player. But when her team made runner-up in their division tournament and the state soccer association learned Jazz had played without being registered, her "coach got in serious trouble, and the team was almost disqualified."[17]

At nine years old, Jazz had already been living as her authentic self for four years. Learning that the state soccer association stood in the way of her fully realizing her potential as a girl was hurtful, but she didn't let that stop her from playing a sport she loved. Jazz went back to playing for the rec team where she could play as a girl. With her parents actively advocating on her behalf, the US Soccer Federation (USSF) eventually "stepped in and took the unprecedented action of demanding that the state soccer association issue [her] a female player card."[18] With assistance from the National Center for Lesbian Rights, the USSF then wrote a transgender-inclusive policy for all state soccer associations.

Like Jazz, Nicole Maines and her parents had to negotiate with a regulatory board to play K–12 sports as a male-to-female young person. (Read more about Nicole in chapter 9, "Restroom Wars." Nicole transitioned publicly upon entering fifth grade.) At age nine, when Nicole was still known as Wyatt, the Maines twins began to play sports on single-sex teams. Nicole's mom reached out to an Equality-Maine attorney, and then wrote to her local Little League office in Maine. Without waiting for an answer, she wrote to the regional Little League office in Connecticut. Within weeks, following much communication, Wyatt was granted a waiver and deemed eligible to play softball. As positive as this outcome was, Wyatt still felt separated—now by the uniform: "No matter how female he felt, under his uniform he had to wear what no other girl did: a cup and an athletic supporter."[19] As Nicole matured, her interests changed. By the time high school graduation rolled around, the college plans for both Maines children included concentrations in theater.

In a June 2018 article for *Outsports*, Cyd Zeigler writes about how the successes of transgender high school sophomore athletes Andraya Yearwood and Terry Miller were causing controversy.[20] At the recent Connecticut state championship races, Miller set Connecticut state open meet records in both the 100-meter and 200-meter races, while Yearwood finished second in the 100-meter race. Miller also won the New England regional championship 100-meter and 200-meter races.

In schools, Title IX provides guidelines for allowing equal access to restrooms and locker rooms in line with a student's gender identity (see chapter 9). Single-sex organized sports, played outside of school, each have their own regulatory boards. Parents and transgender youth must navigate each challenge as it is encountered. As more transgender youth come forward, policies around athletics will doubtlessly improve.

Intersex Athletes

During the 2016 Summer Olympics in Rio, Caster Semenya, an outstanding South African middle-distance runner, and Dutee Chand, an extraordinary sprinter from India, made headlines because they are world-class intersex athletes competing as women yet have testosterone levels higher than what is considered "normal" for females. Some believe this gives them an unfair advantage. After competing brilliantly in Taiwan when she was eighteen, Chand was sent to see a doctor in Delhi for what she thought was a doping test. In reality, competitors in Taiwan had questioned her gender, saying she appeared "too masculine." The doctor in Delhi performed an ultrasound, and shortly thereafter Chand was sent to Bangalore for a gender verification test. There, she had blood drawn for testosterone levels, a chromosomal analysis, an MRI, and a "mortifying" gynecological exam that included palpation and measurement of the clitoris, labia, and vagina, and also evaluation of pubic hair and breast size. The results showed elevated testosterone, and Chand was told she could no longer race. Chand, who was raised in a poor rural village by illiterate parents, had never heard of intersex and did not understand her gender being questioned. Also, although the details of her case were kept private, the media was made aware that Chand had "failed" a gender test—and she was humiliated publicly.[21]

Convinced to fight the ruling, Chand was soon at the center of a legal case in which the judge ruled the International Association of Athletics Federation (IAAF) had to stop sex-testing athletes.[22] Chand ultimately qualified for the 2016 Summer Olympics in Rio and "became the first female Indian sprinter in thirty-six years to qualify for the Olympics."[23]

Concurrently, Caster Semenya's story was unfolding. Like Chand, Semenya is a runner from a poor rural village who was similarly challenged after a spectacular win, Semenya's being the "800-meter race at the 2009 African Junior Championships."[24] Semenya also assumed she was being tested for doping. The press and social media found out about the sex testing and had a field day, remarking on Semenya's stature, physique, and the depth of her voice. Semenya's performance fell off after the IAAF introduced a testosterone limit in 2011, and she was beaten in the 2011 World Championships and the 2012 Olympics.[25] After Chand's legal challenge resulted in a suspension of the IAAF rules, Semenya stopped medically suppressing her testosterone levels, and "she has been unstoppable ever since."[26]

In March 2018, the IAAF approved new "Eligibility Regulations for the Female Classification" of intersex athletes—whom they refer to as athletes having differences of sexual development—which will take effect in November 2018. The regulations are specific to track events from 400 meters to one mile in length and require female athletes to meet low-level testosterone benchmarks.[27]

Although the IAAF defends its regulations as being about fairness, South Africa has slammed it with the charge that the rules are "blatantly racist" because all the women targeted are from the global south.[28]

Dr. Stéphane Bermon, head of the IAAF's health and science department, predicts that within five to ten years a category will be added to athletic competitions specifically for intersex athletes. Bermon says the issue is far more prevalent than the public realizes: "In elite female athletics the number of intersex athletes is one hundred forty times more than what you might find in the normal female population."[29]

What do you think about transgender and intersex athletes? For youth sports, does it matter on which team a transgender or intersex youth plays? For adult athletics, where the stakes are higher, should transgender or intersex athletes have separate rules—even teams? Although this chapter has not provided enough information for you to make a fully informed decision, it has given you a place from which to begin further research. If sports are near and dear to your heart, you may want to give these questions some further consideration.

Spiritual/Religious

Another aspect of a well-rounded, healthy person is an element of faith, a sense that all is right with the world—even when it's not. Some find this in religion, and some find it in spirituality. Others, especially members of the LGBTQ+ community, find their attempts to be included in a religious community are unsuccessful, often hurtfully so. Religious communities can be particularly hard-lined about interpreting whichever doctrine they follow, although a movement for LGBTQ acceptance is underway. This section does not delve into what is right or wrong about any religion or set of religious beliefs. Nor does it purport to advocate for any religious path. Instead, it attempts to offer hope to those seeking a more inclusive body of worshippers, because these bodies exist, and their numbers are growing.

Additionally, some people who do not ascribe to a religion, nonetheless embrace a spiritual side. Perhaps prayers are said to a Higher Power, Supreme Being, the Universe, or Gaia. Perhaps there is simply the internal assurance that the entire earth is connected—trees, rocks, animals, humans, and oceans of water and air. The ability to turn one's personal woes over to an all-knowing,

"God has a purpose for creating diversity as a feature of human life. And God has compassion, especially, for the despised and rejected. Treating badly those who are different from ourselves offends God far more than using the name of God to condemn those who cannot fulfill traditional models of sexual expression. Our sexual orientation is a gift of God's creativity."—Rev. Dr. James A. Forbes Jr., founder and president of the Healing of the Nations Foundation[b]

Contemporary Literature: Autoboyography by Christina Lauren (2017)

Christina Lauren's young adult novel *Auto-boyography* is set in Provo, Utah, where the culture of the Church of Jesus Christ of Latter-day Saints (also known as the LDS Church and the Mormon Church) saturates the landscape. In this coming-of-age story, Tanner is a bisexual senior in high school who falls for Sebastian, a teaching assistant in one of Tanner's classes. *Autoboyography* is an amazing, incredible love story filled with laughter and tears, angst and simmering rage (at a religion that refuses to accept gay love).

---

omniscient Other can help lessen stress, especially when sensing the weight of the world on one's shoulders. Hida Viloria, whose memoir was mentioned in chapter 5, repeatedly and unabashedly prays to the Universe. Without ascribing to any religious practice, she demonstrates a mastery of spiritual practice that serves her well. This ability to ask for help, even from an unknown and unknowable being, or to express gratitude to the same, feeds our sense of well-being and is good for mental health.

Admitting a lack of control and asking for help are the first two steps of twelve-step programs like Alcoholics Anonymous. People who don't have a religious connection sometimes struggle with the second step because it involves turning to a Higher Power for help. The ability to call on God, Allah, Buddah, or a Higher Power by any other name is a pivotal step in these programs and allows participants to relinquish the need to feel fully in control of their own destiny. On one hand we must be responsible for our own actions; on the other hand, turning over our troubles—and giving thanks for our blessings—provides a relief from the stresses of the world.

As I understand it, the basis of all world religions is that whatever Supreme Being you ascribe to is, by definition, love. Love for the earth and for humanity. Love for all people, including the following: the poor, the sick, the downtrodden, the criminal, the mentally ill, the crippled, the healthy, the wealthy, the wise, the feeble, the kind, the malicious, the tenderhearted, and, yes, the lesbian, gay, bisexual, transgender, two-spirit, gender nonconforming, genderqueer, gender fluid, queer, questioning, intersex, asexual, and straight. Love for all of humanity. Love and stewardship are universal messages. Love everyone, and care for one another and the planet that sustains our life.

Yet, various sects within each world religion, and often broad swaths of these religious groups, study their texts and ferret out messages that they feel give them license to discriminate, to exclude, and even to hate. Right-wing Christian group members often cite verses from the book of Leviticus, such as Leviticus 20:13, which says, "If a man has sexual intercourse with a man as he would with a woman, the two of them have done something detestable. They must be executed; their blood is on their own heads."[30] While, on its face, this is a strong admonition, realize that it is taken out of context. Elsewhere in the book of Leviticus are prohibitions against charging interest on loans of money or selling food at a profit. Here is Leviticus 25:35–37:[31]

> If any Israelites living near you become poor and cannot support themselves, you must provide for them as you would for a hired worker, so that they can continue to live near you. Do not charge Israelites any interest, but obey God and let them live near you. Do not make them pay interest on the money you lend them, and do not make a profit on the food you sell them.

Today we operate in a world of banks and credit lending, driven by interest rates. The idea of making a loan without charging interest is almost laughable—

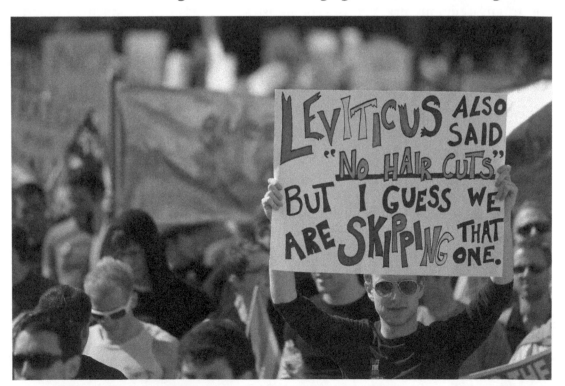

At the National Equality March on October 11, 2009, in Washington, DC, a protester holds up a sign to show selective reading of the Bible when it comes to gay rights. © iStock / Pfrederiksen

Contemporary Literature: Georgia Peaches and Other Forbidden Fruit *by Jaye Robin Brown (2016)*

Jaye Robin Brown's young adult novel *Georgia Peaches and Other Forbidden Fruit* is the story of Jo, the much-loved, out-and-proud lesbian daughter of a well-known radio evangelist in Atlanta, Georgia. This is a story of attraction and romance complicated by promises and secrets; it is also a story of faith. In a note at the end of the book, the author writes, "I wanted this to be something a young queer person of faith could hold on to as a bright spot while they navigate the waters of finding themselves."[c]

---

yet, there you see the biblical prohibition. Which prohibitions are we to take verbatim? The answer lies outside the covers of this book. Although a prohibition exists in a text written some two thousand years ago that is said to contain the Word of God, understand that it may bear further study.

Excluding people from a congregation for whatever reason runs counter to the idea of worshipping a universally loving Supreme Being, as I see it. Even if one's interpretation of a sacred text declares a behavior or way of life to be wrong, doesn't judgment belong to the God—by whatever name you worship Him or Her? As my late mother-in-law used to remind me, it is not our place to judge others. We are just beings on this earth.

A growing number of houses of worship welcome LGBTQ+ parishioners (for example, read about an LGBTQ+ friendly mosque in Chicago here: www.npr. org/2018/04/15/602605271/a-mosque-for-lgbtq-muslims), and LGBTQ+ clergy are being accepted and ordained by an increasing number of denominations. Are you looking for an LGBTQIA-friendly place to worship? Look in "Resources" at the back of this book to find a section devoted to religious resources. While far from exhaustive, it provides you a place to start your search and includes organizations in the United States focused broadly on LGBTQ-inclusive organizations within the Christian, Jewish, and Muslim religions.

Even if you do not live in an area of the country that is welcoming to LGBTQ persons, know that certain faith groups will be accepting, even if their parent denomination is exclusionary. The Family Acceptance Project materials mentioned earlier in this chapter address issues of faith within families; the trailer for their short documentary *Families Are Forever* speaks to the experience of a Mormon family with a queer son—and a mother who loves him just as he is. There is hope.

Remember, whole-person health is important. Throughout life we must care for our bodies, minds, families, and communities. Learn to develop the skills you need to become resilient—a survivor. Help others to do the same. It all begins with acceptance and love.

11

ALLIES ARE DEFINED BY ACTIONS

How You Can Make a Difference

Now that you've educated yourself about the intricacies of gender, how can you make a difference in the world? First and foremost, speak out! Breaking the silence around such taboo topics as intersex children or transgender persons' positions on the broad spectrum of gender identity and expression is necessary to normalize the existence of such persons. In biology classrooms, ask about chromosomal structures beyond XX and XY. Although your teacher may not feel either prepared or empowered to teach information outside the norm, you can appeal to your teacher's scientific curiosity. Ask for extra credit and offer to bring in information yourself. When you provide information to your teacher about the Intersex Campaign for Equality and the Accord Alliance, you are educating one person who will, in turn, educate many others over the years. In health classrooms, ask questions that encourage inquiry into and discussions about the multifaceted nature of gender identity and expression (and sexual orientation, if your teacher is willing and allowed to address it). Raise the possibility that these aspects of our personhood exist on a broad spectrum, not just the duality of male-female or the categories of heterosexual, bisexual, and homosexual. Share information about days of visibility (see table 11.1); you can start by asking whoever does the announcements at your school to add a bit about them, or place posters in visible locations in your school and town.

In 1987, when the AIDS epidemic was decimating the gay community and an AIDS diagnosis was almost certainly a death sentence, the AIDS activist group ACT UP (the AIDS Coalition to Unleash Power) was born and adopted the motto "Silence=Death." The reasoning behind the equation was that by maintaining

Table 11.1. Calendar Dates

February 7	National Black HIV/AIDS Awareness Day
First full week of March	Black Church National Week of Prayer for the Healing of AIDS
March 10	National Women and Girls HIV/AIDS Awareness Day
March 20	National Native HIV/AIDS Awareness Day
March 31	International Transgender Day of Visibility
April 10	National Youth HIV and AIDS Awareness Day
April 18	National Transgender HIV Testing Day
April 19	National Day of Silence
April 26	Lesbian Visibility Day
May 17	International Day against Homophobia, Transphobia and Biphobia
May 18	HIV Vaccine Awareness Day
May 19	National Asian and Pacific Islander HIV/AIDS Awareness Day
May 19	Hepatitis Testing Day
May 22	Harvey Milk Day
May 24	Pan Visibility Day (pansexual and panromantic)
Month of June	GLBTQ Pride Month
June 5	HIV Long-Term Survivors Day
June 27	National HIV Testing Day

June 28	Stonewall Riots Anniversary
September 18	National HIV/AIDS and Aging Awareness Day
September 23	Celebrate Bisexuality Day
September 27	National Gay Men's HIV/AIDS Awareness Day
Month of October	LGBT History Month
October 11	National Coming Out Day
October 15	National Latinix AIDS Awareness Day
October 20	Spirit Day
Last full week of October	Asexuality Awareness Week
October 26	Intersex Awareness Day
First two full weeks of November	Transgender Awareness Week
November 8	Intersex Day of Solidarity/Intersex Day of Remembrance
November 28	Transgender Day of Remembrance
December 1	World AIDS Day
First Sunday in December	World AIDS Sunday

Sources:
www.aids.gov/news-and-events/awareness-days/index.html
www.therainbowbabies.com/Holidays.html
www.algbtical.org/2A%20DAYS.htm
en.wikipedia.org/wiki/List_of_LGBT_awareness_days

silence around difficult or taboo sexual topics, the spread of HIV (the virus that causes AIDS) would continue, permitting the AIDS epidemic to continue to flourish and more people to die. If people would discuss their HIV status or risks before becoming sexual partners, unnecessary deaths could be averted. The ACT UP posters featured a pink triangle (the emblem used by Nazis to denote homosexuals) on a black background accompanied by these words "Silence=Death."[1]

In a similar way, intersex individuals who have suffered at the hands of the medical establishment (albeit at the hands of physicians who sought to improve the person's life circumstances through "normalizing" surgeries) realize that society's silence about intersex conditions will result in the death of sexual pleasure or other problems for many more intersex persons. Although the medical community is making strides toward understanding intersex conditions and in postponing surgeries, the practice of performing genital surgeries on infants with atypical genitalia is far from eradicated. While Americans express outrage about female circumcisions routinely practiced by other cultures, we remain mute about treatment of intersex infants here in the United States. Also, the practice of male circumcision on infants is fairly normal in the United States, while other countries are outlawing the practice as barbaric. Make a difference by breaking the silence around the issue of intersex genital mutilation.

The ACT UP slogan eventually grew. "Knowledge=Power; Silence=Death" soon appeared on posters for good reason. People discuss what they know. We learn from these discussions. Armed with knowledge, we can make intelligent, informed decisions and effect change upon our own lives and the lives of those in our community. The treatment of intersex conditions as medical emergencies serves to preserve the silence of taboo topics. Concerned physicians seeking to make newborns "normal" are—in the eyes of some who have received such "care"—depriving the individuals from making informed decisions about their own bodies and their futures as sexual beings. The Intersex Society of North America (ISNA) was formed in 1993 in opposition to that standard of care. They began the momentum that led to the changes that have already happened; the groups that came after them and continue the work today, and you can continue that work. Speak out, share what you know, to ensure that the existence of intersex conditions and their relative frequency of occurrence (see table 5.1 in chapter five for numbers) is understood in your community.

Other places to speak out include social science (history) and language arts (English) classrooms. Make statements and ask questions about the power of language. Introduce your teachers to the Teaching Tolerance campaign of the Southern Poverty Law Center (SPLC), which is dedicated to providing free curriculum materials for teachers. Introduce your peers to Mix It Up, the SPLC resource for student activists. The website, Tolerance.org, provides materials with lesson plans developed for elementary and secondary classrooms that teachers can

Intersex Information to Share

- In 2017, Human Rights Watch (HRW) published a six-minute video titled "US: End Irreversible Genital Surgeries on Intersex Infants," which focuses on the practice of performing medically unnecessary surgeries on intersex infants that continues in the United States. The video can be found at www.hrw.org/video-photos/video/2017/07/25/video-end-irreversible-genital-surgeries-intersex-infants-us or on You Tube at www.youtube.com/watch?v=KeAVdOJOfKk.
- The HRW also published a report titled *"I Want to Be Like Nature Made Me": Medically Unnecessary Surgeries on Intersex Children in the U.S.*, which can be downloaded from www.hrw.org/sites/default/files/report_pdf/lgbtintersex0717_web_0.pdf.
- Kyle Knight, a researcher in HRW's LGBT Rights Program, published an article titled "Intersex Infant Surgery Settlement Highlights Regulatory Gaps: Such Surgeries Should be Banned for Children," which can be found at www.hrw.org/news/2017/08/01/intersex-infant-surgery-settlement-highlights-regulatory-gaps.
- The trailer for filmmaker Pidgeon Pagonis's documentary *The Son I Never Had: Growing Up Intersex* can be found at www.pidgeonismy.name/documentary/.

use to enhance their curricula. By introducing teachers to these materials (or renewing their interest in them), you will definitely make a difference. Remember, education is a powerful tool. You serve your community by making others aware of the existence of intersex conditions; of the differences among gender roles, identity and expression, physical or biological sex, and sexual orientation; and of the power language has to influence the world. Armed with such knowledge, each person is better prepared to decide for him- or herself what stance to take on these issues.

Always watch your language. Work to be inclusive. Avoid the rigid male-female and lesbian, gay, and bisexual categories alone and include *intersex* and *trans* in your working vocabulary. True, no one can, or wants to be, politically correct 100 percent of the time. Policing our own language can be tiring; it may

Scholarship Opportunities

Scholarship opportunities for LGBTQ students and activists are available. You may have to look to find them all, but here are two places to start.

- The Stonewall Community Foundation offers two scholarships: the Traub-Dicker Rainbow Scholarship supports women-identified lesbians in their pursuit of higher education, and the Levin-Goffe Scholarship provides a measure of financial stability to undergraduate students who are both LGBTQ or intersex and undocumented immigrants. For more information visit www.stonewallfoundation.org/scholarships/.
- The Human Rights Campaign website has a scholarship database, which it admits is not exhaustive, but I counted ninety possibilities under the "National" tab. The database is also searchable by state. Visit www.hrc .org/resources/scholarship-database.

even strain friendships. By simply being aware of the words you speak and hear, and choosing your own words with care (or correcting yourself when you hear you have misspoken), you will effect change in the world around you.

Start a GSA

Does your school have a GSA? Although this acronym once stood for Gay-Straight Alliance, as awareness and inclusivity have grown, the meaning has changed. Sometimes it stands for Genders and Sexualities Alliance. Similar groups—which do not align with the acronym, admittedly—include Queer Students Alliance and Pride Club. Currently, such groups work for racial and gender justice. Social justice is at the heart of LGBTQ activism, and adding in the racial component, which is new since the first edition of this book, makes sense since LGBTQ people of color are targeted for harassment and violence at a greater rate than are white members of the community. Whatever the name of your club, your school (and the administration, obviously, as you will likely need their approval to start an official entity) needs to know that it's an inclusive group—straight allies are welcome, as are students with LGBTQI parents—and that the club does not promote homosexuality, heterosexuality, bisexuality, or sexuality of any kind. Nor does it instruct attendees in the intricacies of sex—although if your members are of age to be sexually active, it may well include information on safer sex practices and promote the use of condoms (male and female) to reduce the chances of sexually transmitted illnesses. Having a GSA on campus means that your school and its administration support schools as being centers of education, where open minds can gain valuable information and where students can question the order of the universe—and your local cultural climate—in safety. Through the process of listening and questioning in a safe space, people grow to be healthy, thinking citizens, ready to take action (large or small) in their communities.

For more information on starting a GSA on your campus, check out the GSA Network at gsanetwork.org/. In addition, explore the resources at the back of this book to find materials that will empower the youth activists in your GSA to welcome gender-expansive youth, and to fight homophobia, transphobia, racism, and more. Print or purchase posters, buttons, or stickers to expand visibility. Use the designs you find to jump-start your own creativity—art is a powerful way to spread your message; student-designed posters and murals will carry weight in your community. The Trans Student Educational Resources (www.transstudent. org/), True Colors Fund (truecolorsfund.org/), and downloadable materials from interACT Advocates (www.interactadvocates.org) are a great place to start.

Campus Activism

College and university campuses are good places to exercise one's ideals. While campuses may provide academic havens from the community at large, they are still microcosms of society—complete with hierarchical government structures. Beyond encouraging discussions of genders and sexualities in the lecture hall and promoting inclusive language, activists on campus might consider the admissions and employment practices of their college or university and the toilet, bathing, sleeping, and locker room facilities available to students and faculty. Schools with nondiscrimination policies that include gender identity and expression are more likely to be supportive of gender-variant students and faculty. Some schools provide unisex or gender-neutral toilets, bathrooms, and locker facilities. Some offer gender-neutral housing options. Although the number of campuses that address these issues is growing, campus activists will find many opportunities to work for change. As always, visibility is critical. Campuses offer a wealth of locations to post information and artwork. Think: the more eye-catching the design, the more minds you can reach!

To learn how far your school will go to support gender identity and expression, ask to see the school's nondiscrimination policy. When shopping for schools,

Shop for Workplace Equality with HRC

Each year the Human Rights Campaign (HRC) releases a buyer's guide titled "Buying for Workplace Equality" that empowers shoppers to patronize businesses that support LGBTQI equality. HRC polls businesses through its Corporate Equality Index (CEI), where it asks about LGBT-related policies, benefits, and corporate practices; the buyer's guides are based on corporations' responses to the CEI. Buyer's guides can be downloaded as PDF documents or searched online; HRC even has a mobile phone app where you can text the company or product name to HRC. Get started at www.hrc.org/apps/buyersguide/#.

inquire about the school's dormitory facilities and room assignment policies. Do not assume that schools with coed dorms or bathrooms are sensitive to the needs of androgynous or gender-variant students; ask directly. The more admissions offices field such questions, the sooner schools will seek to accommodate the needs of students whose gender identity or expression does not match with the sex they were assigned at birth.

Educate Your Community

Don't leave the discussion of genders and sexualities to the gender-variant people in your community. Whether you are straight, gay, bisexual, intersex, transgender, queer, or questioning, you have a responsibility to act as an ally for other groups. If you are not present to stand up for the rights of others, how can you expect others to defend your rights should they ever come into question? *Bending the Mold: An Action Kit for Transgender Youth* is an excellent resource for advocates of transgender teen issues, written specifically for transgender youth. Available from Lambda Legal (see "Resources" section), the thirty-two-page booklet includes provocative ideas with which you can arm yourself for action.

Beyond talking about gender issues, you can make a difference just encouraging others to consider the topic. If your school does not yet have a GSA, locate individual teachers, counselors, youth clergy, and other adults who would be willing to post "GLBT Safe Zone" or "Diverse, Inclusive, Accepting, Welcoming, Safe Space for Everyone" stickers or posters, advertising their openness to discussing the issues. Obtain permission to hang LGBTQ-friendly notices and posters

Five members of interACT Advocates for Intersex Youth attend the annual Creating Change Conference hosted by the National LGBTQ Task Force in Detroit, Michigan, in January 2017. The interACT Advocates attended to discuss intersex issues. Persons depicted: (rear) AJ; (front—left to right): Koomah, Jonathan Legette, Emily Quinn, Ali Crivelli. *Courtesy of interACT Advocates for Intersex Youth*

around campus. Little signs of acceptance can make an enormous difference for someone who feels marginalized in his, her, or their community. Everyone likes to be recognized and to see reflections of himself or herself on campus; each person has the right to feel welcome in school and a community. Help make all students feel at home in your school.

Consider waging a campaign at your local library. Befriend a librarian. (They are outstanding people!) Create a wish list of titles you would like to have available and present it to your local librarian. Ask to have *Gender Identity: The Ultimate Teen Guide*, second edition, and some of the other resources you have found made available for circulation. Since school and library funds are always tight, consider holding a bake sale or car wash, or donating a weekend's wages to accompany your request. If you do, be sure to earmark your donation for gender identity resources and include a list of titles you would like to see added to the collection.

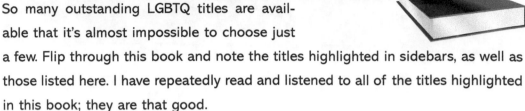

Titles to Suggest for Library Wish Lists

So many outstanding LGBTQ titles are available that it's almost impossible to choose just a few. Flip through this book and note the titles highlighted in sidebars, as well as those listed here. I have repeatedly read and listened to all of the titles highlighted in this book; they are that good.

- Kirstin Cronn-Mills's *Beautiful Music for Ugly Children* (2012) is narrated by Gabe, who was born Elizabeth, and now hosts his own radio music show.
- Meredith Russo's *If I Was Your Girl* (2016) is narrated by Amanda, who moves to live with her dad after surviving an antitrans attack. There she finds romance but cannot find the opportunity to voice her truth to Grant—the boy who has captured her heart.
- Brian Katcher's *Almost Perfect* (2009) is narrated by Logan, a straight guy on the rebound after being dumped who falls for the beautiful, mysterious, new girl—Sage.

One last thought on spreading enlightenment through sharing books. While I am an advocate of buying full-price directly from publishers and independent bookstores to ensure authors get their full share of the royalties, I know authors write to get their stories read. As such, consider buying used works to spread your dollars further. While used books won't be shelved in libraries, they can be placed on public libraries' "Free Books" tables and racks when you are finished. Or you can place them in little neighborhood library boxes found in some communities across the United States and even in the entrances of some supermarkets. For a small investment, you can get books out into circulation—and people who pick up such free books may be more inclined to continue a book's circulation after reading. Or consider pooling funds with a friend and gathering ten or twelve copies of the same title and then sharing them with a local book group (or start your own book group).

Exercise Your Political Voice

When you become aware of a legislative issue about which you feel strongly, speak out. If your life feels too busy to seek out these issues, you can subscribe to mailing lists with some of the organizations mentioned in this chapter and at the end of the book. Although many will send calls to sign online petitions, realize that personal letters and phone calls are more powerful ways to get your voice heard. Take the key talking points from the original email, newsletter, or online petition and use them to craft your own letter. If you're too busy for that, consider copying the text from the online petitions, pasting this into a blank document, and then writing your own letter using the pertinent information from the original. Legislators do listen to their constituents. If you receive already-prepared postcards or letters from an organization that only require your signature and a stamp, stop and think about how it will be received. Individual handwritten or typed letters, into which the writer obviously invested time and thought, carry far more weight than cookie-cutter postcards sent out in mass mailings. Phone calls, emails, faxes, postcards, and letters pour into legislators' offices on a daily basis. The more effort a sender takes to generate a message, the more weight it will carry in the recipient's office.

If you wish to be politically active without adding your name to mailing lists, visit your local library; surf the websites of the legal and political organizations listed in the "Resources" section; and read newspapers, magazines, and blogs. You can draft correspondence and make phone calls independently of any organization. Beyond becoming a registered voter and going to the polls on voting days, our political system has room for every citizen's voice; however, only those who speak out are heard. Your opinion matters; make sure your views are heard.

While several states have implemented Safe Schools program initiatives, others still lag behind. Check the legislative docket in your state to see whether Safe

HRC Advocacy Training

Visit HRC's Equality Voter Action Center. Join its Equality Action Academy to attend the online activist training series that promises to sharpen your advocacy skills. Sign up for the Mobile Action Network to be alerted when there are opportunities to contact elected officials, sign petitions, and take other actions. Join the Dialer Team to help call and text like-minded voters about issues as they arise. Visit takeaction.hrc.org/.

Schools programs are being considered, then be sure to make your legislators aware of your stance on the issue. If the state in which you reside already has a Safe Schools plan in place, find out about it. What is the reporting mechanism? Where should someone direct his or her gender-related Safe Schools concern? How effective is the program? By doing what you can to ensure that any Safe Schools laws in your state are enforced, you can make schools safer for all.

Make a Difference, Starting Today

Today is a great day to begin your campaign to raise awareness of gender- and sexuality-related issues in your school and community. Look around. Do you see unisex or family restrooms in many places? Take note when completing any standard form: must applicants list a gender, and are there only two—male and female—from which to choose? If you are not ready to launch into an educational lecture, try simply leaving that question blank. Or you might write in a suggestion that the form leave a blank for gender, which each person can complete in a manner with which they are comfortable. Whenever you encounter a person whose gender appears ambiguous or otherwise appears "different" from the norm, do remember to smile and nod hello; the act of welcoming one of society's marginalized citizens is simple enough and may be powerful for the recipient. However you approach the issue, resolve to make a difference in your world—starting today.

Appendix: WPATH Identity Recognition Statement

www.wpath.org
wpath@wpath.org

phone: 1+(847) 752-5328
fax: 1+(224) 633-2166

2575 Northwest Parkway
Elgin, IL 60124

STAFF

Executive Director
Sue O'Sullivan
sue@wpath.com

**Executive Director of Global
Education & Development**
Donna Kelly
donna@wpath.org

EXECUTIVE COMMITTEE

President
Gail Knudson, MD, FRCPC

President-Elect
Vin Tangpricha, MD, PhD

Secretary
Randi Ettner, PhD

Treasurer
Walter Pierre Bouman, MD

Past-President
Jamison Green, PhD

BOARD OF DIRECTORS

Tamara Adrian, JD
Tone Marie Hansen
Dan Karasic, MD
Baudewijntje Kreukels, PhD
Katherine Rachlin, PhD
Loren Schecter, MD
Sam Winter, PhD

Student Representative
Luke Allen, MA

EPATH Representative
Griet De Cuypere, MD

For Immediate Release

November 15, 2017

This statement replaces WPATH's Identity Recognition Statement of January 19, 2015.

WPATH Identity Recognition Statement

The World Professional Association for Transgender Health (WPATH) recognizes that, for optimal physical and mental health, persons must be able to freely express their gender identity, whether or not that identity conforms to the expectations of others. WPATH further recognizes the right of all people to identity documents consistent with their gender identity, including those documents which confer legal gender status. Such documents are essential to the ability of all people to enjoy rights and opportunities equal to those available to others; to access accommodation, education, employment, and health care; to travel; to navigate everyday transactions; and to enjoy safety. Transgender people, regardless of how they identify or appear, should enjoy the gender recognition all persons expect and deserve.

Medical and other barriers to gender recognition for transgender individuals may harm physical and mental health. WPATH opposes all medical requirements that act as barriers to those wishing to change legal sex or gender markers on documents. These include requirements for diagnosis, counseling or therapy, puberty blockers, hormones, any form of surgery (including that which involves sterilization), or any other requirements for any form of clinical treatment or letters from doctors. WPATH argues that marital and parental status should not be barriers to recognition of gender change, and opposes requirements for persons to undergo periods living in their affirmed gender, or for enforced waiting or 'cooling off' periods after applying for a change in documents. Further, court and judicial hearings can produce psychological, as well as financial and logistical barriers to legal gender change, and may also violate personal privacy rights or needs.

WPATH advocates that appropriate gender recognition should be available to transgender youth, including those who are under the age of majority, as well as to individuals who are incarcerated or institutionalized. WPATH recognizes that there is a spectrum of gender identities, and that choices of identity limited to Male or Female may be inadequate to reflect all gender identities. An option of X, NB (non-binary), or Other (as examples) should be available for individuals who so choose.

WPATH urges governments to eliminate barriers to gender recognition, and to institute transparent, affordable and otherwise accessible administrative procedures affirming self-determination, when gender markers on identity documents are considered necessary. These procedures should be based in law and protect privacy.

Glossary

5-alpha-reductase pseudohermaphrodite: a rare genetic disorder where the person's external genitals are of normal size for females, but who also have Wolffian ducts and testes

a-: prefix meaning "without"

affirmed female: a term for someone who identifies as female but was not labeled female at birth; a transwoman

affirmed male: a term for someone who identifies as male but was not labeled male at birth; a transman

agender: genderless or gender neutral; a new and quickly evolving term to describe people who do not have a gender

ally: a friend or advocate, in this case to the GLBTQIA community or a portion thereof, as demonstrated by actions

ambigender: presenting ambiguous gender; genderqueer

ambiguous genitalia: external genitals that are neither clearly male or clearly female, but could be either or both

anatomical sex: *See* biological sex

androgen: a male sex hormone

androgen insensitivity syndrome: a genetic condition that is the most common diagnosis of male pseudohermaphroditism

androgen resistance syndrome: *See* androgen insensitivity syndrome

androgynous, androgyny: having the characteristics of both sexes; someone who appears both male and female at once

aromantic: not experiencing romantic inclination

asexual: sexless; not experiencing sexual attraction

assigned male at birth or **assigned female at birth**: birth sex; the sex (male or female) assigned at birth

assigned sex: the sex assigned at birth

berdache: a male who dresses and behaves in the role of a female in some Native American cultures; term used derogatorily by European colonizers for Native persons who did not fit their expectations of gender (*see also* two-spirit)

bi-: prefix meaning "two"

bigendered: one who has a gender identity that encompasses both male and female

binary genders: two options (*male* and *female*) given for gender in cultures that subscribe to the gender binary system in which all people are either male or female

binding: *See* chest binding

biological sex: a term used to classify one as male, female, or intersex based upon physical, genetic, biological, and hormonal characteristics, including genitalia

birth sex: biological sex as determined at birth

bisexual: of or pertaining to two sexes; one sexually attracted to both males and females

body dysmorphia: emotional distress experienced when one's external body does not match one's gender identity or internal image

boi: alternative spelling for *boy*, used mostly by alternative boys, FTM gender benders

"bottom" surgery: genital reconstruction as part of sexual or gender reassignment surgery

brain sex: the organizational structure of a person's brain, which is said to differ between male and female brains

breast augmentation: surgical enlargement of the breast tissue

butch: displaying masculine characteristics or appearing more masculine than feminine; generally used in conjunction with *lesbian*

chest binding: tight wrapping of the chest area designed to flatten breasts, creating a more masculine appearance in the body

Chicago Consensus: the 2006 consensus statement regarding medical treatment protocols that had language usage related to intersex conditions

chromosomes: biological structures in cell nuclei that carry genetic information; most humans have twenty-three pairs of chromosomes, with the standard female having two X chromosomes (XX) in the last pair and the standard male an X and Y chromosome (XY)

circumcision: (male) removal of the foreskin of the penis; often performed as a religious rite by Jews or Muslims; generally performed on infants for religious, hygienic, or aesthetic reasons; presently practiced on adult males in some African countries as prevention against disease transmission, specifically HIV

cis-: a prefix from the Latin *cis*, meaning "on this side of," used as an abbreviation of cisgender; the opposite of *trans-*

cisgender: one who presents as the same gender assigned at birth

cismale or **cisfemale, cisman** or **ciswoman**: one who was assigned at birth the sex correlating to his or her gender identity/expression

cisnormative: the cissexist practice of excluding or overlooking the experiences of trans persons when considering gender

cissexism: bias against transgender persons; transphobia

clitorectomy, clitoridectomy: (female) surgical removal of the clitoris (*see also* female genital cutting)

clitoroplasty: plastic surgery on the clitoris

closeted: hiding one's gender identity/expression or sexuality from public view and only sharing information deemed acceptable by society (*see also* stealth)

coming out: revealing one's gender identity/expression or sexual orientation to others (as in "coming out of the closet"), not to be confused with "outing" or "being outed"; for one who has fully transitioned, coming out can mean disclosing that the sex they were assigned at birth was different from the sex in which they live now

congenital adrenal hyperplasia: an inherited condition that causes the malfunction of the fetal adrenal gland resulting in an excess of androgen; the most common form of intersexuality

cross-dresser: a person of one physical sex or assigned gender who dresses in the clothing of the opposite sex or gender

dead name: the name a transgender person used with his, her, or their gender assigned at birth; "dead-naming" a person, or intentionally using the person's dead name, is defamatory

demi-: prefix meaning "half" or "partially"

demisexual: a person who feels sexual attraction only after forming an emotional connection

detransition: process of returning to one's former gender presentation; may be as simple as changing wardrobes and pronouns or as complex as involving cosmetic surgery

drag: the clothing/attire of the opposite sex; to be *in drag* is to be dressed as a person of the opposite sex

drag king: a woman dressed as a man, often a lesbian appearing or performing as a man

drag queen: a man dressed to appear or perform as a woman

dyke: derogatory term for a lesbian

dysmorphia, dysmorphic: *See* body dysmorphia

dysphoria, dysphoric: emotional distress, in this case experienced when one's gender identity does not match one's physical body structure

epispadias: a birth difference where the urethra exits on the upper side of the penis

ex-gay movement: a movement that attempts to convince LGBTQ individuals to become straight by undergoing conversion or reparative therapy

faggot: derogatory term for a gay man

female circumcision: *See* female genital cutting

female genital cutting, female genital mutilation: clitoridectomy; surgical altering of the female genitals, especially as a cultural rite, to remove the clitoris and sometimes the labia

femme: from *effeminate*; displaying feminine characteristics, often used in contrast with the word *butch*

FTM, F2M: female-to-male transsexual or transgender person; someone assigned a female gender at birth but who identifies as a male

gay: (slang) technically, a man whose sexual preference is for men, that is, a male homosexual; the preferred term for a reference to a homosexual; may be used to describe a woman (as in "a gay woman" or "she's gay")

gender: one's sex; usually either male or female, but intersex does occur

gender ambiguity: when one's gender is not easily discernible by others

gender attribution: others' perception of one's gender

gender bender: a person who dresses and behaves like a member of the opposite sex; in the twenty-first century the more commonly used terms include *genderqueer*, *gender nonconforming*, or *gender fluid*

gender binary: the concept that there are only two genders: male and female

gender confirmation surgery: surgery to transform one's genitals; carries the connotation that one might not "be" the chosen gender until it is "confirmed" through surgery (*see also* genital reconstruction surgery)

gender dysphoria: psychiatric term used to describe a person who is unhappy with his or her gender role in society, specifically when one's *gender identity* differs from one's *gender*

gender expression: the gender role one plays; the way one expresses gender through dress, movement, speech, and behavior (*see also* gender role)

gender fluid, genderfluid: genderqueer; when one's gender expression moves between and across genders

gender identity: the gender with which one identifies internally, whether or not this matches the body's physical sex or genitalia

gender identity disorder: a psychiatric term used to describe a person who is unhappy with hir gender role in society, who feels greatly at odds with the gender zee was assigned at birth and the associated gender role expectations

gendermap: a term coined by Dr. John Money to refer to the entity, template, or schema within the mind and brain unity that codes masculinity, femininity, and androgyny

gender nonconforming: persons crossing the boundary lines of gender who may or may not consider themselves transgender (*see also* trans and gender nonconforming)

genderqueer, GenderQueer, gender queer: a slang term for a person crossing the boundary lines of gender expression; often used by persons who may or may not be transgender, but who feel their gender falls outside the male-female dichotomy

gender reassignment surgery: *See* genital reconstruction surgery; sex reassignment

gender role: the role one plays (or is expected to play) within society as dictated by gender-specific behaviors and one's gender assignment at birth

gender suppressing drugs: medications prescribed by physicians for prepubescent transgender children in order to stave off puberty of the birth sex

gender transitioning: *See* transition

gender variant: *See* gender nonconforming

genital reconstruction surgery, gender reassignment surgery: surgery to transform one's genitals; remaking a penis into a urethra, clitoris, and vagina (vaginoplasty) or surgically constructing a penis using the clitoris, labia, and vagina (phalloplasty)

genital surgery: surgery to change the appearance of one's genitals, as may be done when sex determination is made difficult by ambiguous genitalia; not to be confused with genital reconstruction surgery

genotype: the genetic makeup of an organism

gestation: the period of time when a fetus is developing in the uterus

GLBTQI: gay, lesbian, bisexual, transgender, queer or questioning, intersex; variations may swap the positions of the first two (LGBTQI), double the Q, or leave off portions such that they are implied without being stated (LGBT)

gonad: organ that produces gametes for sexual reproduction; in humans, testes and ovaries

greygender: one who feels indifferent to their gender identity

gynecomastia: abnormal enlargement of the breast tissue in males; in slang, "man boobs"

HBIGDA: the Harry Benjamin International Gender Dysphoria Association which, in 2006, became WPATH or the World Professional Association for Transgender Health

heredity: also called "nature"; that which is passed on through genes to offspring

hermaphrodite: an outdated term for a person with both male and female sex characteristics; today called "*intersex*"

he-she: (slang) an outdated term for a butch (or masculine) lesbian or a transman; a person whose gender expression is male and whose birth sex is female

hetero-: prefix meaning "other," "different," or "opposite"

heteronormative: a stance on sexual orientation wherein heterosexual is considered normal

heterosexism: a bias toward heterosexuality and heterosexuals, and against non-heterosexual persons

heterosexual: a person (male or female) who is sexually attracted to persons of the opposite sex

hijras: the people in India deemed neither men nor women

hir, hirs: gender-neutral pronoun to replace *her/hers* and *him/his* (*see also* xyr)

homo-: prefix meaning "same"

homophobia: an irrational fear or dislike of same-gender-loving persons

homosexual: a person who is sexually attracted to another of the same gender

hormone therapy, hormone replacement therapy: the introduction of hormones to a body to treat a condition; for transgender individuals, HRT is employed specifically to develop characteristics of a gender other than the one assigned

hypospadias: a birth difference where the urethra forms an opening on the underside of the penis

hysterectomy: surgical removal of female sex organs; removal of the uterus, at a minimum, and possibly also including removal of the cervix, ovaries, and vagina

intergender: *See* genderqueer

inter phobia: an irrational fear or dislike of or prejudice against intersex people

intersex: a person born with an anatomy or physiology different from the cultural norm of male or female and who displays both male and female sex characteristics; sometimes erroneously called a hermaphrodite

intersex genital mutilation: the practice of surgically "correcting" atypical genitalia of intersex babies before they can give meaningful informed consent

ISNA: Intersex Society of North America

karyotype: blood test used to detect a chromosomal anomaly

Klinefelter syndrome: a common chromosomal variation in which males have an extra X chromosome (usually written as 47, XXY), which may cause sterility, breast development, and incomplete masculine body build

lesbian: a woman who is sexually attracted to other women; a homosexual woman

LGBTQIA: lesbian, gay, bisexual, transgender, queer or questioning, intersex, asexual

mammoplasty: plastic surgery performed on one or both breasts to alter the shape or size, which may include augmentation or enlargement, reduction or removal, or reconstruction

mastectomy: surgical removal or one or both breasts

Mayer Rokitansky Kuster Hauser syndrome: a congenital variation in typical XX females, MRKH girls are born without a completely formed uterus, fallopian tubes, and/or vagina; also known as congenital total or partial absence of the uterus or vagina, Müllerian agenesis, vaginal agenesis, and MRKHauser syndrome; sometimes written as Mayer-Rokitansky-Kuster-Hauser syndrome

metaoidioplasty: plastic surgery to enlarge the clitoris to resemble a penis

misgendering: the act of identifying a trans person using incorrect gender markers

MSM: men who have sex with men

MTF, M2F: male-to-female transsexual or transgender person; someone assigned a male gender at birth but who identifies as a female

Mullerian duct: either of a pair of embryonic ducts parallel to the Wolffian ducts and giving rise in the female to the fallopian tubes, uterus, cervix, and upper portion of the vagina

Mx.: a gender-neutral title of address

nature: heredity, as used in reference to growth and development; natural, inborn characteristics that are unchanged by environment

nonbinary, non-binary: one whose gender is not wholly male or female

nurture: environment, as used in reference to growth and development; those aspects formed in response to one's living conditions and life experiences

omnisexual: a person who is sexually attracted to persons of all genders; also pansexual

out: visible to the public; to not be in hiding; also, to reveal one's own or another's undisclosed sexual orientation (from the phrase *out of the closet*)

outing: the act of revealing or making visible to the public

ovotestis: a gonad containing both testicular and ovarian tissue

packing: (slang) giving the appearance of a penis by inserting an object into a person's pants

passing: (slang) being perceived as other than what one is (for example, a lesbian might pass as straight, or a transgender person may pass as being the gender ze desires); carries the connotation that passing is a lie, whereas the person with gender identity disorder is actually portraying hir true self

phallic reconstruction: the surgical reconstruction of a (damaged) penis

phalloplasty: plastic surgery on the penis or the building of a penis by plastic surgery

phallus: penis

phenotype: the observable makeup of an organism

phimosis: a condition of the penis that prevents retraction of the foreskin

postoperative transsexual: a transgender or transsexual person who has had her or his body's physical structure surgically altered to create the genitals of the sex opposite from that assigned at birth

preferred pronouns, preferred gender pronouns: those pronouns by which a person prefers to be identified

preoperative transsexual: a transgender or transsexual person planning or preparing to have his or her body's physical structure altered to incorporate the genitals opposite those with which he or she was born

primary sex characteristics: those determinants of sex present and observable at birth, including the external genitals and internal sexual parts

progestin induced virilization: a condition where an XX (female) baby has an enlarged clitoris and no testes

pseudohermaphroditism: outdated terminology for a condition whereby a person's chromosomal and external genital makeup do not match; *intersex* is the preferred terminology (*see also* hermaphrodite)

queen: (slang) an effeminate homosexual male

queer: strange or odd from a conventional viewpoint; unusually different; unconventional; slang for homosexual (*see also* genderqueer)

questioning: the state of being uncertain of one's sexual identity or orientation

secondary sex characteristics: those determinants of sex that appear with puberty, including (for females) development of breasts and hips, a softer feminine physique, maturation of genitals, appearance of body hair, and the onset of menstruation and (for males) development of a more masculine build, maturation of genitals, deepening voice, protrusion of the Adam's apple, and appearance of body hair

sex: one's gender as determined by the presence (or absence) of gender-specific genitalia (*see also* biological sex)

sex reassignment, sexual reassignment surgery: surgery altering a person's body, specifically the genitalia or secondary sex characteristics, to that of another sex; sought to bring one's gender identity and one's body into alignment (*also* gender reassignment surgery)

sexual behavior: sexual actions, what one does sexually; not to be confused with sexual identity or sexual orientation

sexual identity: the sex that you recognize as your self; sometimes explained as "who you go to bed *as*" (*see also* gender identity)

sexual orientation: the sex toward which one feels carnally attracted; sometimes explained as "who you go to bed *with*"

she-he: (slang) an outdated term for a transwoman or a drag queen; a person whose gender expression is female and birth sex is male

sie: (pronounced "see") a gender-neutral pronoun to replace *she* and *he*; sie provides an alternate spelling and is synonymous with *xe*, *ze*, or *zee*

SRY: acronym for the sex-determining region of the Y chromosome

Standards of Care: Standards of Care; originally referred to the HBIGDA SOC established in the 1970s; the seventh version of the WPATH SOC became effective in 2011

stealth, living stealth: the trans community's equivalent to the gay community's *closeted*; living in one's chosen gender identity without detection; surviving "under the radar"; passing completely

straight: slang for heterosexual

testicular feminization: an outdated name for the condition now called androgen insensitivity (or resistance) syndrome

"top" surgery: breast reduction or augmentation as part of sexual reassignment surgery

tranny boy, tranny boi: someone who identifies as a female-to-male transgender person; the spellings vary and may include hyphens or be written as a single word

trans and gender nonconforming: transgender and persons crossing the boundary lines of gender who may or may not consider themselves transgender

transfeminine: term for a person who was assigned male at birth and who now identifies as feminine, or mostly feminine

transgender, trans: one who crosses the boundary of the sex assigned at birth; this person may choose to undergo sexual reassignment surgery and/or treatment with hormones

transition: the period of change when a trans person begins to live more fully as a person of his or her true gender, possibly including a required period of full-time living before sexual reassignment surgery

transman, TransMan: female-to-male transsexual or transgender person

transmasculine: a term for a person who was assigned female at birth and who now identifies as masculine, or mostly masculine

transmasculine birth: when a baby is born to a transman, a person who identifies as male but has female anatomy

transphobia: irrational fear of persons whose gender does not fit within the binary system of male-female

transsexual: one who crosses the boundary of the sex assigned at birth; the person may or may not opt to undergo sexual reassignment surgery or treatment with hormones

transvestite: a public cross-dresser; one who wears the clothing of the opposite sex and appears before others dressed in this fashion, but who identifies with the gender corresponding to the sex assigned at birth

transwoman, TransWoman: male-to-female transgender or transsexual person

trimester: a period of three months, often used with reference to human gestation or academic calendars

Turner's syndrome: a condition describing females who carry the genetic code XO (rather than the standard XX), lack ovaries, and demonstrate exaggeratedly female behavior accompanied by sterility

two-spirit: Native American name for transgender people and those who identify outside the binary male-female, also called two-soul people; also known as *berdache* or, in the Crow nation, *badé* (or *boté*); among the Maricopa, *kwiraxame'*; among the Chumash, *joya*; among the Cocopa, *warhameh*; or among the Zuni, *Ihamana*

urethra: the tube that extends from the bladder to the outside, through which urine passes and, in men, through which semen travels

urethroplasty: surgical extension of the urethra, the result of which allows a person to urinate while standing up

vaginectomy: surgical removal of the vagina

vaginoplasty: plastic surgery on the vagina, especially the building of a vagina by surgery

Wintke: a common shortening of *Winyanktecha*, or Two-Souled person; recognition as a third gender in parts of Native American culture

Wolffian duct: the duct of the mesonephros that persists in the female chiefly as part of a vestigial organ and in the male as the duct system leaving the testes and including the epididymis, vas deferens, seminal vesicle, and ejaculatory duct

womyn, wimmin: alternative spelling for *woman* or *women*, removing the male root of the word

WPATH: World Professional Association for Transgender Health, formed in 2006 from the HBIGDA

xe: gender-neutral pronoun to replace *she* and *he* (*see also* sie, zee)

xyr: gender-neutral pronoun to replace *her* and *his* (*see also* hir)

ze, zee: gender-neutral pronoun to replace *she* and *he* (*see also* sie)

Notes

Chapter 2

1. *Men Are from Mars, Women Are from Venus* (New York: HarperCollins, 1992) was the first in a series of similarly titled self-help books about relationships written by psychologist and author John Gray, PhD.
2. Judy Foreman, "The Biological Basis of Homosexuality," *Boston Globe*, Health/Science section, December 2, 2003.
3. "Transgender Teens," Discovery Health Channel, 2003.
4. Dhruv Marwha, Meha Halari, and Lise Eliot, "Meta-Analysis Reveals a Lack of Sexual Dimorphism in Human Amygdala Volume," *NeuroImage* 147 (February 15, 2017), 282–94, www.sciencedirect.com/science/article/pii/S1053811916307431. Accessed May 10, 2018.
5. Rosalind Franklin University of Medicine and Science, "Mounting Challenge to Brain Sex Differences," *Science Daily*, January 17, 2017, https://www.sciencedaily.com/releases/2017/01/170117135943.htm. Accessed May 8, 2018.
6. All quotes in this paragraph come from Carl W. Bushong, "What Is Gender and Who Is Transgendered?" *Labioplasty* (blog), January 2008, labiaplastyblog.blogspot.com/2008/01/what-is-gender-and-who-is-transgendered_19.html. Accessed May 5, 2018.
7. Andrew R. Flores, Jody L. Herman, Gary J. Gates, and Taylor N. T. Brown, *How Many Adults Identify as Transgender in the United States?* (Los Angeles: Williams Institute, 2016), williamsinstitute.law.ucla.edu/wp-content/uploads/How-Many-Adults-Identify-as-Transgender-in-the-United-States.pdf. PDF publication. Accessed January 12, 2018.
8. Lesley Rogers, *Sexing the Brain* (New York: Columbia University Press, 2001).
9. Debra W. Soh, "Cross-Cultural Evidence for the Genetics of Homosexuality," *Scientific American*, April 25, 2017, www.scientificamerican.com/article/cross-cultural-evidence-for-the-genetics-of-homosexuality/. Accessed May 6, 2018.
10. Francisco R. Gómez, Scott W. Semenyna, Lucas Court, and Paul L. Vasey, "Familial Patterning and Prevalence of Male Androphilia among Istmo Zapotec Men and Muxes," *PLoS ONE*, 13(2): e0192683, www.researchgate.net/publication/312051698_Recalled_Separation_Anxiety_in_Childhood_in_Istmo_Zapotec_Men_Women_and_Muxes. Accessed May 12, 2018.
11. Siddhartha Mukherjee, *The Gene: An Intimate History* (New York: Scribner, 2016), 366.
12. Mukherjee, *The Gene*, 368.
13. Mukherjee, *The Gene*, 368.
14. Melissa Hogenboom, "Are There Any Homosexual Animals?" *BBC Earth*, February 6, 2015, www.bbc.com/earth/story/20150206-are-there-any-homosexual-animals. Accessed May 5, 2018.

15. Jack Drescher, "Out of *DSM*: Depathologizing Homosexuality," *Behavioral Sciences* 5, no. 4 (December 2015), www.ncbi.nlm.nih.gov/pmc/articles/PMC4695779/. Accessed May 13, 2018.

16. Madeline H. Wyndzen, "DSM-IV, All Mixed Up: A Transgendered Psychology Professor's Perspective on Life, the Psychology of Gender, and 'Gender Identity Disorder,'" (written prior to the 2013 *DSM-5* release). www.genderpsychology.org/transsexual/dsm_iv.html. Accessed May 27, 2018.

17. Wyndzen, "DSM-IV."

18. "DSM-IV-TR Diagnostic Criteria for Gender Identity Disorder," *Psychiatric News*, July 18, 2003, psychnews.psychiatryonline.org/doi/10.1176/pn.38.14.0032. Accessed May 27, 2018.

19. Francine Russo, "Where Transgender Is No Longer a Diagnosis," *Scientific American*, January 6, 2017, www.scientificamerican.com/article/where-transgender-is-no-longer-a-diagnosis/. Accessed May 27, 2018.

20. Wayne Parry, "Gender Dysphoria: *DSM-5* Reflects Shift in Perspective on Gender Identity," *Huffington Post*, June 4, 2013, updated August 4, 2013, www.huffingtonpost.com/2013/06/04/gender-dysphoria-dsm-5_n_3385287.html. Accessed May 27, 2018.

21. Julia Reischel, "See Dick Be Jane," *Broward-Palm Beach New Times*, May 18, 2006. Accessed May 28, 2018.

22. Julia Reischel, email message to the author, July 3, 2006.

23. Tom Verdin, "Calif. Governor Signs Transgender-Student Bill," *USA Today*, August 12, 2013, www.usatoday.com/story/news/nation/2013/08/12/calif-transgender-bill/2645435/. Accessed May 28, 2018.

24. Lane Brown, "Gender Neutrality: Why Teachers Won't Ask Boys and Girls to Line Up in Lincoln, Nebraska," October 9, 2014, www.csmonitor.com/The-Culture/Family/Modern-Parenthood/2014/1009/Gender-neutrality-Why-teachers-won-t-ask-boys-and-girls-to-line-up-in-Lincoln-Neb. Accessed December 17, 2017.

25. Peter and Emily's names have been changed to protect their identity and that of their family.

---

a. Caroline T., "Gender Dysphoria, Abuse," March 2016.

b. *Call Me Malcolm* is available on DVD and from some streaming services, but the original links to a website for the film and a page for Filmworks are no longer active. The United Church of Christ maintains a web page with information—although some links on the page were inactive when visited I last visited them. www.ucc.org/lgbt_callmemalcolm. Accessed June 7, 2018.

c. *Being Me*, a 2015 feature documentary film by Journeyman Pictures, is available from the filmmaker and through various streaming services. Visit www.journeyman.tv/film/6341/being-me. Accessed December 25, 2018.

Chapter 3

1. New Revised Standard Version Bible: Anglicized Edition (New York: National Council of the Churches of Christ in the United States of America, 1995). bible.oremus.org/?ql=412834564, bible.oremus.org/?ql=412834795. Accessed December 26, 2018.

2. This paragraph draws from Joyce Tyldesley's biography *Hatchepsut: The Female Pharaoh* (New York: Viking, 1996).

3. *The Trial of Joan of Arc: Being the Verbatim Report of the Proceedings from the Orleans Manuscript*, translated by W. S. Scott (Westport, CT: Associated Booksellers, 1956), quoted in Les-

lie Feinberg, *Transgender Warriors: Making History from Joan of Arc to Dennis Rodman* (Boston: Beacon Press, 1996), 37.

4. Vanessa Baird, *The No-Nonsense Guide to Sexual Diversity* (Toronto: New Internationalist Publications and Between the Lines, 2001), 121.

5. Andrew Matzner, in his book *'O Au No Keia: Voices from Hawaii's Mahu and Transgender Communities* (2001), shares the stories of contemporary *mahu* and their attempts to reflect the diversity of the community.

6. Baird, *No-Nonsense Guide to Sexual Diversity*, 114.

7. This section draws extensively from "Gender Benders," a 2004 episode of the National Geographic Channel series *Taboo*. See also "Aruvani—A Day in the Sun," a compilation of three BBC articles from 2001 to 2003, WE News Archive, thewe.cc/contents/more/archive/aruvani .html. Accessed June 6, 2017.

8. "India's Eunuchs Seek New Way," BBC News World Edition, June 5, 2006, thewe.cc/wc planet/news/asia/india/aravani_seek_new_way.htm. Accessed June 6, 2017.

9. Kate Bornstein, *Gender Outlaw: On Men, Women, and the Rest of Us* (New York: Routledge, 1994), 23.

10. Walter Williams, *The Spirit and the Flesh: Sexual Diversity in American Indian Culture* (Boston: Beacon Press, 1986), 178–81.

11. Feinberg, *Transgender Warriors*, 21.

12. You can read more about Christine Jorgensen in her book *Christine Jorgensen: A Personal Autobiography* (San Francisco: Cleis Press, 2001).

13. Gypsey Teague, "The Increase of Transgender Characters in Movies and Television," *Transgender Tapestry* 102 (Summer 2002): 31.

14. Walter Scott, "Personality Parade," *Parade*, August 8, 2004.

15. This paragraph draws extensively from Nazila Fathi, "As Repression Eases, More Iranians Change Their Sex," *New York Times*, August 2, 2004.

16. This paragraph draws extensively from "Sexuality," a 2002 episode of the National Geographic series *Taboo*.

17. Oriana Schwindt, "Netflix Revives 'Queer Eye for the Straight Guy,'" *Variety*, January 24, 2017, variety.com/2017/tv/news/queer-eye-for-the-straight-guy-netflix-revival-1201968887/. Accessed July 18, 2017.

18. This paragraph draws from Alison Glock, "She Likes to Watch," *New York Times*, February 6, 2005, www.nytimes.com/2005/02/06/arts/television/she-likes-to-watch.html, and *Wikipedia*, s.v. "*The L Word*," en.wikipedia.org/wiki/The_L_Word. Accessed August 1, 2017.

19. Scott Collins, "Corporate Giant Viacom to Roll Out Gay Cable Channel Tonight," *Baltimore Sun*, June 30, 2005, articles.baltimoresun.com/2005-06-30/features/0506300101_1_viacom -gay-cable-network. Accessed August 1, 2017.

20. Diane Anderson-Minshall, "Why You Should Watch *Orange Is the New Black*," Advocate.com, July 10, 2013, www.advocate.com/print-issue/current-issue/2013/07/10/why-you -should-watch-orange-new-black?page=full. Accessed September 10, 2017.

21. Taffy Brodesser-Akner, "Can Jill Soloway Do Justice to the Trans Movement?" *New York Times Magazine*, August 29, 2014, www.nytimes.com/2014/08/31/magazine/can-jill-soloway-do -justice-to-the-trans-movement.html?Src=longreads&_r=0. Accessed November 5, 2017.

22. Jacqueline Spendlove, "Career Revival: Katherine Heigl Takes Another Crack at TV Success," decoy.tvpassport.com/news/career-revival-katherine-heigl-takes-another-crack-tv -success. Accessed November 5, 2017.

23. Raina Deerwater, "Must-See LGBTQ TV: Don't Miss the 'Pose' Premiere, 'Sense8' and 'The Fosters' Finales, 'Alex Strangelove,' and More!" GLAAD blog, June 3, 2018, www.glaad.org/blog/must-see-lgbtq-tv-dont-miss-pose-premiere-sense8-and-fosters-finales-alex-strange love-and-more. Accessed July 1, 2018.

24. James Poniewozik, "Review: 'Pose' Demands to Be Seen," *New York Times*, June 1, 2018, www.nytimes.com/2018/06/01/arts/television/pose-review-fx-ryan-murphy.html. Accessed July 1, 2018.

25. Deerwater, "Must-See LGBTQ TV."

26. Human Rights Campaign and Trans People of Color Coalition, "Addressing Anti-Transgender Violence: Exploring Realities, Challenges and Solutions for Policymakers and Community Advocates," hrc-assets.s3-website-us-east-1.amazonaws.com//files/assets/resources/HRC -AntiTransgenderViolence-0519.pdf. Accessed November 5, 2017.

27. Mildred L. Brown and Chloe Ann Rounsley, *True Selves: Understanding Transsexualism . . . for Families, Friends, Coworkers, and Helping Professionals* (San Francisco: Jossey-Bass, 1996), 29.

28. The Audre Lourde Project, "Trans Day of Action for Social and Economic Justice—Points of Unity," alp.org/trans-day-action-social-and-economic-justice-points-unity. Accessed November 7, 2017.

29. Dan Frosch, "Murder and Hate Verdict in Transgender Case," *New York Times*, April 22, 2009, www.nytimes.com/2009/04/23/us/23transgend.html. Accessed November 7, 2017.

30. US Department of Justice Office of Public Affairs, *Attorney General Holder Directs Department to Include Gender Identity Under Sex Discrimination Employment Claims*, December 18, 2014, www.justice.gov/opa/pr/attorney-general-holder-directs-department-include-gender -identity-under-sex-discrimination. Accessed November 9, 2017.

31. US Department of Justice Office of Public Affairs, *Attorney General Holder Directs Department.*

32. Staff, "Milestones in the American Transgender Movement" (editorial), *New York Times*, August 28, 2015, www.nytimes.com/interactive/2015/05/15/opinion/editorial-transgender -timeline.html. Accessed November 16, 2017.

33. Emma Talkoff, "Will 2017 Be the Year of the Transgender Candidate?" *Time*, July 6, 2017, time.com/4846082/transgender-political-candidates/. Accessed November 16, 2017.

34. The following articles provide more details on the candidates who made history: Courtney Connley, "Meet the 15 People Who Made History in the 2017 Election," CNBC, November 8, 2017, www.cnbc.com/2017/11/08/meet-the-15-people-who-made-history-in -the-2017-election.html. Accessed November 16, 2017. Nico Lang, "New Jersey Elects First-Ever Intersex Person to Hold Public Office in U.S." Intomore, November 9, 2017, into more.com/impact/New-Jersey-Elects-FirstEver-Intersex-Person-to-Hold-Public-Office-in -US/3b58450f57784745. Accessed November 16, 2017. Evan Minsker, "Danica Roem, Metal Vocalist, Become's Virginia's First Openly Transgender Legislator," Pitchfork.com, November 8, 2017, pitchfork.com/news/danica-roem-metal-vocalist-becomes-virginias-first-openly -transgender-legislator/. Accessed November 21, 2017. Cerys Beckwith and Jay Wu, "The Eight Trans Officials Who Made History Tuesday Night," National Center for Transgender Equality via Medium, November 8, 2017, medium.com/@TransEquality/the-seven-trans -officials-who-made-history-last-night-53920bbbc5d1. Accessed November 21, 2017.

a. Aaron, "5 Black Trans Women Who Paved the Way," Massachusetts Transgender Political Coalition, February 21, 2014, www.masstpc.org/5-who-paved-the-way/. Accessed July 1, 2018.

b. Solange Reyner, "NBC: Twenty Transgender Candidates Running for Office in US," Newsmax, June 12, 2017, www.newsmax.com/Politics/transgender-candidates-20-running/2017/06/12/id/795637/. Accessed March 6, 2018.

c. Logan S. Casey and Andrew Reynolds, "Standing Out: Transgender and Gender Variant Candidates and Elected Officials Around the World," LGBTQ Representation and Rights, October 2015, lgbtqrightsrep.files.wordpress.com/2015/10/lgbt_report_trans_v4.pdf. Accessed March 6, 2018.

d. This poem was initially posted on Facebook by the poet, Pamela, with this caveat, "I wrote this for all of us. I felt as if I were only a conduit, a channel for it as I wrote this. It all came out at once, and I feel it was my response to Trump's anti trans in the military stance. I felt as if I were standing on a mountain top when it was complete. All may feel free to copy, print, and post as you please; you may insert you names in lew [*sic*] of mine; This is for all of us!" When the author attempted to obtain further permission for this book, the poet replied, "Go ahead and use it. You have my permission. Print this response. Asking for info that predators could use is futile on your part. 'I am Trans' is free and open for the world."

e. This section borrows heavily from the International Transgender Day of Remembrance website, "About TDoR" section, tdor.info/about-2/. Accessed March 6, 2018.

Chapter 4

1. Patricia T. O'Conner and Stewart Kellerman, "All-Purpose Pronoun," On Language, *New York Times Magazine*, July 26, 2009, nytimes.com/2009/07/26/magazine/26FOB-onlanguage-t.html. Accessed September 27, 2016.

2. Leslie Feinberg, *Transgender Warriors: Making History from Joan of Arc to Dennis Rodman* (Boston: Beacon Press, 1996), x.

3. Katy McColl, "Don't Lose Your Head over That Normal Dude," *Jane*, June/July 2004, 142–45.

4. *The New Shorter Oxford English Dictionary*, s.v. "phobia."

5. Abigail Garner, *Families Like Mine* (New York: HarperCollins, 2004).

6. Bruce Coville, "Am I Blue?" in *Am I Blue? Coming Out from the Silence*, ed. Marion Dane Bauer (New York: HarperCollins Children's Books, 1994), 6.

7. Jakobi E. Williams, "The Original Rainbow Coalition: An Example of Universal Identity Politics," Tikkun, posted online November 12, 2013, www.tikkun.org/nextgen/the-original-rainbow-coalition-an-example-of-universal-identity-politics. Accessed March 13, 2018.

8. Casey Hoke, "Michael Page—Bisexual Pride Flag (1998)," Queer Art History, August 25, 2017, www.queerarthistory.com/love-between-women/michael-page-bisexual-pride-flag-1998/. Accessed January 27, 2018.

9. Emma Gran and Anna Vagianos, "We Have a Navy Veteran to Thank for the Transgender Pride Flag," *Huffington Post* Queer Voices, July 26, 2017, www.huffingtonpost.com/entry/we-have-a-navy-veteran-to-thank-for-the-transgender-pride-flag_us_5978c060e4b0e201d57a711f. Accessed January 27, 2018.

10. Hoke, "Michael Page."

11. "About the Flag," Genderqueer and Non-Binary Identities, updated 2013, genderqueerid.com/about-flag. Accessed December 10, 2017.

12. *Merriam-Webster Online*, s.v. "Mx.," www.merriam-webster.com/dictionary/mx. Accessed March 11, 2018.

13. "A Gender-Neutral Honorific," *Merriam-Webster Online*, www.merriam-webster.com/words -at-play/mx-gender-neutral-title. Accessed March 11, 2018.

a. Hida Viloria, "Caught in the Gender Binary Blind Spot: Intersex Erasure in Cisgender Rhetoric," HidaViloria.com, August 18, 2004, hidaviloria.com/caught-in-the-gender-binary-blind -spot-intersex-erasure-in-cisgender-rhetoric/. Accessed March 15, 2018.

Chapter 5

1. Elizabeth Reis, *Bodies in Doubt: An American History of Intersex* (Baltimore, MD: Johns Hopkins University Press, 2009).

2. Cheryl Chase, "What Is the Agenda of the Intersex Patient Advocacy Movement?" *Endocrinologist* 13, no. 3 (May–June 2003): 240–42; also available at www.isna.org/drupal/agenda. Accessed December 11, 2017.

3. Johns Hopkins Medicine, "Hopkins Research Shows That Nature, Not Nurture, Determines Gender," press release, EurekaAlert!, May 12, 2000, www.eurekalert.org/pub_re leases/2000-05/JHMI-Hrsn-1205100.php. Accessed February 22, 2018.

4. "What Is the American Academy of Pediatrics' Stance on the Treatment of DSD?" Accord Alliance, www.accordalliance.org/learn-about-dsd/faqs/. Accessed July 12, 2017.

5. "How Common Are These Conditions?" Accord Alliance, www.accordalliance.org/learn -about-dsd/faqs/. Accessed February 22, 2018.

6. Emi Koyama, *Introduction to Intersex Activism: The Second Edition* (Portland, Oregon: Intersex Initiative Portland, 2003), 3. www.ipdx.org/publications/index.html. Accessed July 31, 2016.

7. M. Blackless, A. Charuvastra, A. Derryck, A. Fausto-Sterling, K. Lauzanne, and E. Lee, "How Sexually Dimorphic Are We? Review and Synthesis," abstract. *American Journal of Human Biology* 12, no. 2 (March 2000):151–66, available at www.ncbi.nlm.nih.gov/ pubmed/11534012. Accessed June 13, 2017.

8. "How Common Are These Conditions?"

9. Mary Emily O'Hara, "'Nonbinary' Is Now a Legal Gender, Oregon Court Rules," *Daily Dot*, June 10, 2016, www.dailydot.com/irl/oregon-court-rules-non-binary-gender-legal/. Accessed July 10, 2016.

10. "Physicians for Human Rights Publish 'Unnecessary Surgery on Intersex Children Must Stop!'" Intersex Campaign for Equality, October 20, 2017, www.intersexequality.com/ physicians-for-human-rights-call-for-moratorium-on-nonconsensual-intersex-surgeries/. Accessed February 22, 2018.

11. This section draws from "Intersex across the Animal Kingdom," by the SciShow channel, published October 10, 2016, www.youtube.com/watch?v=Jxs2yHP6K2E. Accessed March 6, 2018.

12. John Colapinto, *As Nature Made Him: The Boy Who Was Raised as a Girl* (New York: HarperCollins, 2000), 25.

13. "Sex Unknown," NOVA Online, PBS Television, 2001. Additional related resources are available at www.pbs.org/wgbh/nova/gender. Accessed March 6, 2018.

14. To protect the Reimer family's privacy, Money used the pseudonyms John and Joan in place of Bruce and Brenda.

15. Rick Groleau, "How Is Sex Determined?" NOVA Online, www.pbs.org/wgbh/nova/gender/determined.html. Accessed March 6, 2018.

16. This section draws from a combination of sources including Klinefelter Syndrome Information and Support, klinefeltersyndrome.org, and US Department of Health and Human Services, "Klinefelter Syndrome (KS)," Eunice Kennedy Shriver National Institute of Child Health and Human Development, www.nichd.nih.gov/health/topics/klinefelter/Pages/default.aspx. Accessed August 8, 2017.

17. This section draws from Turner Syndrome Society of the United States, "Patient and Family Resources," www.turnersyndrome.org/copy-of-patient-and-family-resource. Accessed February 20, 2018.

18. This section draws from both the Boston Children's Hospital's Center for Young Women's Health, "MRKH: General Information for Teens," updated December 4, 2014, youngwomenshealth.org/2013/10/02/mrkh, and MRKH.org, www.mrkh.org. Accessed August 10, 2017.

19. Alex Rees, "Why This Woman Is Proud to Be Known as 'The Pageant Queen without a Uterus,'" *Cosmopolitan.com*, January 20, 2015. www.cosmopolitan.com/entertainment/celebs/news/a35462/jaclyn-schultz-mrkh-syndrome-miss-michigan-survivor/. Accessed August 8, 2017.

20. Lindahl, email communication.

21. This section draws from a combination of sources including "Androgen Insensitivity Syndrome" in the Genetics Home Reference from National Institutes of Health, ghr.nlm.nih.gov/condition/androgen-insensitivity-syndrome#, and "Living with Androgen Insensitivity Syndrome," on the United Kingdom's National Health Service site, www.nhs.uk/conditions/androgen-insensitivity-syndrome/treatment/#. Accessed December 31, 2018.

22. Christine M. Trapp and Sharon E. Oberfield, "Recommendations for Treatment of Nonclassic Congenital Adrenal Hyperplasia (NCCAH): an Update," abstract, *Steroids* 77, no. 4 (March 10, 2012): 342–46. doi.org/10.1016/j.steroids.2011.12.009. Accessed March 8, 2018.

23. "What Is Congenital Adrenal Hyperplasia (CAH)?" the CARES Foundation, www.caresfoundation.org/what-is-cah/. Accessed December 31, 2018.

24. This section draws from two sources: "Progestin Induced Virilization" in the FAQs section of the ISNA website, www.isna.org/faq/conditions/progestin, and "What Is Progestin-Induced Virilization?" in the FAQs section of the Accord Alliance website, www.accordalliance.org/faqs/what-is-progestin-induced-virilization/. Accessed October 3, 2017.

25. This section draws from the Accord Alliance website's FAQs section, www.accordalliance.org/faqs/what-is-5-alpha-reductase-deficiency-5-ard/. Accessed October 3, 2017.

26. This section draws from an email communication with Hans Lindahl on March 6, 2018, and "Hypospadias: Patient's Guide to Surgery," www.isna.org/node/81. Accessed March 8, 2018.

27. Patricia Anstett, "A Different Kind of Normal: MSU Professor Leads a Change for Children with Physical Abnormalities," *Free Press* (Detroit), July 10, 2004.

28. Ruth Padawer, email message to the author, June 6, 2005. Her articles "Intersexuals Struggle to Find Their Identity" and "A 10-Year-Old's Decision: Will I Be Kelli or Max?" appeared in the *Record* (New Jersey) on July 25 and 26, 2004.

29. "Unnecessary Surgery on Intersex Children Must Stop," press release, Physicians for Human Rights, October 20, 2017, physiciansforhumanrights.org/press/press-releases/intersex-surgery-must-stop.html. Accessed October 26, 2017.

---

a. *Merriam-Webster Collegiate Dictionary*, 11th ed., s.v. "hermaphrodite."

b. Hans Lindahl, email communication with the author, March 6, 2018.

c.   "What Is Useful about the Terminology of DSD? What Is Unhelpful?" Accord Alliance, www.accordalliance.org/learn-about-dsd/faqs/. Accessed October 10, 2017.

d.   Hida Viloria and Dana Zzyym, "How Intersex People Identify," Intersex Campaign for Equality, July 10, 2015, www.intersexequality.com/how-intersex-people-identify/. Accessed March 6, 2018.

e.   Intersex advocates take issue with the novelist's language choices, disliking the historically accurate use of *hermaphrodite* and *pseudohermaphrodite* instead of *intersex*.

f.   This section draws from information on and linked to the Intersex Day website, including Betsy Driver, "The Origins of Intersex Awareness Day," intersexday.org/en/origin-intersex -awareness-day/, and the archived web page "Celebrate Intersex Awareness Day: October 26, 2004," web.archive.org/web/20050407222911/http://www.intersex-awareness-day.org/ index.html. Both sites accessed March 8, 2018.

Chapter 6

1.   Andrew R. Flores, Jody L. Herman, Gary J. Gates, and Taylor N. T. Brown, *How Many Adults Identify as Transgender in the United States?* (Los Angeles: Williams Institute, 2016), williamsinstitute.law.ucla.edu/wp-content/uploads/How-Many-Adults-Identify-as-Trans gender-in-the-United-States.pdf. Accessed January 12, 2018.

2.   GLAAD Media Institute, *Where We Are on TV, 2017–2018 Season: GLAAD's Annual Report on LGBTQ Inclusion* (New York: GLAAD, 2017), glaad.org/files/WWAT/WWAT_GLAAD_2017-2018.pdf. Accessed January 15, 2018.

a.   Loki Leigh, email communications with author, 2016. A version of this essay appeared on Medium but no longer does. Follow Loki's transition at medium.com/search?q=loki%20 leigh. Accessed December 31, 2018.

Chapter 7

1.   Jaimie Seaton, "Homeless Rates for LGBT Teens Are Alarming, but Parents Can Make a Difference," *Washington Post*, March 29, 2017. www.washingtonpost.com/news/parenting/ wp/2017/03/29/homeless-rates-for-lgbt-teens-are-alarming-heres-how-parents-can-change -that. Accessed February 13, 2018.

2.   Mildred L. Brown and Chloe Ann Rounsley, *True Selves: Understanding Transsexualism . . . for Families, Friends, Coworkers, and Helping Professionals* (San Francisco: Jossey-Bass, 1996), 134.

3.   "Transgender Voice Tutor," Gender Life, www.genderlife.com/free-transgender-voice -resources/voice-tutor/. Accessed February 11, 2018.

4.   Megan Rauscher, "Illicit Silicone Injections Can Be Lethal," Reuters, January 20, 2007. www.reuters.com/article/us-silicone-injections/illicit-silicone-injections-can-be-lethal -idUSCOL05920520061130. Accessed May 6, 2018.

5.   Natalie Kita, "Are Liquid Silicone Injections Safe?" VeryWell, updated March 26, 2017. www .verywell.com/are-liquid-silicone-injections-safe-2710243. Accessed May 6, 2018.

6.   World Professional Association for Transgender Health, *Standards of Care for the Health of Transsexual, Transgender, and Gender Nonconforming People*, version 7, released September 25, 2011.

7. This section on puberty blockers draws from "How Parents and Doctors Can Support Transgender Children" by Rafi Letzter, found on the Live Science website at www.livescience .com/62893-transgender-kids-puberty-blockers-hrt-hormones.html. Accessed December 31, 2018.

8. The sections on hormone treatments and surgeries draw heavily from "Medical and Surgical Options" in Brown and Rounsley, *True Selves*, 196–211, and from the WPATH *Standards of Care*, version 7.

9. WPATH *Standards of Care*, 20.

10. WPATH *Standards of Care*, 36.

11. WPATH *Standards of Care*, 36.

12. WPATH *Standards of Care*, 57.

13. WPATH *Standards of Care*, 57–58.

14. WPATH *Standards of Care*, 27.

15. National Center for Transgender Equality, "What Does Medicare Cover for Transgender People?" transequality.org/know-your-rights/medicare. Accessed February 15, 2018.

16. Human Rights Campaign, "State Maps of Laws and Policies: Transgender Healthcare," www.hrc.org/state-maps/transgender-healthcare. Accessed February 15, 2018.

17. Olivia Petter, "Gender Reversal Surgery Is More In-Demand Than Ever before but What Are the Consequences?" *Independent*, October 3, 2017. www.independent.co.uk/life-style/gender-reversal-surgery-demand-rise-assignment-men-women-trans-a7980416.html. Accessed February 17, 2018.

18. Samantha Allen, "How the Non-Binary Revolution Hit the West Coast," *Daily Beast*, February 8, 2018. www.thedailybeast.com/how-the-non-binary-revolution-hit-the-west-coast. Accessed February 10, 2018.

19. Allen, "How the Non-Binary Revolution Hit the West Coast."

20. Brown and Rounsley, *True Selves*, 130–31.

21. WPATH *Standards of Care*, 59–60.

---

a. William Shakespeare, *The Tragedy of Hamlet, Prince of Denmark*, act 1, scene 3, lines 78–80, in *The Norton Shakespeare* (New York: Norton, 1997).

Chapter 8

1. *Brown v. Board of Education*, 347 U.S. 483 (1954) (USSC+), opinion delivered by Chief Justice Warren for the Supreme Court of the United States, May 17, 1954, nationalcenter.org/brown .html. Accessed June 14, 2018.

2. Randy Hedlund, "Segregation by Any Other Name: Harvey Milk High School," *Journal of Law and Education*, July 2004.

3. J. Hirby, "How Much Does It Cost to Change Your Name?" *Law Dictionary*, thelawdictionary.org/article/how-much-does-it-cost-to-change-your-name/. Accessed June 23, 2018.

4. National Center for Transgender Equality, *The Report of the 2015 U.S. Transgender Survey* (Washington, DC: National Center for Transgender Equality, 2016), www.transequality.org/sites/default/files/docs/USTS-Full-Report-FINAL.PDF. Accessed December 30, 2018.

5. Lauren Dake, "Jamie Shupe Becomes First Legally Non-Binary Person in the US," *Guardian*, June 16, 2016, updated July 14, 2017, www.theguardian.com/world/2016/jun/16/jamie -shupe-first-non-binary-person-oregon. Accessed June 24, 2018.

6. Jamie Shupe, "I Am the First Official Genderless Person in the United States," *Guardian*, June 16, 2016, www.theguardian.com/commentisfree/2016/jun/16/i-am-first-official-genderless -person-united-states. Accessed September 27, 2016.

7. Ryan Masters, "Santa Cruz Gender Change: First Californian to Be Declared 'Nonbinary'" *Santa Cruz Sentinel*, October 5, 2016, www.mercurynews.com/2016/10/05/santa-cruz-gen der-change-first-californian-to-be-declared-nonbinary/. Accessed October 8, 2016.

8. James Michael Nichols, "California Becomes First State to Legally Recognize a Third Gen- der," *Huffington Post*, October 17, 2017, www.huffingtonpost.com/entry/california-third -gender-option_us_59e61784e4b0ca9f483b17b9. Accessed June 24, 2018.

9. The information in this paragraph is based upon Fae Patton, "The Future of Gender Desig- nation in U.S. Legal Documents," *Journal of Gender, Social Policy & the Law*, November 13, 2017, www.jgspl.org/future-gender-designation-u-s-legal-documents/#_ftn2. Accessed June 24, 2018.

10. Tenn. Code Ann. § 68–3–203, as found on the National Center for Transgender Equality Identity Document Center, transequality.org/documents/state/tennessee. Accessed June 23, 2018.

11. *Transgender People and the Social Security Administration*, National Center for Transgender Equality, June 2013, transequality.org/know-your-rights/social-security. Accessed June 23, 2018.

12. "Know Your Rights: Social Security," National Center for Transgender Equality, transequal- ity.org/know-your-rights/social-security. Accessed June 23, 2018.

13. Lambda Legal, "Zzyym v. Pompeo (formerly Zzyym v. Tillerson & Zzyym v. Kerry)," www .lambdalegal.org/in-court/cases/co_zzyym-v-tillerson. Accessed June 24, 2018.

14. Alex Swoyer, "Intersex Person Can't Be Denied Passport for Not Identifying as Male or Female, Judge Rules," *Washington Times*, September 19, 2018, www.washingtontimes.com/ news/2018/sep/19/dana-zzyym-intersex-person-cant-be-denied-passport/. Accessed De- cember 31, 2018.

15. National Center for Transgender Equality, *The Report of the 2015 U.S. Transgender Survey: Executive Summary*, December 2016, page 7, transequality.org/sites/default/files/docs/usts/ USTS-Executive-Summary-Dec17.pdf. Accessed June 24, 2018.

16. Alice Little, "A Legal Sex Worker on What It's Really Like to Work in a Brothel," *SheKnows*, January 17, 2018, www.sheknows.com/love-and-sex/articles/1137779/what-its-like-to-work -in-brothel. Accessed June 24, 2018.

17. www.lambdalegal.org/states-regions/in-your-state. Accessed June 24, 2018.

18. The data in this paragraph comes from National Center for Transgender Equality, *The Report of the 2015 U.S. Transgender Survey: Executive Summary*, 3.

19. "What Are My Employment Rights?" National Center for Transgender Equality, transequal- ity.org/know-your-rights/employment-general. Accessed June 24, 2018.

20. Naval Institute Staff, "Key Dates in U.S. Military LGBT Policy," *Naval History Blog*, March 26, 2018, www.navalhistory.org/2018/03/26/key-dates-in-u-s-military-lgbt-policy. Accessed June 24, 2018.

21. Naval Institute Staff, "Key Dates in U.S. Military LGBT Policy."

22. "Federal Court Denies Renewed Attempt to Implement Transgender Military Ban," Lambda Legal, June 15, 2018, www.lambdalegal.org/blog/20180615_trans-military-ban-stay-denied. Accessed June 28, 2018.

23. "Know Your Rights: Fair Housing and Transgender People," National Center for Transgender Equality, March 2012, transequality.org/know-your-rights/housing-and-homeless-shelters. Accessed June 28, 2018.

24. Rachel Hope Cleves, *Charity and Sylvia: A Same-Sex Marriage in Early America* (New York: Oxford University Press, 2014).

25. *Richard John Baker v. Gerald R. Nelson*, 291 Minn. 310, 191 N.W.2d 185 (1971), scholar.google.com/scholar_case?case=14283825888588258352&hl=en&as_sdt=400006&as_vis=1. Accessed June 19, 2018.

26. Information in this paragraph is sourced from "'Baker v. Nelson' Same-Sex Marriage Pioneer Hails U.S. Supreme Court Ruling," *LGBTQ Nation*, June 28, 2015, www.lgbtqnation.com/2015/06/same-sex-marriage-pioneer-hails-u-s-supreme-court-ruling/. Accessed July 24, 2018.

27. "Other Parental Recognition Laws," Movement Advancement Project, www.lgbtmap.org/equality-maps/other_parenting_laws/. Accessed June 28, 2018.

28. "Protecting Your Family After Marriage Equality," National Center for Lesbian Rights, 2015, www.nclrights.org/wp-content/uploads/2015/01/Protecting-Your-Family-After-Marriage-Equality.pdf. Accessed July 26, 2018.

29. The data in this paragraph comes from "Adoption Statistics," Adoption Network Law Center, adoptionnetwork.com/adoption-statistics. Accessed June 28, 2018.

30. "Foster and Adoption Laws," Movement Advancement Project, www.lgbtmap.org/equality-maps/foster_and_adoption_laws/. Accessed June 28, 2018.

31. "TMM Update Trans Day of Remembrance 2017," Transgender Europe press release, November 14, 2017, transrespect.org/en/tmm-update-trans-day-remembrance-2017/. Accessed June 28, 2018.

32. The data in this paragraph comes from National Center for Transgender Rights, *The Report of the 2015 U.S. Transgender Survey: Full Report*, 202–4, 191, 195, transequality.org/issues/resources/national-transgender-discrimination-survey-full-report. Accessed April 24, 2018.

---

a. Will Johnson, "Emma Snodgrass: Cross-Dresser," County Historian, May 26, 2010, www.countyhistorian.com/knol/4hmquk6fx4gu-506-emma-snodgrass-cross-dresser.html. Accessed March 10, 2018.

b. Massachusetts Governor's Commission on Gay and Lesbian Youth, *Making Schools Safe for Gay and Lesbian Youth: Breaking the Silence in Schools and in Families*, February 25, 1993, www.massresistance.org/docs/issues/glbt_youth/docs01/CommReport_Making_Schools_Safe_2-93.pdf. Accessed December 31, 2018.

c. Jamie Shupe, "I Am the First Official Genderless Person in the United States," *Guardian*, June 16, 2016, www.theguardian.com/commentisfree/2016/jun/16/i-am-first-official-genderless-person-united-states. Accessed September 27, 2016.

d. Murray Lipp, "'Gay Marriage' and 'Marriage Equality'—Both Terms Matter," *Huffington Post*, May 12, 2013, updated February 2, 2016, at www.huffingtonpost.com/murray-lipp/gay-marriage_b_3249733.html. Accessed 19 June 19, 2018.

e. Trevor MacDonald, "Facing My Fear: I Wanted to Have a Baby. But as a Trans Man, I Was Terrified of Labor," *Guardian*, October 7, 2006, https://www.theguardian.com/commentisfree/2016/oct/07/trans-man-have-baby-labor-terrified-facing-my-fear. Accessed October 9, 2016.

f. *Transparent* synopsis from www.julesrosskam.com/transparent-1/. Accessed June 28, 2018.

Chapter 9

1. Stephanie Pappas, "The Weird History of Gender-Segregated Bathrooms," *Live Science*, May 9, 2016, www.livescience.com/54692-why-bathrooms-are-gender-segregated.html. Accessed April 28, 2018.
2. Terry S. Kogan, "How Did Public Bathrooms Get to Be Separated by Sex in the First Place?" Conversation, May 26, 2016. theconversation.com/how-did-public-bathrooms-get-to-be-separated-by-sex-in-the-first-place-59575. Accessed January 28, 2018.
3. This paragraph draws from "University of Vermont Adds 'Gender-Neutral' Bathrooms," by the Associated Press, published by Fox News, August 26, 2007, www.foxnews.com/story/2007/08/26/university-vermont-adds-gender-neutral-bathrooms.html. Accessed April 22, 2018.
4. This paragraph draws from "A Very Brief Timeline of the Bathroom Wars," by Kevin Drum, published by *Mother Jones*, May 14, 2016. www.motherjones.com/kevin-drum/2016/05/timeline-bathroom-wars/. Accessed November 15, 2017.
5. Suzi Parker, "Transgender Students Just Got New Rights, Thanks to the Federal Government," TakePart, May 1, 2014. www.takepart.com/article/2014/05/01/discrimination-against-transgender-students/. Accessed April 29, 2018.
6. "U.S. Departments of Education and Justice Release Joint Guidance to Help Schools Ensure the Civil Rights of Transgender Students," archived press release of the US Department of Education, May 13, 2016. www.ed.gov/news/press-releases/us-departments-education-and-justice-release-joint-guidance-help-schools-ensure-civil-rights-transgender-students. Accessed April 6, 2018.
7. Amy Ellis Nutt, *Becoming Nicole: The Transformation of an American Family* (New York: Random House, 2015), 126.
8. Jazz Jennings, *Being Jazz: My Life as a (Transgender) Teen* (New York: Crown, 2016), 34.
9. Jennings, *Being Jazz*, 35.
10. The information in this paragraph is based closely upon the reporting in Moriah Balingit's August 30, 2016, *Washington Post* story, "Gavin Grimm Just Wanted to Use the Bathroom. He Didn't Think the Nation Would Debate It."
11. Matt Stevens, "Federal Judge Sides with Transgender Student in Lawsuit over Bathroom Policy," *New York Times*, May 23, 2018.
12. Lawrenz Fares, "Federal Judge: Maryland Transgender Student May Use Facilities That Align with Gender Identity," *Jurist*, March 14, 2018. www.jurist.org/paperchase/2018/03/maryland-district-court-says-transgender-student-may-use-facilities-that-aligns-with-gender-identity-1.php. Accessed April 29, 2018.
13. The material in this section, up to this point, is closely based upon reporting by Michael Gordon, Mark S. Price, and Katie Peralta in "Understanding HB2: North Carolina's Newest Law Solidifies State's Role in Defining Discrimination," *Charlotte Observer*, March 26, 2016, updated March 30, 2017, www.charlotteobserver.com/news/politics-government/article68401147.html. Accessed April 24, 2018.
14. Lester Lyle, personal communication, Nashville, TN, August 17, 2017.
15. Hannan Adely and Matt Kadosh, "'All-Gender' Bathrooms under Fire," *North Jersey Record*, Bergen edition, May 22, 2018.

a. "Title IX and Sex Discrimination," US Department of Education, Office for Civil Rights, revised April 2015, www2.ed.gov/about/offices/list/ocr/docs/tix_dis.html. Accessed April 6, 2018.

Chapter 10

1. "Ending Conversion Therapy: Supporting and Affirming LGBTQ Youth," Substance Abuse and Mental Health Services Administration (SAMHSA), October 2015, store.samhsa.gov/product/Ending-Conversion-Therapy-Supporting-and-Affirming-LGBTQ-Youth/SMA15-4928. Accessed June 17, 2018.
2. "Ending Conversion Therapy."
3. Christy Mallory, Taylor N.T. Brown, and Kerith J. Conron, "Conversion Therapy and LGBT Youth," Williams Institute at UCLA School of Law, January 2018, williamsinstitute.law.ucla.edu/wp-content/uploads/Conversion-Therapy-LGBT-Youth-Jan-2018.pdf. Accessed July 3, 2018.
4. Mallory, Brown, and Conron, "Conversion Therapy and LGBT Youth."
5. Mallory, Brown, and Conron, "Conversion Therapy and LGBT Youth."
6. Mallory, Brown, and Conron, "Conversion Therapy and LGBT Youth."
7. "Ending Conversion Therapy."
8. Caitlin Ryan, "Supportive Families, Healthy Children: Helping Families with Lesbian, Gay, Bisexual and Transgender Children," Family Acceptance Project at San Francisco State University, 2009, familyproject.sfsu.edu/sites/default/files/FAP_English%20Booklet_pst.pdf. Accessed July 3, 2018.
9. Movement Advancement Project, Johnson Family Foundation, and American Foundation for Suicide Prevention, "Suicide and LGBT Populations, Second Edition," Movement Advancement Project, 2017, lgbtmap.org/file/talking-about-suicide-and-lgbt-populations-2nd-edition.pdf. Accessed July 3, 2018.
10. Chapin Hall at the University of Chicago, Voices of Youth Count, *Missed Opportunities: LGBTQ Youth Homelessness in America*, 2018, https://voicesofyouthcount.org/brief/lgbtq-youth-homelessness/. Accessed December 30, 2018.
11. "Is Intense Sport Making You Infertile?" *Dreaming of Baby* (blog), CCRM Fertility Clinics, November 26, 2017, www.ccrmivf.com/news-events/intense-sport-infertility/. Accessed June 17, 2018.
12. Cyd Zeigler, *Fair Play: How LGBT Athletes Are Claiming Their Rightful Place in Sports* (New York: Akashic Books, 2016), 15.
13. Zeigler, *Fair Play*, 55.
14. "Ex-Seton Hall Player Derrick Gordon: NBA Blackballed Me Because I'm Gay," CBS News New York, August 17, 2016, newyork.cbslocal.com/2016/08/17/derrick-gordon-nba-gay/. Accessed June 17, 2018.
15. Christina Kahrl, "Chris Mosier Becomes First Known Transgender Athlete in World Duathlon Championship," ESPN.com, June 23, 2016, www.espn.com/sports/endurance/story/_/id/15976460/chris-mosier-becomes-first-known-transgender-athlete-compete-world-duathlon-championship. Accessed June 30, 2018.

16. Jazz Jennings, *Being Jazz: My Life as a (Transgender) Teen*, Kindle edition (New York: Random House Children's Books, 2016), 51.

17. Jennings, *Being Jazz*, 53.

18. Jennings, *Being Jazz*, 59.

19. Amy Ellis Nutt, *Becoming Nicole: The Transformation of an American Family*, Kindle edition (New York: Random House, 2015), 112.

20. Cyd Zeigler, "As Trans High School Athletes Win State Titles, Parents Petition to Ban Them," *Outsports*, June 14, 2018, www.outsports.com/2018/6/14/17458696/trans-athlete-connecti cut-high-school-ban-petition. Accessed June 17, 2018.

21. Ruth Padawer, "The Humiliating Practice of Sex-Testing Female Athletes," *New York Times Magazine*, June 28, 2016, www.nytimes.com/2016/07/03/magazine/the-humiliating-practice -of-sex-testing-female-athletes.html. Accessed September 15, 2016.

22. Padawer, "The Humiliating Practice of Sex-Testing Female Athletes."

23. Associated Press, "Indian Sprinter Dutee Chand, Reinstated, Wants Olympic Final," *USA Today*, June 28, 2016, www.usatoday.com/story/sports/olympics/2016/06/28/indian-sprinter -dutee-chand-reinstated-wants-olympic-final/86466352/. Accessed July 31, 2018.

24. Padawer, "The Humiliating Practice of Sex-Testing Female Athletes."

25. Sean Ingle, "IAAF Doctor Predicts Intersex Category in Athletics within Five to 10 Years," *Guardian*, April 27, 2018, www.theguardian.com/sport/2018/apr/26/iaaf-doctor-calls-for -intersex-category-athletics-caster-semenya. Accessed July 3, 2018.

26. Ingle, "IAAF Doctor Predicts Intersex Category."

27. "IAAF Introduces New Eligibility Regulations for Female Classification," press release, IAAF, April 26, 2018, www.iaaf.org/news/press-release/eligibility-regulations-for-female -classifica. Accessed June 16, 2018.

28. Amanda Shalala, "IAAF Female Classification Rules Slammed as 'Blatantly Racist,'" ABC News, April 28, 2018, mobile.abc.net.au/news/2018–04–28/critics-say-iaaf-testosterone -rules-blatantly-racist/9706744?pfmredir=sm. Accessed June 16, 2018.

29. Ingle, "IAAF Doctor Predicts Intersex Category."

30. Leviticus 20:13, *Common English Bible*, Bible Gateway, www.biblegateway.com/passage/?search =lev+20%3A13&version=CEB. Accessed June 30, 2018.

31. Leviticus 25:35–37, Good News Translation, Bible Gateway, www.biblegateway.com/passage /?search=Leviticus+25%3A35%E2%80%9337&version=GNT. Accessed January 17, 2019.

a. Clare K., email communication with the author, October 13, 2016.

b. James A. Forbes Jr., *Whose Gospel? A Concise Guide to Progressive Protestantism* (New York: New Press, 2010), 43.

c. Jaye Robin Brown, *Georgia Peaches and Other Forbidden Fruit* (New York: Harper Teen, 2016), 423.

Chapter 11

1. Avram Finkelstein, "The Silence=Death Poster," *New York Public Library LGBT* blog, November 22, 2013. www.nypl.org/blog/2013/11/22/silence-equals-death-poster. Accessed May 5, 2018.

Resources

This book is meant to provide an introductory overview of gender identity issues. To learn more, venture beyond the covers of this book. Living in the information age affords us advantages like an ever-growing wealth of resources providing information and support in various media. Here is a list to get you started; it is far from exhaustive. Each source has the potential for providing you with other sources. Resources included here are mostly national or international in scope and reach. Local resources are numerous; use the information here to help you find what resources may be available near where you live. The resources listed here are current as of August 2018.

Crisis Hotlines

Life can be difficult for myriad reasons, inclusive of gender identity and sexual orientation. As such, crisis intervention and suicide prevention services are extremely important. If you are in crisis, or know someone who is, please reach out for help.

LGBT National Youth Talkline
LGBT National Youth Talkline provides peer support for teens and young adults up to age twenty-five via telephone, chat, and email for eight hours on weekdays and five hours on Saturday. Dial 1 (800) 246–7743 Monday through Friday from 4:00 p.m. to midnight Eastern Time/1:00 p.m. to 9:00 p.m. Pacific Time; on Saturday, telephones are staffed from noon to 5:00 p.m. Eastern Time/9:00 a.m. to 2:00 p.m. Pacific Time. To check for changes, visit www.glbthotline.org/talkline.html.
The LGBT National Youth Talkline is a program of the LGBT National Help Center. Visit www.glbthotline.org/ for links to online chat, weekly moderated group discussions for trans teens (Wednesday afternoons) and LGBTQ teens (Tuesday afternoons), phone lines for LGBTQ persons of all ages, a phone line dedicated to senior citizen callers, and a wealth of other material including factual information and local resources for cities and towns across the United States.

Trans Lifeline

The Trans Lifeline serves transgender people in crisis, eighteen hours a day, seven days a week. In the United States, call 1 (877) 565–8860; in Canada, dial 1 (877) 330–6366. Phones are staffed from 11:00 a.m. to 5:00 a.m. Eastern Time/8:00 a.m. to 2:00 a.m. Pacific Time.

Funded by contributions, the Trans Lifeline is staffed entirely by transgender persons; with additional funding, the Trans Lifeline would provide services 24/7.

Trevor Project

The Trevor Project serves LGBTQ persons ages thirteen to twenty-four and provides three forms of remote assistance in times of crisis.

TrevorLifeline provides free telephone support around the clock at 1 (866) 488–7386.

TrevorChat provides seven hours of service daily via a secure instant messaging service for computer users. Please note that callers can often expect to wait a few minutes to chat with a counselor, and that during busy times the wait may extend to a half hour. Chat hours are daily from 3:00 p.m. to 10:00 p.m. Eastern Time/noon to 7:00 p.m. Pacific Time. Go to www.thetrevorproject.org/get-help-now/ and click on "TrevorChat."

TrevorText provides seven hours of service daily Monday through Friday. Text hours are weekdays from 3:00 p.m. to 10:00 p.m. Eastern Time/noon to 7:00 p.m. Pacific Time. Text "Trevor" to 1 (202) 304–1200.

Organizations

Organizations change over time. Several of those listed in the first edition of this book no longer exist. They may have merged with others, changed their names, or simply closed. Sites that provide solid historical information, but not the most current news or research, appear in the "Historically Important Internet Resources" section.

Gender-Related Organizations

Accord Alliance
531 Route 22 East #244
Whitehouse Station, NJ 08889
Tel: 1 (908) 349–0534
www.accordalliance.org/

Accord Alliance, the successor organization to the Intersex Society of North America, opened its doors in 2008 and serves public health around disorders of sex development (DSD) with a website designed to be a central informational hub "for those working to improve the quality of outcomes in DSD through enhanced healthcare and research" and public education. The site provides information for families, clinicians, and researchers and is suitable for those seeking to learn more about DSD.

The Asexual Visibility and Education Network
www.asexuality.org/
    The Asexual Visibility and Education Network hosts the world's largest online asexual community and archive or resources on asexuality.

Family Acceptance Project
San Francisco State University
fap@sfsu.edu
familyproject.sfsu.edu/
    The Family Acceptance Project at San Francisco State University is a research, intervention, education, and policy initiative that works to prevent health and mental health risks for LGBT children and youth, including suicide, homelessness, and HIV. They are developing a new family model to increase family support, decrease risk, and promote the well-being of LGBT children and youth in the context of their families, cultures, and faith communities. Print publications (familyproject.sfsu.edu/publications) and videos (familyproject.sfsu.edu/family-videos) to this end are available through their website.

Gender Identity Research and Education Society (GIRES)
Melverly
The Warren
Ashtead
Surrey
KT21 2SP
England
Tel: (011) (44) 01372 801554
www.gires.org.uk
    GIRES is a research and education charity based in the United Kingdom whose purpose is to "improve the lives of trans and gender non-conforming people, including those who are non-binary and non-gender." Beyond the many UK-specific resources, its website offers online resources and e-learning modules for physicians about gender variance, for other health-care providers about working with gender non-conforming youth, and for employers and service providers of trans people. Its downloadable guide "Inclusivity: Supporting BAME Trans People" is specific to serving black, Asian, and minority ethnic (BAME) populations. Extensive archives include a wealth of information for educators, physicians, families, and more.

GLSEN
110 William Street, 30th Floor,
New York, NY 10038
Tel: 1 (212) 727–0135
info@glsen.org
www.glsen.org

GLSEN (pronounced "glisten") was founded in 1990 by a group of Massachusetts teachers as the Gay, Lesbian and Straight Educators Network. Now a national organization, GLSEN focuses on ensuring safe and affirming schools for all, including LGBTQ students. Extensive support for educators and schools, including lesson plans and curriculum guides, are available through GLSEN.

LGBT National Help Center
2261 Market Street, #296
San Francisco, CA 94114
help@LGBThotline.org
www.glbthotline.org/

The LGBT National Help Center provides a wealth of resources for LGBTQ persons of all ages, including separate hotlines for teens and young adults, adults, and seniors; weekly moderated group discussions for trans teens (Wednesdays) and LGBTQ teens (Tuesdays); and factual information and local resources for cities and towns across the United States.

PFLAG National Office
1828 L Street, NW, Suite 660
Washington, DC 20036
Tel: 1 (202) 467–8180
info@pflag.org
www.pflag.org/

Formerly Parents, Families, and Friends of Lesbians and Gays, the organization officially changed its name in 2014 to PFLAG (pronounced "P-flag"). After marching with her son in the 1972 Christopher Street Liberation Day March in New York City, the precursor to today's Pride parade, Jeanne Manford was approached by numerous gays and lesbians begging her to speak to their parents. Manford decided to start a support group, which then became PFLAG. In 1981 PFLAG became a national organization. The website states that PFLAG National speaks out on issues critical to creating a world where diversity is celebrated, and all people are respected, valued, and affirmed.

Safe Schools Coalition (SSC)
c/o Equal Rights Washington
P.O. Box 2388
Seattle, WA 98111
Tel: 1 (206) 451–7233
www.safeschoolscoalition.org/

The SSC began in 1988 as a Washington State initiative and expanded until in 2001 it recognized itself as an international public-private partnership. According to its mission statement, the SSC serves families, schools, and communities with the goal of supporting LGBTQ youth and "working to help schools become safe places where every family can belong, where every educator can teach, and where every child can learn, regardless of gender, gender identity or sexual orientation."

Sexuality Information and Education Council of the United States (SIECUS)
1012 14th Street, NW, Suite 1108
Washington, DC 20005
Tel: 1 (202) 265–2405
info@siecus.org
siecus.org/

Incorporated in 1964, SIECUS is a national nonprofit organization that affirms sexuality is a natural and healthy part of living. The website is a clearinghouse for information about sexuality, specifically for professionals, parents, and the public.

Stonewall Community Foundation
1270 Broadway, Suite 501
New York, NY, 10001
Tel: 1 (212) 457–1341
stonewall@stonewallfoundation.org
www.stonewallfoundation.org/

The Stonewall Community Foundation is a grant-making organization that strengthens the LGBTQ movement by making smart, values-driven investments in dynamic organizations, projects, and leaders. And as a public foundation, it does this in partnership with donors and the people working on the front lines of progress. It funds over one hundred nonprofits each year, in more than thirty issue areas. Additionally, it provides scholarship programs, including the largest in the country created to support LGBTQ refugees and asylum seekers, and runs intensive capacity-building and training programs to equip local leaders with the tools needed to be effective change agents.

TransAthlete

www.transathlete.com

Founded in 2013 by Chris Mosier, a transgender athlete, coach, and educator, TransAthlete is an online compendium of resources for students, athletes, coaches, and administrators to find information about trans inclusion in athletics at various levels of play. Included are documents from such varied sources as the Transgender Law and Policy Institute, the National Collegiate Athletic Association, the Women's Sports Foundation, and Campus Pride. Guidelines for transgender inclusion at the K–12 level include the LGBT Sports Foundation's "All 50": The Transgender-Inclusive High School Sports and Activities Policy and Education Project, which was funded by a grant from Nike. The project's Proposed Model High School Policy, completed in 2016 and available on TransAthlete.com, is clear, straightforward, and brief—at only five pages. Student athletes, their families, coaches, and administrators are encouraged to visit this site for guidance around transgender inclusion.

Transkids Purple Rainbow Foundation (TKPRF)

www.transkidspurplerainbow.org

Jazz Jennings's mom started TKPRF when she realized that other parents of transgender and gender nonconforming youth needed the information that she had trouble finding. A multifaceted organization, TKPRF "is committed to enhancing the future lives of TransKids by educating schools, peers, places of worship, the medical community, government bodies, and society in general, in an effort to seek fair and equal treatment for all transyouth," and provides financial assistance to transyouth through scholarships and other support.

Transvivor

www.transvivor.com

Started in 2017 by two young people trying to change the way that transgender people are treated and to help them get equal access to affirming care, Transvivor is an easy-to-navigate, straightforward online resource for transgender persons, parents, and allies. Transvivor's stated mission is to provide professional resources for the transgender community and their allies to foster acceptance, through refined education, exemplary advocacy, and thoughtful listening.

TransYouth Family Allies, Inc. (TYFA)

P.O. Box 1471

Holland, MI 49422–1471

Tel: 1 (888) 462–8932 (IMA-TYFA)

info@imatyfa.org

imatyfa.org/

TYFA empowers children and families by partnering with educators, service providers, and communities to develop supportive environments in which gender may be expressed and respected. Working to create a society in which all children are respected and celebrated, TYFA strives to educate and inform schools, health-care professionals, day care centers, courts and legal representatives, child welfare agencies, and communities about discrimination based on gender identity or gender expression. It informs citizens, including legislators, about advances in medical science and current standards of care regarding the legal status of transgender and gender variant children. Finally, it forms alliances to help achieve support services for the gender variant children of America, so that they and their families may find the services and support that they need to live their lives free of harassment and obstruction.

TRUTH

ourtranstruth.org/

TRUTH, a trans youth storytelling project whose name is derived from TRans yoUTH, is a joint venture of the Transgender Law Center and the GSA Network that launched in 2015. This youth-led program for trans and gender-nonconforming young people aims to build public understanding and empathy through storytelling, and a movement for liberation through sharing these stories. Find their stories, connect with others, and learn how to share your own story at ourtranstruth.org/youth/.

World Professional Association for Transgender Health (WPATH)

www.wpath.org/

Formerly the Harry Benjamin International Gender Dysphoria Association, WPATH is an organization devoted to transgender health. Its mission is to promote evidence-based care, education, research, advocacy, public policy, and respect in transgender health. WPATH publishes the Standards of Care and Ethical Guidelines concerning the emotional, medical, and surgical management of gender dysphoria.

Legal and Political Organizations

American Civil Liberties Union (ACLU)

125 Broad Street, 18th Floor

New York, NY 10004

Tel: 1 (212) 549–2500

www.aclu.org/

The ACLU's main focus is defending the Bill of Rights. Founded in 1920, this nonprofit organization actively defends student rights in several areas, and the

ACLU LGBT Project helps protect young people's right to express themselves, start gay-straight alliance clubs, have their gender identity respected, and be taught in a safe environment.

Equality Federation
818 SW 3rd Avenue #141
Portland, OR 97204–2405
TEL: (929) 373–3370
www.equalityfederation.org

Founded in 1997, Equality Federation serves as a movement builder and strategic partner to state-based organizations that serve LGBTQ people. Believing that change is possible in every community, Equality Federation empowers local leaders to build strong movements for equality that can succeed in elections at every level.

GLAAD
www.glaad.org

Originally the Gay & Lesbian Alliance Against Defamation, an organization of writers formed in the 1980s in response to virulently defamatory writing in the age of AIDS, GLAAD works to promote fair, accurate, and inclusive representation of people and events in the media as a means of eliminating homophobia and discrimination based on gender identity and sexual orientation.

GLBTQ Legal Advocates & Defenders (GLAD)
18 Tremont Street, Suite 950
Boston, MA 02108
Tel: 1 (617) 426–1350
gladlaw@glad.org
www.glad.org

Founded in 1978, GLAD is New England's leading civil rights organization dedicated to ending discrimination based on sexual orientation, HIV status, and gender identity and expression. This is the nonprofit that filed and won the "freedom to marry" case in Massachusetts.

Human Rights Campaign (HRC)
1640 Rhode Island Avenue, NW
Washington, DC 20036
Tel: 1 (202) 628–4160
www.hrc.org

The Human Rights Campaign Fund was established in 1980 as one of the first gay and lesbian political action committees, rising to prominence after its first election cycle in 1982 to be the seventeenth largest political action committee in the United States; however, in 1995, the organization dropped "fund" from its name and the HRC was born. The HRC actively works for LGBTQ equal rights through the political arena, and organizes and educates at the grassroots level. Visit its site for resources including an LGBTQ scholarship database, the annual "Buying Guide for Workplace Equality," a guide to finding insurance for transgender related health care, and much more.

Intersex Campaign for Equality (IC4E)
info@intersexequality.com
www.intersexequality.com
Founded by intersex activist and author Hida Viloria, the IC4E, once known as OII-USA or the United States affiliate of the Organisation Intersex International, has a strong internet presence with information about current issues pertinent to intersex issues.

Intersex & Genderqueer Recognition Project (IGRP)
40087 Mission Boulevard, #275
Fremont, CA 94539
Tel: 1 (510) 585–3052
info@ intersexrecognition.org
www.intersexrecognition.org
IGRP is the first, and leading, organization in the United States whose work addresses the right of nonbinary adults to self-identify on legal documents. Email for assistance on obtaining government documents identifying you as nonbinary.

Lambda Legal National Headquarters
120 Wall Street, 19th Floor
New York, NY 10005-3919
Tel: 1 (212) 809–8585
www.lambdalegal.org
Lambda Legal was founded in 1973 as the nation's first legal organization dedicated to achieving full recognition of the civil rights for LGBTQ people. The organization's legal, education, and advocacy work touches nearly every aspect of life for lesbians, gay men, bisexuals, transgender people, and everyone living with HIV.

Movement Advancement Project (MAP)
MAP Administrative Office
3020 Carbon Place, Suite 202
Boulder, CO 80301
Tel: 1 (303) 578–4600
www.lgbtmap.org
MAP is an independent think tank providing research, insight, and analysis working for equality for LGBT people. Founded in 2006, MAP has three main

areas of focus: policy and issue analysis, movement capacity, and effective messaging. For those researching any area of LGBT equality, the MAP website is a resource worth visiting.

National Center for Lesbian Rights (NCLR)
870 Market Street, Suite 370
San Francisco, CA 94102
Tel: 1 (415) 392–6257
www.nclrights.org

Founded in 1977, NCLR is a national legal organization committed to advancing the civil and human rights of LGBT people and their families through litigation, legislation, policy, and public education. NCLR's campaign #BornPerfect: The Campaign to End Conversion Therapy already achieved protection for youth in ten states from such "remedies," and will continue working to effect change in other states in 2018.

National Center for Transgender Equality (NCTE)
1133 19th Street, NW, Suite 302
Washington, DC 20036
Tel: 1 (202) 642–4542
ncte@transequality.org
transequality.org

Founded in 2003 by transgender activists who saw the urgent need for policy change, the NCTE is now a solid network with an extensive record of winning change for transgender people. It offers resources about how to interact with transgender people, and information about transgender political and health issues, rights, identity documentation, and ways to take action.

National Coalition of Anti-Violence Programs (NCAVP)
New York City Anti-Violence Project
116 Nassau Street, 3rd Floor
New York, NY 10038
Tel: 1 (212) 714–1141
avp.org/ncavp

NCAVP, a project of the New York City Gay and Lesbian Anti-Violence Project, Inc., provides national advocacy for local LGBTQ communities. A national coalition of local member programs and affiliates who work to create systemic and social change, NCAVP fights to end all forms of violence against and within the LGBTQ community. NCAVP releases two annual national reports: one on LGBTQ hate violence and one on LGBTQ intimate partner violence. To find member programs in your area, visit avp.org/ncavp-members/.

National LGBTQ Task Force
1325 Massachusetts Avenue, NW, Suite 600
Washington, DC 20005
Tel: 1 (202) 393–5177
www.thetaskforce.org

Founded in 1973 as the National Gay Task Force and later known as the National Gay and Lesbian Task Force, the LGBTQ Task Force is the country's oldest national LGBTQ advocacy group. With five offices around the country, this national organization seeks civil rights for LGBTQ people. Its Trans/Gender Non-Conforming Justice Project started in 2001 and seeks to expand rights through the legislative and policy arenas.

OutServe-SLDN
P.O. Box 65301
Washington, DC 20035–5301
800–538–7418
admin@outserve-sldn.org
www.outserve-sldn.org

OutServe-SLDN is a legal defense network for service members that represents the US LGBT military community worldwide. Its mission includes the following: educating the community, providing legal services, advocating for authentic transgender service, providing developmental opportunities, supporting members and local chapters, communicating effectively, and working toward equality for all.

Southern Poverty Law Center (SPLC)
400 Washington Avenue
Montgomery, AL 36104
Tel: 1 (334) 956–8200
www.splcenter.org

Dedicated to fighting hate and promoting tolerance, the SPLC is a national nonprofit organization. Founded in 1971 as a small civil rights firm, it is now respected for its many programs and projects. Teaching Tolerance is a program established in 1991 that provides free curriculum materials to teachers; visit www.tolerance.org. Mix It Up is a project geared to breaking the walls of division within school communities.

Transgender, Gender Variant, Intersex Justice Project (TGIJP)
Physical Address: 234 Eddy Street
San Francisco, CA 94102

Mailing Address: 370 Turk Street #370
San Francisco, CA 94102
Tel: 1 (415) 554–8491
info@tgijp.org
www.tgijp.org

TGIJP was initiated in 2004 to provide legal services for transgender and gender variant/nonconforming people, primarily those in California prisons, jails, and detention centers. The mission of TGIJP is to challenge and end the human rights abuses committed against transgender, gender variant, and intersex people in California prisons, jails, detention centers, and beyond.

Transgender Law Center (TLC)
P.O. Box 70976
Oakland, CA 94612–0976
Tel: 1 (510) 587–9696
Legal Assistance: (415) 865–0176 or transgenderlawcenter.org/legalinfo
info@transgenderlawcenter.org
transgenderlawcenter.org

TLC is the largest national trans-led organization advocating self-determination for all people. Grounded in legal expertise and committed to racial justice, TLC employs a variety of community-driven strategies to keep transgender and gender-nonconforming people alive, thriving, and fighting for liberation.

The Williams Institute
Physical Address: 337 Charles E. Young Drive East
Public Policy Building Room 2381
Los Angeles, CA 90095
Mailing Address: c/o UCLA School of Law
P.O. Box 951476
Los Angeles, CA 90095-1476
Tel: 1 (310) 267–4382
williamsinstitute@law.ucla.edu
williamsinstitute.law.ucla.edu

The Williams Institute on Sexual Orientation and Gender Identity Law and Public Policy at the UCLA School of Law advances law and public policy through rigorous, independent research and scholarship, and disseminates its work through a variety of education programs and media to judges, legislators, lawyers, other policy makers and the public. These studies can be accessed at the Williams Institute website.

Religious Organizations

Affirmation: LGBT Mormons, Families & Friends
P.O. Box 898
Anoka, MN 55303
contact@affirmation.org
affirmation.org

Although it existed quietly in pre-Stonewall days, Affirmation proclaimed itself in 1979 beginning with Los Angeles Pride and spreading to Affinity Groups across the United States by year's end. Under the "Especially for You" tab, the website includes resource pages specifically for teens, transgender persons, women, family and friends, church leaders, and more. It also includes affinity groups for people of color, millennials, fathers in affirmation, mixed orientation families, and friends and family.

Believe Out Loud
c/o Intersections International
145 West 28th Street, 11th Floor
New York, NY 10001
team@believeoutloud.com
believeoutloud.com
believeoutloud.com/take-action/find-your-community

Believe Out Loud was formed in 2009 to encourage Christian clergy to voice their affirmation for LGBTQIA people. An online community that empowers Christians to work for justice for LGBTQIA people, Believe Out Loud claims to be the leading platform in Christian faith and LGBTQIA advocacy as it reaches over three million online visitors monthly. Use its Welcoming Church Map to find a congregation near you.

GALIP Foundation
P.O. Box 318
Gold Run, CA 95717
www.gaychurch.org
www.gaychurch.org/find_a_church

The GALIP Foundation is a nonprofit organization dedicated to bringing the reconciling message of God's love and reconciliation to the gay, lesbian, bisexual, and transgender community. GALIP stands for God's Agape Love (put) into Practice. Originally begun in 1999, the GALIP website's Affirming Church Directory now claims to be the largest directory of LGBTQ-friendly churches available online. Type a zip code into the search box to find a map with affirming churches pinned across it.

Institute for Judaism, Sexual Orientation & Gender Identity (IJSO)
c/o Hebrew Union College-Jewish Institute of Religion (HUC-JIR)
3077 University Avenue
Los Angeles, CA 90007
ijso.huc.edu

Founded in 2000, IJSO at HUC-JIR is the first and only institute of its kind in the Jewish world. IJSO was created to educate HUC-JIR students on lesbian, gay, bisexual, and transgender issues to help them challenge and eliminate homophobia and heterosexism and to learn tools to be able to transform the communities they encounter into ones that are inclusive and welcoming of LGBT Jews. In time, it expanded to the larger community outside the walls of their four campuses in Los Angeles, Cincinnati, New York, and Jerusalem. IJSO offers consultation to individual professionals, synagogues, and organizations; and seminars and workshops at local, national, and international conferences.

Jewish LGBT Network
contact@jewishable.com
https://jvillagenetwork.com/welcome-jewish-lgbt-network batchgeo.com/map/9541d87512cb17fd5040c3fdcf525b1a

The Jewish LGBT Network was designed to support LGBT Jews based in any part of the world. Its online platform allows visitors to locate and connect with local synagogues, events, social groups, professional groups, and other support-groups catering to the LGBT Jewish Community. The website includes a link to a map of welcoming synagogues and an invitation to submit other such synagogues for inclusion.

Keshet
284 Amory Street
Jamaica Plain, MA 02130
Tel: 1 (617) 524–9227
www.keshetonline.org

Founded in 1996, Keshet is a national organization that works for full LGBTQ equality and inclusion in Jewish life. Keshet envisions a Jewish world in which LGBTQ Jews are not merely tolerated or accepted; it envisions communities where the ethos of justice, caring, and inclusion that encapsulates the best of Jewish tradition is seen and felt by all Jews. Among the many resources on the website is a youth organizing manual for creating a Jewish Gay-Straight Alliance.

Many Voices
3133 Dumbarton Street, NW
Washington, DC 20007
info@manyvoices.org
www.manyvoices.org

Many Voices is a nonprofit organization that bills itself as "a Black church movement for gay and transgender justice." They envision a black church and community that embraces diversity of the human family and ensures that all are treated with love, compassion, and justice. Many Voices works to equip and bring forward influential black leaders to demonstrate that support for LGBT equality and justice is deeply rooted in the black religious experience and entirely consistent with being Christian.

Muslim Alliance for Sexual and Gender Diversity (MASGD)
P.O. Box 33881
Washington, DC 20033–3881
info@muslimalliance.org
www.muslimalliance.org
See also: www.lgbtmuslimretreat.com
MASGD was launched in 2013 at the Creating Change conference in Atlanta, Georgia. The organization works to support, empower, and connect LGBTQ Muslims; to challenge root causes of oppression, including misogyny and xenophobia; to increase the acceptance of gender and sexual diversity within Muslim communities; and to promote a progressive understanding of Islam that is centered on inclusion, justice, and equality. MASGD hosts an annual retreat for LGBTQ Muslims and their partners. The LGBT Muslim Retreat site includes a catalog of books and links to resources for LGBT Muslims around the world.

Muslims for Progressive Values (MPV)
1626 North Wilcox Avenue, Suite 702
Los Angeles, CA 90028
Tel: 1 (323) 696–2678
info@mpvusa.org
www.mpvusa.org
Established in 2007, MPV establishes and nurtures vibrant progressive Muslim communities worldwide. MPV envisions a future where Islam is understood as a source of dignity, justice, compassion, and love for all humanity and the world. Find a wealth of resources for LGBTQI+ Muslims at www.mpvusa.org/lgbtqi-resources.

Soulforce
PO Box 2499
Abilene, TX 79604
Tel: 1 (800) 810–9143
hello@soulforce.org
www.soulforce.org

Founded in 1998, Soulforce, whose tagline is "Sabotage Christian Supremacy," has been working for justice and equity for persons across all marginalized racial, sexual, and gender identities. Soulforce challenges Christian supremacy and strives to end the political and religious oppression of lesbian, gay, bisexual, transgender, queer, and intersex people through relentless nonviolent resistance.

Syndrome-Related Organizations

Androgen Insensitivity Syndrome-Differences of Sex Development (AIS-DSD) Support Group
PO Box 2148
Duncan, OK 73534–2148
aisdsd.org
The website of AIS-DSD Support Group is dedicated to helping those with androgen insensitivity syndrome and differences of sex development (DSD) or who are intersex. Its mission is to promote support, education, and outreach to foster healthy outcomes for adults, youth, children, and families affected by intersex/DSD. The annual AIS-DSD SG Conference includes separate tracks for teens and young adults, for parents, and for clinicians—including accreditation for Continuing Medical Education credits for medical professionals. The website offers materials for research, education, advocacy, and peer support.

Beautiful You MRKH Foundation, Inc. (BYMRKH)
c/o Amy Lossie
13301 Clifton Road
Silver Spring, MD 20904
Tel: 1 (765) 337–8683
BYMRKH@gmail.com
www.beautifulyoumrkh.org
BYMRKH promotes self-esteem and empowerment for women and girls with Mayer Rokitansky Küster Hauser (MRKH) syndrome. Its mission is to create a supportive online community that partners with health-care professionals to increase awareness and empower women of all ages with MRKH to feel beautiful, just as they are. You can also find the organization on Facebook, Pinterest, Twitter, and Instagram.

Klinefelter Syndrome Awareness Council
admin@klinefeltersyndromeaware.com
xxyaware.blogspot.com

The mission of the Klinefelter Syndrome Awareness Council is to deliver awareness of Klinefelter syndrome and educate those who could have it, the families in their lives, the medical community about the prevalence of it, the importance of early detection, available treatment options, and other health issues.

Klinefelter Syndrome Information and Support
klinefeltersyndrome.org
The Klinefelter Syndrome Information and Support website provides links to information about the syndrome including a personal story about living with Klinefelter syndrome, links to educational material, support groups, conferences, a YouTube channel, and more.

Turner Syndrome Society of the United States (TSSUS)
11250 West Road, Suite G
Houston, TX 77065
Toll Free: 1 (800) 365–9944
info@turnersyndrome.org
www.turnersyndrome.org
TSSUS advances knowledge, facilitates research, and provides support for all persons touched by Turner syndrome. Staff answer questions, create resources, plan events, and keep the website up-to-date.

Youth-Oriented Organizations

GenderCool Project
info@gendercool.org
www.gendercool.org
The GenderCool Project is a national storytelling campaign spotlighting stories of transgender young people. Meet the remarkable GenderCool Champions on the website and become inspired!

Gender Spectrum
Tel: 1 (510) 788 4412
info@genderspectrum.org
www.genderspectrum.org
Gender Spectrum works to create a gender-sensitive and inclusive world for all children and teens by helping families, organizations, and institutions to better understand gender and how changing views of gender impact each of us. The Education section has materials on several topics, including understanding

gender, gender-inclusive schools, gender and sports, and more. Visit www.gen derspectrum.org/resources/education-2/.

Genders & Sexualities Alliance (GSA) Network
Tel: 1 (415) 552–4229
info@gsanetwork.org
www.gsanetwork.org

GSA Network is "a next-generation LGBTQ racial and gender justice organization that empowers and trains queer, trans, and allied youth leaders to advocate, organize and mobilize an intersectional movement for safer schools and healthier communities." Founded in 1998 as the Gay-Straight Alliance Network, the organization once worked with forty GSA groups in the San Francisco Bay Area. In 2016, the group changed its name to the Genders & Sexualities Alliance Network, and now works with over four thousand GSA clubs across the United States. Today, the GSA Network has three offices across California, and one in the Southeastern United States. GSA Network operates the GSA Network of California, which connects over nine hundred clubs across the state; the National Association of GSA Networks, which unites forty statewide networks of GSA clubs; and GSAs Unite (unite.gsanetwork.org), an online campaign and petition platform supporting youth organizers across the nation.

Healthy Teen Network
1501 Saint Paul Street NW, Suite 114
Baltimore, MD 21202
Tel: 1 (410) 685–0410
info@healthyteennetwork.org
www.healthyteennetwork.org

Founded in 1979, Healthy Teen Network "fosters a national community where all adolescents and young adults, including youth who are pregnant or parenting, are supported and empowered to thrive." A leading national membership organization for adolescent health professionals and organizations, Healthy Teen Network promotes a holistic perspective to improve the health and well-being of young people with youth-centered, evidence-based strategies designed to educate and empower the whole teen as an individual.

IGLYO
Chaussée de Boondael 6
Brussels B-1050
Belgium
www.iglyo.com

IGLYO—the International Lesbian, Gay, Bisexual, Transgender, Queer & Intersex (LGBTQI) Youth & Student Organisation—is the largest LGBTQI youth and student organization in the world, with over ninety-five members in over forty countries. IGLYO uses cross-cultural exchange and peer-learning to empower and train youth leaders and activists to work in the LGBTQI and human rights arenas. Based in the European Union (EU), it boasts partnerships with organizations in almost every country in the EU. Although not US based, its powerful and far-reaching work is worth studying by persons with similar interests. Find its YouTube channel to view uplifting short videos—including faces from North America—or its Facebook page for myriad opportunities to learn about digital activism.

interACT Advocates for Intersex Youth
365 Boston Post Road, Suite 163
Sudbury, MA 01776
Tel: 1 (707) 793–1190
info@interactadvocates.org
www.interactadvocates.org

Founded in 2006 under the name Advocates for Informed Choice (AIC), this group focused on legal advocacy for the rights of intersex children. interACT was started by AIC in 2013 as a youth-led advocacy program for intersex teens and twenty-somethings. In 2016 interACT announced its new name, developed by its youth leaders, that recognizes and honors the intersex youth voices that are at the core of its mission. The world's first successful youth intersex advocacy group, interACT continues to develop intersex youth advocates, to advance affirming language, and to raise intersex awareness and visibility, while also working to build international advocacy capability and to develop plans focused on healing trauma.

TransActive Gender Center
Mailbox: 1631 NE Broadway Street, #355-T
Portland, OR 97232
Tel: 1 (503) 252–3000
info@transactiveonline.org
www.transactiveonline.org

The TransActive Gender Center is a nonprofit organization providing a holistic range of services to empower transgender and gender diverse young people and their families to live healthy lives, free from discrimination. Their Youth Expressions programming includes In a Bind, a project that distributes new and preowned binders to transmasculine youth in need, and About Face, a project that provides basic makeup kits to transfeminine and gender-diverse youth in need anywhere in the United States, including Puerto Rico. Visit its website to apply.

Trans Student Educational Resources (TSER)
tser@transstudent.org
www.transstudent.org

TSER was cofounded in 2011 by Eli Erlick and Alex Sennello, two sixteen-year-old transgender females. It was and remains the only national organization run by young transgender people. TSER was originally envisioned as an organization for creating safer schools through youth-led action, much of which focused on policy. It now encompasses many programs and services and reaches tens of millions of people around the world with resources, and thousands through workshops, speeches, and events. Its Trans Youth Leadership Summit is a collaborative fellowship program providing young transgender people the opportunity to work toward liberation through collective organizing for solidarity, advocacy, and empowerment. Find printable posters on its site and order buttons for your groups to increase visibility.

Trans Youth Equality Foundation (TYEF)
PO Box 7441
Portland, ME 04112–7441
Tel: 1 (207) 478–4087
contact@transyouthequality.org
www.transyouthequality.org

The Trans Youth Equality Foundation is a nonprofit organization that advocates for trans and gender nonconforming and intersex youth ages two to eighteen. Founded upon the principle that no child or family needs to be alone on this journey, TYEF provides education, advocacy, and support for trans gender-nonconforming children, youth, and their families. Through youth retreats, trainings, workshops, social media, and the podcast *TransWaves*, TYEF works to foster healthy, safe, and caring environments for all transgender young people by sharing information, and partnering with families, schools, and other service providers.

True Colors Fund
311 West 43rd Street, 12th Floor
New York, NY 10036
Tel: 1 (212) 461–4401
truecolorsfund.org

Cofounded by Cyndi Lauper—an American singer, songwriter, actress, and LGBT rights activist—the True Colors Fund is a nonprofit organization working nationally to end homelessness among lesbian, gay, bisexual, and transgender youth. Through public engagement, public policy, youth collaboration, research, and community organizing programs, the True Colors Fund is creating a world in which young people can be their true selves. The website's resources include "On Our Own: A Survival Guide for Independent Youth," and a Learning Community that offers self-paced online courses to establish a common understanding about LGBTQ youth homelessness and what we can all do to make a difference.

Find LGBTQI+ Books

Gay, Lesbian, Bisexual, Transgender Round Table (GLBTRT)
American Library Association (ALA)
50 East Huron Street
Chicago, IL 60611
Tel: 1 (800) 545–2433
www.ala.org/rt/glbtrt
GLBTRT of the American Library Association is committed to serving the information needs of the GLBT professional library community, and the GLBT information and access needs of individuals at large. It encourages and supports the free and necessary access to all information, as reflected by the missions of the American Library Association. It curates a Rainbow Book List of GLBTQ+ books for children and teens. Visit glbtrt.ala.org/rainbowbooks to learn more.

Harmony Ink Press
www.harmonyinkpress.com
Harmony Ink Press is an imprint of Dreamspinner Press publishing "teen and new adult fiction featuring significant personal growth of unforgettable characters across the LGBTQ+ spectrum." Although many LGBTQ-friendly publishers now exist (you can find many through Lambda Literary), Harmony Ink focuses solely on LGBTQ+ titles for teen and new adult readers.

Lambda Literary Foundation
811 West 7th Street, 12th Floor
Los Angeles, CA 90017
Tel: 1 (213) 277–5755
admin@lambdaliterary.org
www.lambdaliterary.org
The Lambda Literary Foundation arose in 1987 with the publication of the *Lambda Book Report (LBR)*—a journal of LGBT literature. In 1989 if hosted the first annual Lambda Literary Awards ceremony. "From the very first year they have made the statement that lesbian, gay, bisexual and trans stories are part of the literature of the nation." Surf the site to learn about the best LGBT books and to find encouragement for writers of LGBT+ books.

Historically Important Internet Resources

The International Foundation for Gender Education
www.ifge.org
This website promoted "acceptance for transgender people" into 2012, including the publication of *Transgender Tapestry* magazine.

Intersex Initiative (IPDX)
www.intersexinitiative.org
This website addressed intersex issues and provided concrete, factual information through 2010. For current information, visit the Intersex Campaign for Equality at www.intersexequality.com and the Organization Intersex International Intersex Network at www.oiiinternational.com.

Intersex Society of North America (ISNA)
www.isna.org
This organization existed from 1993 until 2008, "building a world free of shame, secrecy, and unwanted sexual surgeries." For current information refer to the Accord Alliance or the United States affiliate of the Organization Intersex International. The ISNA website exists for historical purposes.

Index

About the Author

Cynthia Winfield graduated from Lesley College in 1992 with a bachelor of science degree in middle school education and from Emerson College in 2000 with a master of fine arts degree in creative writing. Once a licensed educator in the state of Massachusetts, she adored teaching middle school reading, writing, and language arts in a Boston suburb. Her interest in quiet political activism—mostly around issues of equal rights, health care, literacy, and education—brought her together with the gay community starting in the mid-1980s, when she began volunteering for the AIDS Action Committee of Boston. She later served as volunteer secretary for the McLean Association of Gay, Lesbian, and Bisexual Issues committee of McLean Hospital, in Belmont, Massachusetts. An active participant in Seeking Educational Equity and Diversity (SEED) seminars from 1999 to 2008, Cynthia relished interactions with colleagues at her local SEED seminars, at New England SEED Leaders' seminars, and at gatherings of the national SEED program at the Wellesley College Center for Research on Women. Upon relocating to Tennessee, she left public education for small-scale farming and livestock husbandry—maintaining a farm blog (pandcworganicfarm.blogspot.com) for a few years. After interviewing for the United States Decennial Census in 2010 and serving in an administrative capacity assisting her pastor, she took up writing inspirational fiction set in Middle Tennessee. Cynthia's work on myriad surveys for the US Department of Commerce, the US Department of Health and Human Services, and the US Food and Drug Administration provided her opportunities to interact with a vast array of humanity across middle and east Tennessee, Virginia, and Kentucky. A 2012 graduate of the Institute for Integrative Nutrition, she is passionate about the healing power of unprocessed food and subscribes to alternative health practices. Settled with her family on a few acres outside of Nashville, she practices gratitude daily, enjoying time in nature and among animals, and continuing her quarter-century practice of reviewing books for *VOYA: Voice of Youth Advocates* magazine. She is grateful for the opportunity to educate others through the publication of this book.